The
Madefor Method

Patrick Dossett

A step-by-step guide designed by world-renowned
experts to help you get better at being your best

Dedication

"To those who take action, give grace, and
believe a better world begins within."

Contents

Foreword

I started my professional career, serving as a US Navy SEAL. The path to become a SEAL begins with a 7-month course known as Basic Underwater Demolition SEAL Training ("BUD/s"). My BUD/s class started with 220 highly motivated individuals, each of whom possessed the necessary physical abilities to become a SEAL. However, by the end of our 5th week of training, our class had been reduced to 150 candidates. By the end of the 6th week, our class had 36 candidates left. And, by the end of training, only 17 out of the original 220 remained. What struck me about those 17 individuals wasn't how special they were but rather how unremarkable they were. In fact, all of the biggest, fastest, strongest candidates, those that most looked the part (and certainly those who showed up on day one of training with SEAL tattoos), were some of the first to quit training. Over the course of my career, I came to understand that whether in training or in combat, the common feature amongst SEALs has nothing to do with a physical attribute or natural ability—it has everything to do with a mindset. This mindset is not unique to SEALs—you have it and you have the capacity to strengthen it at any stage of life.

A couple of years after I transitioned from military service, I was sitting in the back of an undergraduate class on Positive Psychology taught by Dr. Angela Duckworth. The field of Positive Psychology posits that in any intervention, be it behavioral, mental, or physical, there are two sides to the equation. One side, where we traditionally focus our attention and effort, deals with minimizing downside risk and reducing negative outcomes—this is the side of avoidance. The other side of the equation, where Positive Psychology focuses, deals with positive pursuits—doing things that are in line with the way our brains and bodies are designed, to grow what's good inside and help us live a more flourishing life. The more I learned about this field and the mountains of evidence-based research to support its findings, the more I knew that one day I'd build a company to help others discover their own capacity to flourish.

In 2017, my friend Blake Mycoskie and I decided to build this company. With the help of Dr. Andrew Huberman and a number of other world-class advisors and teammates, we created a program to get people offline and into action—the result was Madefor.

Madefor has now served thousands of Members across the world, helping each build a better foundation for physical and mental health. The book you're holding in your hands is an adaptation of the original Madefor Program and the summation of our collective effort. At the end of each chapter, I'll offer resources to support you on your journey, including personal reflections to help guide you.

If you take one thing from Madefor, I hope you discover that there isn't one perfect way for everyone to live, but that if you do the work, you can discover your best way to be. Our goal isn't to give you a deliberate checklist of things to do every day to be better. Rather, the goal is to help you reflexively move through life in a way that brings out your best. Listen, trust, and be kind to yourself—with time, you'll become your own best guide on your unique journey.

Cheers,
Pat

P.S. We've produced and reference a lot of great audio and video content to support you on your Madefor journey. You can find all of it on our YouTube page (https://www.youtube.com/@getmadefor).

Welcome

On behalf of the founding team and our global community, welcome to Madefor.

We've put together this _Welcome Video_ (https://youtu.be/ wiOIhn91zS8) to provide you a complete overview of the Madefor Program and a message from Pat and a few of our Alumni—we hope you enjoy it.

If you would like to learn more about how the Madefor Method is designed and how to get the most from this book, we recommend familiarizing yourself with the Program Guide located in the back of this book.

Let's begin.

Madefor onboarding

Welcome to the first step

The fact that you're reading these words means you have an inherent bias for action, even when faced with uncertainty. This is a courageous trait, one from which you'll benefit in the coming months as you engage in small, purposeful challenges that may push you outside your comfort zone.

Chances are, your reasons for doing Madefor are unique. Maybe you want to learn from our experts. Or you're seeking a way to get "back on track." Or maybe you simply want to connect with an exceptional, growth-oriented community. Whatever the reason, you've come to the right place.

Madefor is about you. You are the hero in this journey, because it's you who will do the work and realize the benefits. Our role is to guide you, encourage you, and hold you accountable along the way.

Thank you for taking the first of many pivotal steps. It's our honor to serve you on your journey. In fact, it's our mission, as we believe a better world starts with the best you.

Let's do this,

BLAKE & PAT

The Basics

For more than 150 years, every new cab driver in London has had to pass "the Knowledge," a grueling exam that tests their mastery of central London. To prepare, candidates spend four years studying maps and traversing the city's 25,000 streets, learning every hotel, pub, church—basically, anywhere a passenger might ask to go. About half of all trainees successfully "obtain the Knowledge" and receive a license to operate one of London's famous black cabs.

Researchers at University College London wondered if the Knowledge was something you could actually see if you scanned the cabbies' brains with MRI machines. What they found was fascinating: People who'd obtained the Knowledge had significantly more gray matter (brain tissue) in the posterior hippocampus—an area that governs long-term memory and spatial navigation—than people who didn't.

How to explain this enlarged memory-and-navigation center in cabbies' brains? Did intense study of London's geography actually alter their neuroanatomy? Or was it simply that individuals with plump hippocampi were naturally drawn to driving professions?

To find out, the researchers next scanned the brains of bus drivers, who do not study for the Knowledge. None of them had enlarged hippocampi. Next, they scanned cabbies *before* they began Knowledge training and then *after* their exams. All the subjects had relatively similar brain scans at the start, but by the end, trainees who'd mastered the Knowledge had *larger hippocampi* than those who'd failed or dropped out.

These groundbreaking results showed that when you engage in an endeavor with deliberate intention and attention, it can improve and even alter the anatomy of your brain. In fact, it confirms a growing body of scientific evidence that our brains are much more "plastic" and capable of transformation than previously imagined.

Scientists used to think that our brains were fully developed by age 18, but thanks to improved neuroimaging technology we now know that the adult brain is far from being fixed: It has the power of neuroplasticity.

Neuroplasticity is a scientific concept that refers to the different ways the brain can modify itself in order to process and respond to external stimuli. Put simply, your brain has a vast capacity to grow and learn. It can rewire and reorganize itself to compensate for injuries. It can learn language, music, and other complex skills in old age. It can even be trained to replace poor habits like smoking and gambling with healthier ones such as working out and meditating.

Our minds are capable of much more than we ask of them. You just need to understand and apply the science in order to tap into its natural capacity for plasticity. That's where Madefor comes in.

Madefor is a life-changing program that employs basic tenets of neuroscience, physiology, and positive psychology to help you tap into your best self as you slowly develop healthy habits of body and mind. Over the coming months, we're going to guide you through small *Challenges*, just one per month, that give you a greater sense of authority over your own life. As you tap into your brain's capacity for top-down control, you become more present, aware, and confident about how you move through and operate in the world. The Challenges we're going to guide you through may seem simple at first, but in the collective, they will be transformational.

> **Fig. 1**
> *Neuroplasticity refers to your
> brain's ability to learn and grow.*

Each chapter acts as a **Challenge Guidebook** for the respective month, which explains the science and method behind your new Challenge, along with one or more tools that serve as a reminder and reinforcement to your practice. You can choose to purchase the tools separately or create your own. Either way, the items chosen are simple by design. At Madefor, we don't believe in unnecessary trinkets, trends, or fads. **We believe the truth lies within you. You are the authority.** That's why your Challenges are pared down to the essentials - the minimum tools, energy, and time necessary to unlock your maximum potential.

Madefor was created with an advisory board of neuroscientists, nutritionists, psychiatrists, psychologists, physical therapists, coaches, athletes, authors, and wellness experts, who hail from such distinguished institutes as Harvard, Stanford, and the National Institute of Mental Health. In the months ahead, you'll come to know their groundbreaking work as we help you apply it in your own life. On the surface, we're simply asking you to engage in one new positive habit a month. But dig deeper and you'll discover that the *way* in which you practice these habits is actually training your brain to be better.

"There are essentially two ways to modify the brain to be better," says Madefor's lead advisor Dr. Andrew Huberman, an associate professor of neurobiology and head of the Huberman Lab at Stanford University's School of Medicine. "One way is to engage in a high-attention, high-intensity event for which you'll never forget the feelings and associations—your brain is forever changed."

Think of the oxytocin rush you get from running a marathon or watching the birth of a child. Any new parent will tell you that their brain is forever changed, and it's true: New neural pathways are created that let a mother pick out her child's voice from all others and cause a father to wake up in the middle of the night to check that his baby is breathing.

Oxytocin is just one of the many powerful chemicals in our brains that plays a role in reinforcing novel behaviors around high-intensity events.

"The second way to modify the brain is through small, consistent behavioral changes," Huberman says. "That process isn't associated with any kind of roaring-crowd, finish-line feeling. But there are a series of steps—processes involving attention, reward, and reinforcement—which can lead to a big shift, to true neuroplasticity."

A series of steps; attention-reward-reinforcement; small changes that lead to a big shift: this is the Madefor approach. It's how you'll practice each Challenge. Imagine a Knowledge trainee poring over a map of London and plotting the best routes. Or the way your concentration intensifies when you study a foreign language, play a musical instrument, or memorize the words of a poem. You're activating an attention-reward-reinforcement loop that *slowly* creates new neural connections and strengthens existing ones.

- MEMBER MOMENT -

"What's been most impactful for me is slowing down and focusing on just ONE thing. It's helping me to ease the pressure off myself and be more patient. The result has been an ever-decreasing amount of stress, for which I am SO grateful. So happy to have finally found something that WORKS for me!"

- Yvette H

Here's what that process looks like under the hood: Your brain contains anywhere from 86 billion to 100 billion neurons that communicate with one another using the language of electro-chemistry. Neurotransmitters are the chemical messengers in your brain that carry information from one neuron to the next, and neuromodulators are chemicals that adjust the volume and frequency of that conversation.

Broadly speaking, when you pay close *attention* to something, say, a guitar teacher's hands, a neuromodulator called ace-tylcholine is poured on the synapse (the junction between the neurons), telling the neurons: *This neural conversation is important!* When you experience a reward like when your hands play those chords perfectly—a neuromodulator called dopamine is released, telling your brain: *Good job, do it again!*

Neuroplasticity is anchored in consistent attention (acetylcho-line) and reward (dopamine) over time—it's how a new conver-sation gets chemically reinforced.

So while it may seem harder to pick up a guitar at age 30, with focused attention, your brain reorganizes itself to learn a new skill. When you begin to play the right notes with ease, that dopamine rush of satisfaction fortifies the experience, telling your brain: *This feels good. Do it more.*

The Madefor method hijacks the same process. Over the com-ing months, you're going to intentionally engage in healthy, positive habits while doing **attention** exercises that **reward** and **reinforce** your new behavior.

Your Challenges are designed to set you up for success: Each practice is built on research that's been studied, lab-tested, and peer-reviewed in scientific journals, and then pared down to the smallest thing you need to do in order to reap maxi-mum returns. And by focusing on one practice at a time, you're building a healthier, more successful mindset.

When actor Will Smith talks about the mindset that has helped him to become one of the most successful entertainers in Hollywood, he tells the story of when his father made him build a wall 30 feet long and 16 feet high. Every day after school, 12-year-old Smith worked on the wall, even mixing concrete by hand. It seemed like an impossible assignment, but after about 18 months, he finally laid the last brick.

"I learned very young that you don't set out to build a wall and say, 'I'm going to build the biggest, baddest, greatest wall that's ever been built,'" Smith says. "You say, 'I'm going to lay this brick as perfectly as a brick can be laid.'… You do that every single day. And soon you have a wall."

The one-brick-at-a-time approach isn't rocket science. But it is brain science. And it's one of several crucial strategies that underpin the Madefor method. **Attack one habit at a time, as well as you can, and pretty soon you've become the kind of person who can achieve anything.**

To foster this brain-building approach, we only share the full details of each Challenge when you are ready to start your next Challenge. Just as hopeful London cabbies memorize one street at a time to build their navigational prowess, you're focusing on one habit at a time to build a healthier body and mind. In fact, each Challenge begins when you remove unnecessary distractions, start a timer or flip over an hourglass, and read your Challenge Guidebook.

Science tells us that when we multitask, our frontal lobes— the conductors of cognitive function—have to toggle back and forth among complex tasks, resulting in less focused thinking, increased errors, and decreased mental processing. The reason for this cognitive bottleneck is that our brains are constantly processing a tremendous amount of information in the background.

Imagine it's a beautiful summer day and you're in the backyard starting a barbecue. Your sensory organs are bombarding your brain with data: the smell of burning chicken, the tactile sensation of heat, the sound of your spouse talking, the sight of your dog sniffing at a plate of unguarded franks. Your brain has to instantly decide what to act upon: Save the hotdogs? Listen to my wife? Turn over the chicken? Add to this quandary, the chirps from the phone in your pocket. You may think you're being an effective multitasker, but your overtaxed brain is hard-pressed to perform any one of these tasks with integrity.

When you pursue one goal at a time, your brain rewards you with clearer thinking, better strategies, and less stress. This is how Madefor was designed. It won't overtax your brain and it won't disrupt your life—it will become a joyful part of your life.

Each Challenge redirects your attention away from digital distractions and externally generated rewards, and back to the internal rewards we create for ourselves when we slow down and connect our actions to our feelings. So we'll never ask you to log on to a tracking device to count your footsteps or compare yourself to others. On the contrary, we're going to help you carve out time to unplug and check in with yourself.

Each monthly Challenge is paired with a **Challenge Card** (available in the Tools & Resources section). The Challenge Card was designed to help reward effort and track progress, as you cross off steps each day. We recommend finding a second tool, like a bracelet, to serve as a reminder of your practice and your intention—a visual cue for the moments when you forget that you're on a journey. While using the Challenge Card & finding a **Challenge Bracelet** isn't required, we highly recommend using a visual cue each month and have provided additional options to use within the **Tools & Resources** section.

Next, having something to write in throughout the program *is required*. Get a **Journal** (identify your own) to help you harness the power of plasticity—just putting pen to paper tells your brain: Pay attention.

PRO TIP: *New to journaling? Check out our Journaling Tips & FAQ at the end of the book.*

Best of all, as you move through the Challenges, you'll make incremental changes that slowly elevate your mental and physical *baselines*—those elemental indicators of overall health that bring a greater sense of inner strength and wellbeing. Raising your baselines gives you the capacity to do *everything* better. You know, for instance, that practicing free throws will make you a better basketball player, but it won't help you to make wiser career moves or relationship decisions. When you raise your baselines, however, you feel more alert, capable, connected— you're better equipped to take on whatever life throws at you.

"We know that most mental and physical wellbeing comes from having your baselines elevated," says Huberman. "Waking up feeling rested, moving through the day with energy and focus, being able to engage and disengage with things freely, feeling socially connected, feeling tired and being able to go right to sleep—all these things sound pedestrian, but there's nothing pedestrian about having that kind of life experience. It's what most people are seeking."

On the flip side, we've all seen what happens when people who are hyperfunctional in one area of their lives fail to attend to their mental and physical baselines. Picture any number of famous athletes, tech titans, students, CEOs, or entertainers who work super hard, day in and day out. "You can predict with certainty that they're going to have a health crash, or an emotional crash, or a relationship crash," Huberman says. "Some sort of crash is inevitable."

Madefor raises your baselines to an optimal state so you can avoid crashes, be fully present, and make good choices. With each new Challenge, you're not only feeling better, you're cultivating the most powerful tool of all: *your mindset.*

As simplistic as it sounds, our brains are like muscles. When habits fade, their corresponding neural connections wither away. But when you intentionally engage in a practice repeatedly, even at the smallest level, you create deep neural patterns that result in lasting change. That's why we take you through plenty of journaling in each Challenge. Just a couple sentences of daily reflection rewards your brain and reinforces your new habit. You're affirming your innate ability to learn—to be more plastic. And that lays the groundwork for something called a "positive growth mindset."

Stanford University psychology professor Dr. Carol Dweck coined the terms "fixed mindset" and "growth mindset" more than 30 years ago while studying the way students tackled challenging puzzles. Some students grunted, groaned, and gave up. But others rubbed their hands together in anticipation and excitement for a harder puzzle. They weren't discouraged by failure because they didn't think they were failing—they thought they were *learning.*

As Dweck explains in her bestselling book, *Mindset: The New Psychology of Success*, individuals with a growth mindset believe that their talents can be cultivated through greater effort, new strategies, and help from others. These people tend to live happier, more meaningful lives than those who believe that their intelligence and abilities are *fixed*.

Everyone knows someone who embodies a positive growth mindset. They tend to persist when others quit. They can reframe failure as an opportunity to learn. They're open to hearing criticism because it may help them to be better. They value progress over perfection.

> **Fig. 2**
> *Elevated baselines promote overall wellbeing.*

On the other end of the spectrum, those with a fixed mindset think that test scores define the boundaries of our abilities. If something feels too hard, they lose interest. When bested by a competitor, they're apt to say the other person is smarter or more naturally gifted, rather than considering that they could have used better strategies, practiced longer, or worked harder.

"These beliefs... strongly affect what we want and whether we succeed in getting it," Dweck writes. "Much of what you think of as your personality actually grows out of this 'mindset.' Much of what may be preventing you from fulfilling your potential grows out of it."

The truth is, we all have fixed and growth tendencies and they tend to kick in when we confront uncomfortable and unfamiliar situations: the last stretch of an arduous workout, an emotional fight with a friend, a creative project that failed to take shape. We can quit and throw up our hands in frustration or we can lean in and savor the adventure.

The Madefor method helps you achieve a growth mindset because you tackle new goals slowly, with small wins right out of the gate. As the monthly practices become more challenging, you have a reservoir of courage, resilience, and energy to take them on.

"When things become difficult, you prevail. When things become confusing, you reflect and persist," says Huberman. "You get the benefit of all these new practices that make your brain and body feel good. But the way in which you adopt these habits actually makes your brain fundamentally better at going after new, bigger challenges—which is the process that gets you to a positive growth mindset."

This is the Madefor end game:

1. You've taught your brain the art of forming and reinforcing positive habits.
2. You can see how the science maps to other areas of your life that you want to improve.
3. Without even thinking, you lean toward a positive growth mindset.

In other words, you no longer need Madefor—you've successfully obtained the knowledge.

# The Challenge

You're almost ready to start your first Challenge. But before you do, let's set an intention.

Research shows that writing out goals and intentions helps you to realize them. In a study at Dominican University of California, participants who wrote down their goals had a 42% higher rate of success than subjects who simply thought about them. That's because it puts your brain on notice: *This is important; take steps to achieve it.*

It also helps to keep your mind attuned to useful information. For example, if your intention is to be more present with your children, then you're more likely to recognize the calm, patient behaviors of other parents—and mirror them to good effect during toddler meltdowns in the grocery store.

Remember, an intention is not really a goal. Goals are specific things you want to accomplish, like: *I want to lose 50 pounds; earn a graduate degree; get married in the next five years.*

Intentions are the hopes and dreams behind these goals, your true north: *I want to be more physically fit; prime my mind for greater success; become the kind of person who is ready for a healthy, committed relationship.*

Take the next few days to think about why you're doing Madefor. Where do you want to see yourself, and what kind of person do you want to be at the end of this journey? We suggest you take a 360-degree view—**present, past, future**—in order to achieve a deep cognitive imprint.

For example:

- **Present**: *Identify your intention.*
- **Past**: *Reflect on the reasons behind it. What life experiences and decisions brought you to this point?*
- **Future**: *Imagine a future in which you've realized your intention. In what meaningful ways will it change your life? How will you honor this new you?*

When you tie these three levels together, you create more attention around your intention, which translates to enhanced brain rewards that fortify your experience. In practice, setting an intention might look like this:

- **Present**: *My intention is to be more physically fit.*
- **Past**: *For a while now, I've channeled stress in unhealthy ways, putting me in a place where I'm not happy with my body. At times, this has made me feel isolated and depressed.*
- **Future**: *If I move my body more, I'll have increased energy and confidence, which will allow me to take part in physical activities I used to enjoy and to feel more sociable. Maybe it will even put me on the path to finding a life partner, which would bring me great joy.*

- **Intention:** *Connect with my body to better understand how to serve it and rediscover all of the joy and benefits that moving my body delivers.*

Once you've determined your intention, be sure to write it down inside your Journal as a visual reminder of the future that awaits you.

Let's Do This

Now, you're ready. You are about to embark on an incredible adventure, a series of small steps that lead to big change. Very soon, you're going to feel stronger, healthier, more engaged, and more creative. Like cab drivers who rewire their brains to navigate the city with ease, you're going to rewire your brain to get you where you want to be, effortlessly.

It might seem hard at first, but we've witnessed thousands and thousands of Members complete Madefor. In fact, somewhere in the world right now a Member is going through the exact same Challenge as you—they're experiencing the same joys, frustrations, and changes, too. Whether you're connecting with another Member or building your own Madefor team, it's important to know that you're not alone.

This program is for you.

So imagine the best possible version of yourself and reach for it. You can reclaim the power you've always had: The power to achieve extraordinary things.

- - -

A reminder: Madefor is a program that engages your mind and body in positive practices that are safe and effective for the vast majority of people. But if you have any medical issues or health concerns, consult with your primary care doctor before beginning this or any program.

Looking for a way to track your progress? Take your Metrics of Change Survey!

Track key areas of change throughout the Madefor Program by completing the short five-question survey provided in the Program Guide (back of the book) - *it will only take 5 minutes to complete!* For the most accurate results, we recommend completing the survey before your Month 1: Hydration Challenge, Month 5: Breath Challenge, and Month 10: Vision Challenge (3 times total).

Pat's Onboarding Guidance

A Member once described Madefor to me as offensively simple, yet highly effective—it's true.

But, this program is only as effective as the intention you set at the outset. Don't rush this crucial step. Your intention will serve as a source of motivation and a marker of progress, signaling whether you're moving closer towards or further away from what matters most to you.

For additional support, check out my <u>Perspectives video</u>* for more information on how to get the most out of the Madefor Program. Or, listen to this quick <u>Campfire Story</u>* for a little inspiration.

*Madefor Videos and Audio recordings can be found on our YouTube page (https://www.youtube.com/@getmadefor)

Madefor hydration

Ready to start?

***PRO TIP:** Wait to begin the Hydration Challenge until AFTER you complete Onboarding & Intention Setting.*

If you've been anticipating the first Challenge for a while, you may want to just breeze through the materials and get started! However, we recommend slowing down and carving out 45 to 60 minutes with no distractions. You deserve to begin your Madefor journey with calm, focused attention. When you're ready, follow these 3 simple steps:

- Step 1: Remove distractions and start a timer for 1 hour.
- Step 2: Read the Founders Letter from Pat & Blake.
- Step 3: Read the rest of your Guidebook.

NOW, YOU'RE READY.

Each month, you'll start with the same 3 steps: remove distractions, letter, guidebook. Let's go!

Bottoms up!

Welcome to your first Madefor Challenge.

We hope you found value in reflecting on and crafting your unique intention for this program. If not, don't worry. The benefits will be revealed in due time.

This month, we are going to ask you to do something that may appear overly simplistic at first (and maybe even second) glance: Pay attention to the water you drink and how it makes you feel.

But trust in the science and experts working on your behalf. Madefor was designed to give you small wins early. So drink up and have fun—the best you awaits.

Let's begin,

BLAKE & PAT

The Basics

For anyone who dreams of becoming a US Navy SEAL, all hope is typically dashed during a six-month training program called Basic Underwater Demolition/SEAL, or BUD/S. Widely considered to be the most challenging military training in the world, BUD/S pushes about 75% of candidates to quit during Hell Week—a grueling trial of increasingly difficult physical challenges that leave you cold, wet, sandy, and miserable.

"For five days, you're rarely still. The entire week feels like a really long bad day," recalls Madefor co-founder and former SEAL Pat Dossett, who completed Hell Week in 2002.

"You transition from one physical task to the next, often while carrying a boat on your head," Dossett says. "Everything from timed races to obstacle courses. And then, my personal favorite, 'surf torture,' where you march into the Pacific Ocean, get pummeled by the waves, and then lie down in the water until you're just shy of hypothermia."

By the end of the week, trainees have had four hours of sleep. Some are hallucinating and passing out in their food. Most have already quit. But Dossett was among 36 candidates (out of 220) who did not quit. And he credits his military training for helping him to recognize powerful internal tools he didn't even know he possessed—the same tools you're going to develop on your Madefor journey, no surf torture necessary.

"Going through BUD/S reveals an internal source of strength that you didn't realize you had," Dossett says. "At some point, a switch flips in your head, and you know: 'They're not going to break me.'"

But there is one fundamental thing that can break him—and almost did. On the third day of a five-day training exercise in the forests of Northern Virginia, Dossett ran out of water. Two days later, as he and a teammate were crawling through thick brush to their final extraction point, Dossett realized that he'd stopped sweating, his head ached, and his muscles were cramping—all symptoms of severe dehydration.

"I could feel this big, heavy blanket starting to envelop me," he recalls. And that's when they discovered that they'd gone about a mile in the wrong direction—a small mistake that now had potentially fatal consequences.

Aborting the exercise, his buddy radioed in their coordinates for emergency support. Medics arrived just as Dossett began to shake and convulse. His veins were so constricted from dehydration, they couldn't get an IV in him. After six tries, they finally found a vein in his hip, placed the IV, and his body sucked down 4 liters of fluid.

Over the next few days, as Dossett and his team packed their gear and headed home, his brain felt completely scrambled. Simple cognitive tasks—finding the tiny serial numbers on a pair of night-vision goggles, taking the correct highway exit, counting out the right toll change—seemed to unfold in slow motion and required extraordinary mental effort. He tired quickly when he tried to swim, run, or lift weights. It took a while before he felt normal again.

"Even in the worst of Hell Week, I'd never felt anything like that," Dossett says. "There are a lot of limits that I can push: I can give up food for 10 days; go without sleep for a week; be cold and wet for a very long time. But I know now that if I don't have water, everything else stops. I really underestimated how much I needed it."

He's not alone. Studies show that we all tend to underestimate or ignore our sensations of thirst. **That's why Hydration is the focus of your first Madefor Challenge.** Over the next three weeks, you're going to develop a greater awareness around thirst and how it feels to meet your body's need for water. Using an action-reward-reinforcement approach, your daily Hydration practice taps into the power of neuroscience to fundamentally change the way you think about the simple act of drinking water. In the process, you'll open channels for even more positive behaviors, like taking more time for self-care, moving your body more, and eating more nutritiously.

You may be thinking: Just drink water? Too easy. After all, you know you need water. But sometimes, like Dossett, you may underestimate the crucial role it plays in the effective functioning of your body and brain. Water, for example, comprises 45% to 75% of your body weight and 80% of your brain composition. Water transports nutrients, regulates your temperature, lubricates your joints and internal organs, gives structure to your cells and tissues, and helps to keep your heart pumping. You can go for a month or two without food, but you won't last for more than a week without water.

While most people will never experience the severe body-water loss that Dossett did, nearly half of all Americans are operating in a state of chronic dehydration. To be clear: Dehydration occurs when you use or lose more water than you take in. The average adult releases the equivalent of 6 to 13 cups a day just through sweat, urine, respiration, and normal body processes. So it's particularly troubling that a study by the Centers for Disease Control and Prevention found that 43.7% of Americans drink less than 4 cups of water a day—including 7% who drink none.

Clearly, we are a chronically dehydrated nation, and yet we have no official recommendations for daily water consumption to lean on. Health-advice columns have been admonishing us for years to "drink at least eight glasses daily"—which is fine, but it's not based in science.

In 2004, the Institute of Medicine of the National Academies (IOM) published "Dietary Reference Intakes: Water, Potassium, Sodium, Chloride, and Sulfate," a 600-page report that did not provide a single measurement for daily water consumption. Instead, the panel offered confusing "Adequate Intake" guidelines: for adult women, about 11 cups a day is adequate; for men, it's 15 cups. But those figures also include the water we consume in our food and beverages. How does one begin to measure the water content in a turkey sandwich or a milkshake?

Part of the reason no one can provide general recommendations about how much water you should drink is that requirements vary greatly based on your age, gender, activity level, diet, medical conditions, and the climate and altitude you live in. For instance, a new mom who's nursing needs significantly more water than a couch-potato dad, and a football player in Arizona needs more water than an office worker in Minnesota.

The IOM report contends that most people can meet their daily needs if they simply let thirst be their guide, which sounds reasonable until you consider that thirst is triggered in the brain when you experience a body-water loss of 1% to 2%—the same range at which you begin to suffer cognitive side effects such as memory loss, lowered concentration, and poor mood, according to a new and growing body of evidence.

"Fatigue, brain fog, headaches, mood swings—this is what most people report when they don't drink enough water," says Dr. Lisa Mosconi, a neuroscience nutritionist and associate director of the Alzheimer's Prevention Clinic at Weill Cornell Medicine in New York. In her book, *Brain Food: The Surprising*

Science of Eating for Cognitive Power, Mosconi points to studies indicating that dehydration may even accelerate the brain shrinkage associated with aging and dementia.

"MRI studies show that when we are dehydrated, several parts of the brain appear to get thinner and lose volume," Mosconi writes. "Clearly this is a much more pressing issue than many might have thought."

If our brains are the first casualties of water deficiency, our bodies are not far behind. The early signs of mild dehydration include dry mouth, chapped skin, headaches, and cramps. Chronic dehydration—enough water to function on a daily basis but not enough to flourish—leaves one vulnerable to constipation, urinary tract infections, and kidney stones.

In severe cases—the kind that land exhausted entertainers (see: Rihanna, Lady Gaga, Tim McGraw) in the hospital— additional symptoms may include dizziness, rapid heartbeat, sunken eyes, lack of energy, confusion, fainting, and an imbalance of electrolytes, the essential minerals that help to carry electrical signals from cell to cell, essentially powering your body. When Dossett began to convulse and shake after nearly two days without water, he was experiencing a severe electrolyte disturbance. For athletes, as little as a 2% loss of body weight in sweat during challenging workouts or competitions can result in decreased endurance, increased fatigue, poorer ability to regulate body temperature, and reduced motivation.

The good news (finally!) is that establishing a proper hydration routine can quickly reverse negative side effects and bring about enhanced concentration, increased energy, improved digestion, better moods, and more.

As Mosconi writes in Brain Food: "Simply drinking more water... could be one of the healthiest changes you make to bring about better health and greater cognitive power in your life."

The Challenge

Your Hydration Challenge Exercises:

Drink:
For the next 21 days, drink all your water from your Madefor Water Bottle.

Track:
Track your daily water consumption by moving a bead every time you finish a bottle.

Reflect:
Each night, cross off a water icon on your Challenge Card. Then record in your Journal how many bottles you drank and write a few sentences about your experience that day. Connect the dots between the act of drinking water and how it made you feel. Just a few sentences is sufficient, but be as specific as possible.

Your first Madefor Challenge is to **Drink, Track, and Reflect.** This month's recommended tool is a water bottle (identify your own). For the next 21 days, you're going to **Drink** all your water from the same bottle. Each day, make a checkmark in your Journal whenever you finish a bottle to **Track** your progress. Each night, cross off a water icon on your **Challenge Card** to finish the day and take a moment to **Reflect** on how the practice made you feel in your **Journal**.

Take time to note how many ounces of water your bottle holds. If you drink three bottles a day, you're likely to notice positive mental and physical changes right away. But if one or two bottles is all you need to feel good, that's totally fine too. With time, you'll begin to notice sensations of thirst more readily, and you will drink the right amount for you, naturally, and without effort.

This is important and bears repeating:

The point of this Challenge is not to drink a specific amount of water each day. Your goal is to create greater awareness around the act of drinking water.

If you're already vigilant about water consumption, you may be tempted to skip or skimp on the practice. But you'd be missing a powerful opportunity to teach your brain new tricks—to harness its plasticity. To put it another way: When you **Drink**, **Track**, and **Reflect**, you're engaging in an attention-reward-reinforcement loop—the neuroplasticity trifecta—that strengthens the neural conversation around your hydration routine, thereby forging stronger habits. But your brain has to be engaged to create neural-level change.

"After age 25 or so, in order to really modify your brain, in a good way, you have to pay attention to what you're doing. Awareness is absolutely key," says Madefor's lead advisor Dr. Andrew Huberman, an associate professor of neurobiology and head of the Huberman Lab at Stanford University's School of Medicine.

As Huberman notes, the best way to sharpen your brain's awareness is to pay attention to the sensory experience of drinking water: You can glance at your **Challenge Bracelet** and remember to check in with your body; you notice a feeling of thirst, so you lift the bottle to your mouth and taste clean water on your palate; you hear the bubbly sound of liquid rising as you refill your empty bottle; you feel a sense of accomplishment as you track your progress. All of these sensory inputs tell your brain: This feels good; do it more.

Surprisingly, the bracelet has really been a game changer for me. There have been many busy days when I would just lose focus on the challenge—until I'd glance down and see the bracelet. Right away, I'd grab my bottle and get some water in. It is a great tool! - Mary Anne K

Granted, we're talking about drinking, tracking, and journaling. Pretty simple stuff. And yet the associations and rewards you're generating when you connect to your body's internal cues are game-changing.

"The brain is a never-ending associative machine," Huberman says. "It's constantly trying to link up how you feel with things that you've done, that you're doing, and what you're planning to do."

Think of how it feels when your hand gets a little too close to a sizzling frying pan. Or when you run into a former sweetheart on the street. Your brain holds a trove of data—strong neural associations—about hot pans and old flames. Chances are, before you even realize what you're doing, your brain has already signaled to your body to recoil (danger: back away) or move in closer (reward!). But the difference here is that the associations and rewards you're creating around water are all internally generated.

Most of us go through life focused on external rewards—things outside ourselves that bring us a dopamine hit of joy. From that first gold star in math class, to unexpected praise from the boss, to the surprise of 70 new "likes" on Twitter—we crave external rewards. But they're not the most effective motivators of positive, long-lasting change because they're not within our control.

"External incentives will always be very strong determinants of behavior. But internal ones bring about more stable and durable changes in behavior," Huberman notes. "A big dopamine rush followed by nothing doesn't lead to stable changes in our neural circuitry."

In other words, rewards that come from outside of us are unpredictable and can disappear. Even worse, they keep us from experiencing true wellbeing. In the extreme, think of a parent whose sole happiness depends on the returned love of a child or a comedian who's depressed unless she's on- stage getting laughs from an audience. External validation can be powerful, but it can also make us miserable. This is why the Madefor method places you at the center. You listen to your body's sensations of thirst. You decide how much water to drink. You are in charge of what's best for you.

"No one's going to give you a trophy and say, 'Wow, good job drinking more water!'" Huberman says. "You're rewarding yourself. And that means your brain is changing in positive ways around this new behavior."

Drinking water, tracking, checking off another day, reflecting in your Journal—these may not seem like big payoffs, but your brain experiences them as major strides. Then, next month, you tackle a new Madefor Challenge. It's a little harder, but you've got this. Pretty soon, you've racked up a half-dozen positive habits, your mental and physical baselines are elevated, and you feel stronger, healthier, more rested, more confident. You direct your own life, through your own internal compass, and not at the whim of external rewards that are out of your control.

Fig. 2A
*Most of us go through life
focused on external rewards.*

➤ **Fig. 2B**
*But internal rewards create
positive, long-lasting change.*

All of which is to say that this practice is 50% about helping you to better hydrate and 50% about teaching you how to direct your brain's attention-reward-reinforcement system so that you can achieve anything you set your mind to. And your nightly Journaling practice is the most effective and durable way to achieve the mental strength and internal tools that Dossett describes at the beginning of this **Guidebook**.

"Every time you journal, you increase the probability that your awareness, and therefore the plasticity around the event, will be reinforced," Huberman says. "It's circular: behavior-attention-awareness-reward; behavior-attention-awareness-reward. It feeds back on itself and becomes self-amplifying."

We know that some people love to write, others not so much. Keep in mind that it doesn't really matter how many lines you produce. The key is to put pen to paper and get your thoughts and feelings down. Describe your experience as vividly as possible, which helps to "raise the volume" of the neural conversation. And don't worry if you don't notice changes right away. This is a slow, steady voyage toward greater mental and physical health.

PRO TIP: Journaling is a challenge! Check out our Journaling Tips & FAQ at the end of the book for more inspiration.

21 Days of Hydration:
Journaling prompts to help you get started

How did your Challenge experience go today?

Did you have any insights about your approach to Hydration?

Any changes in the way you moved through your day?

Did your concentration improve?

Were you in a better mood?

Did you experience sensations of thirst sooner then you might have in the past?

Did you drink fewer non-water beverages?

Did any new feelings or interesting observations around water come up for you today?

If you didn't feel good about your practice today, are there better strategies you can try tomorrow?

You may have some questions and concerns about hydration before you begin. Like, what kind of water is best? And are you going to have to pee all the time?

To the latter question: It depends. If you consume more than you did before, you'll probably urinate more too. But remember that you're ridding your kidneys of waste and toxins, a beneficial effect of proper hydration. We suggest you avoid drinking water an hour or two before bedtime if getting up in the middle of the night to use the bathroom is going to prevent you from falling back asleep.

As for type of water, you needn't buy expensive bottled water. Filtered tap water is more than adequate. Mosconi, for example, has a filtration system in her home that removes impurities but doesn't trap the minerals.

- MEMBER MOMENT -

"My work season just started back up, and I was caught off guard. I did end up missing a couple days, but analyzing the days in which I had missed journaling has showed me what negative habits are staring me in the face."

– Robert S

"The goal is for your filter to get rid of harmful chemicals like asbestos, chlorine, lead, benzene, and trichloroethylene—all of which can be found in tap water," Mosconi says. If your tap water is so unsafe that you must purchase it, try to avoid "purified" water, which has been stripped of mineral content, leaving it nutritionally void.

When it comes to temperature, Mosconi prefers warm water as it helps to dilate the blood vessels and improve blood circulation. But cold water can also help lower body temperature after a hard workout.

Bottom line: Preferences run the gamut and you should hydrate however it works best for you. If you're a staunch advocate of reverse osmosis filtration, that's fine; if you need to drink water that's been blessed by holy men, more power to you; if a little cayenne and lemon juice makes your water more enticing—go for it.

A general rule of thumb with the Madefor method is to do whatever helps you stick with the Challenge.

Keep in mind, however, that although water is vital, it's not magical. Water pseudoscience can be found anywhere you look, and it powers a lot of misconceptions around hydration.

While there's no one-size-fits-all experience, this month's Challenge is unlikely to raise your IQ or prevent cancer, so let's dispel a few common myths upfront.

Common Hydration Myths:

Drinking water sheds pounds.
There's no direct evidence that water consumption triggers weight loss. But more importantly, losing weight isn't the focus of a hydration practice—or your Madefor journey. The goal is to create greater awareness of how drinking water makes you feel so that your brain and body are in positive alignment.

Dark urine is a sure sign that you're dehydrated.
In the urine-color spectrum, anything from pale straw–colored to yellow is considered normal and healthy. Dark urine may signal dehydration, but it can also occur from eating certain foods, like berries, beets, rhubarb, and anything containing dyes. Multivitamins and medications can also cause urine discoloration. Your doctor can help you make the best determination.

Water is the secret to beautiful skin.
Skin cells, like every other cell in your body, are made of water and need it to function. But water reaches all your other organs before it meets your skin. So until research finds differently, the best way to a radiant glow might just be a good moisturizer.

Only water can hydrate me properly.
Actually, water-rich foods (e.g., fruits and vegetables, especially watermelon, strawberries, cucumbers, and lettuce) are an important part of your diet and can be very hydrating. The Institute of Medicine estimates that we meet about 20% of our hydration needs from foods and liquid beverages. In other words, there are plenty of roads to proper hydration, but water is one of the quickest and easiest routes.

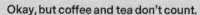

✕ Okay, but coffee and tea don't count.

Actually, they do. But there's a caveat. It was once thought that caffeine was dehydrating because of its diuretic properties, which lead to an increased loss of water and electrolytes in urination. But new studies find that caffeinated beverages are actually not dehydrating. They're just not an effective way to meet your body's fluid needs. So enjoy your morning Joe, but do like the Italians do and have a glass of water with every cup.

✕ How about beer?

An ice-cold beer on a summer day can quench your thirst, but keep in mind the potential trade-offs. Alcohol, depending on the type and amount you consume, can be very dehydrating.

✕ A pinch of salt in my water makes it extra hydrating.

This may benefit marathon runners, ultra-endurance athletes, or individuals who are extremely dehydrated. But that is not the case for most of us. In fact, Americans consume an enormous amount of sodium: 3,400 mg (about 1.5 teaspoons of salt) per day. The Centers for Disease Control and Prevention recommends we consume less than 2,300 mg. So you probably don't need to add more sodium to your diet. However, if a dash of salt in your water helps to keep you on track with the Challenge, go for it.

Again, the key is to do whatever helps you to complete the Challenge. And sometimes hydration hacks, like a pinch of salt, can be valuable tools that let you reclaim control on days when life throws a curveball at your best intentions.

For instance, if you prefer soda and juice to water, an easy hack is to add fresh fruit or herbal tea (lemon, spearmint, hibiscus) to your bottle to enhance the flavor. Some Madefor members fill up their bottle immediately after finishing it, even if they're not thirsty yet, as a way to always be prepared—like never letting your tank run on empty.

Madefor co-founder Dossett used to have a common routine in which he'd wake up and pour himself a cup of coffee to quench his thirst. Although mentally stimulating, caffeine isn't hydrating enough to make up for the water we lose in the form of sweat and exhalation during sleep (and if you're a mouth-breather you lose almost twice as much as a nose-breather). Dossett's water hack is to place a full bottle on his nightstand. Now, he downs a bottle when he wakes up before rewarding himself with coffee.

"I drink water first thing because I know my body really needs it—I've learned that lesson the hard way," he says. A tiny shift in his routine springs him into action, gives him more control over his day, and creates an easy win that sets in motion additional positive habits.

Small changes.

One at a time.

This is how our brain learns best.

This is how you build a growth mindset. Anyone can do it—no military training necessary.

➢ **Fig. 3**
*Small changes, one at a time,
lead to lasting change.*

Let's Do This

You now have everything you need to begin your first Madefor Challenge. This leg of your journey may seem simple, but if you commit to each of the practices, carrying them out just as they were scientifically designed, your destination will be extraordinary.

In fact, we're so excited about your second Challenge that we want to leave you with a hint: If water is crucial for your body to flourish and function at its best, your next Challenge will allow your mind to flourish and function at its best.

We promise, it will be life-changing.

Pat's Hydration Guidance

At the outset of Madefor you set an intention for what you hope to achieve through this program—take a moment now to reflect on and record how engaging this challenge might help serve your intention.

I'm always delighted but never surprised when Members tell me how life-changing the Hydration Challenge is.

Sometimes, it's about the water—*my doctor has been telling me for years to drink more water and I've always ignored her, but this time I actually did it and I'm feeling so much better!!*

But, more often than not, it's about something else—*I never realized how much I ignored my own needs to serve others. I never realized how much of my life was due to inertia. I've grown so disconnected from my body, no more.*

When you force yourself to slow down and pay attention, amazing things happen. As you engage this Challenge, I hope you do so from a place of curiosity, staying open to the connections you might make, be they about water or something much deeper.

If you find yourself disengaging or falling off track this month, I recommend finding the smallest possible step you can take to get back on track—can you fill one bottle, write one sentence? If a step is too hard, revisit your intention for inspiration. You got this.

**I recommend listening to the Basecamp I did with Dr. Ayelet Fishbach or at least reading the summary (Basecamp Highlights Section of Book). One of her central findings is directly applicable to your entire Madefor journey: When it comes to completing your goals and staying motivated, how much you enjoy the process of working toward your goal matters more than how meaningful your goal is. Each of the Madefor Challenges is helping you connect with your capacity to generate rewards and experience joy by engaging small acts within your control. Or, as Dr. Huberman likes to say, true wellbeing is simply feeling good while doing things that are good for you.

For additional support, check out my Perspectives video for more information around how we designed this Challenge, recommendations on how to approach the daily exercises, and real-life experiences and perspectives from Madefor Members that have completed the journey. Or, listen to this quick Campfire Story for a little inspiration.

*Madefor Videos and Audio recordings can be found on our YouTube page (https://www.youtube.com/@getmadefor)

Madefor gratitude

Find the good

We first shared this Challenge in early 2018, with a few close friends and family, some of whom you'll read about shortly. While we knew it would spread joy, we're surprised and delighted that people are still reaching out to share stories about the positive impact this Challenge continues to have.

We're confident that you'll have a similar experience, and we can't wait to hear your stories, too.

This month, as you honor the good in your life, pay close attention to the subtle shifts in how you engage with the world and how the world engages with you. This Challenge may very well change your life.

Go make some waves,

BLAKE & PAT

◆ The Basics

The black-and-tan package sat on Cullen Aderhold's desk, in the study of his Dallas home, for six months. It had arrived, out of the blue, as a New Year's gift from an old friend. Among the enclosures were a note of thanks for his friendship, an essay about gratitude, and a challenge: Pick someone who has had a meaningful and lasting impact on your life, handwrite a letter to this person, then visit them and read your letter aloud.

As a 38-year-old married father of two with a busy career in real estate, Aderhold had so much to be thankful for. But of all the people who had played a meaningful role in his life, how could he pick just one? And when was there time to handwrite a personal letter?

Not now, he thought. Not with his 3-year-old son tugging on his pant leg and his wife needing a break from caring for their 1-year-old daughter. I'll get to this next weekend, he decided.

Next weekend was even busier. Weeks turned to months. Then, one day in June, he ran into the friend who'd sent the package.

"The letter is sitting on my desk right now," Aderhold told him. "I look at it every day. I want to write it to my paternal grandfather, but I just haven't done it yet."

Aderhold explained that Dadpaw, as he called him, was 91 and living in a retirement community with his beloved wife, who was suffering from late-stage Alzheimer's. Dadpaw was a kind, generous man who had a profound influence on his children and grandchildren. Now that he was caring for a spouse who no longer recognized him, he probably needed a reminder of how much his family appreciated him.

"That's amazing," his friend replied. "It's going to mean the world to him. But your window is closing. If he passes away, you'll always regret not telling him how you feel."

Later at home, he couldn't get the words out of his mind: Your window is closing. That Saturday, during a rare stretch when nothing could steal his attention, Aderhold sat alone at his desk to write. He composed for 20 minutes nonstop. When he was done, he called Dadpaw.

"I have something I want to share with you," he said. "Are you free next weekend?" The following Saturday, he buckled up his son in the car and drove to his grandfather's retirement home in Fort Worth. The old man greeted them at his door, wearing his usual uniform of polyester slacks and button-down shirt, his bifocals case snug in his breast pocket. After lunch and a visit with Grandma in the Alzheimer's wing, they sat facing one another at the coffee table while Aderhold's son played with his toys.

"Dadpaw, I wrote you a letter," he said, pulling it out of his pocket. Dadpaw sat up straight. Aderhold cleared his throat and began to read. He explained that he'd been talking to a friend about gratitude, and it got him thinking about the most important people in his life. "I want to tell you some things that I appreciate about you," he read, "which I didn't want to go unsaid."

He thanked Dadpaw for being a virtuous and honest man. For quietly performing good deeds without expecting anything in return. For helping friends and strangers alike, through his church, the local hospital, and the Rotary club. And for modeling to Aderhold's dad the character traits and life lessons that were passed down to him.

"You are the best example of a man," he said, "and I'm so grateful to have you as a role model."

When he got to the end, he folded the letter back into the envelope and handed it to his grandfather. Dadpaw was always pretty stoic—definitely not the crying type. But Aderhold could see that his eyes were misty with pride.

"Thank you," he said as he took the letter and hugged him, adding a tight squeeze at the end, as he always did. When they embraced, Aderhold felt something startling, like a jolt of electricity shooting through his body. "It was like lightning in a bottle," he recently recalled. "That's the only way I can describe it."

There are some things in life—love, hope, faith—that we cannot see and yet we feel them so strongly that we know they exist. In that moment, Aderhold felt as if there were an invisible bond connecting him and his grandfather.

"I felt like I'd just done something so cool that I would remember for the rest of my life," Aderhold says. "And for that couple of hours, it was just between my granddad and me."

While the spiritual impact of their experience is impossible to measure scientifically, we know with scientific certainty that their brains and bodies underwent a profound physiological response. They were under the powerful, life-changing influence of gratitude.

Now, it's your turn to create your own "lightning in a bottle" experience. This month, you're going to develop a simple Gratitude practice that has the potential to bring tremendous life-changing benefits to you and to the people you care about.

In a 2015 Scientific American article, researchers revisited the 24 character strengths and virtues that most contribute to human flourishing, first identified in 2004 by psychologists Christopher Peterson and Martin Seligman. The traits include such heavy-hitters as love, spirituality, creativity, social intelligence, and self-control, and yet the single best predictor of overall wellbeing was gratitude.

Gratitude is the act of giving thanks. In its highest form it's also an orientation—a state of being in which one is able to recognize the good things in life even during difficult times. Philosophers from Buddha to Plato have extolled gratitude as a virtue—and thanks to decades of scientific research, we know that gratitude also exerts a powerful influence over our social, physical, and mental health.

Socially, gratitude is the glue that binds us. In a 2009 study, scientists used functional magnetic resonance imaging on participants as they experienced different emotions. They found that gratitude activates brain regions that govern feelings of reward and the formation of social bonds. Researchers even refer to it as the "find, remind, and bind" emotion: Gratitude helps us "find" people who are good candidates for quality future relationships; it helps "remind" us of the goodness of our existing relationships; and it "binds" us to our partners.

A growing body of literature suggests that being grateful improves our physical health. A 2015 study of 186 people with heart disease found that individuals who scored high on gratitude orientation also reported better moods, sounder sleep, and lower levels of fatigue and the kind of cellular inflammation that can worsen the progression of heart failure.

In a study of 115 women at University College London, participants who started a gratitude diary were rewarded with better sleep and lowered blood pressure. Another study of 962 Swiss adults found that grateful people reported better overall physical health, in part, because of their greater psychological health, their propensity for engaging in healthy activities, and their willingness to seek help for their health problems.

Even more promising are gratitude's proven mental benefits. As Aderhold discovered, gratitude can induce a natural euphoria.

In fact, the electric feeling he experienced didn't start in his arms as he embraced his grandfather—it began in his brain.

In a classic gratitude study from 1998, researchers measured the baseline cortisol and DHEA levels of 45 healthy adults. (DHEA is a naturally occurring hormone that acts like an antidepressant; cortisol, a stress hormone, helps to trigger our fight-or-flight response, yet chronically elevated levels can lead to depression, poor immune function, weight gain, and a host of other health problems.) Next, researchers trained 30 participants on mental techniques to replace negative thought patterns with feelings of compassion and appreciation. The remaining 15 subjects acted as controls and did not undergo gratitude training.

After one month, everyone's hormone levels were retested. The control subjects showed little to no change. **But the subjects who underwent gratitude training had a 23% reduction in cortisol levels and a remarkable 100% increase in the feel-good DHEA hormone.**

"This is the study I always turn to when it comes to gratitude because it's not just about the positive thoughts you're having—it's also about the negative things you're not thinking about," says Madefor advisor and Stanford University neuroscientist Dr. Andrew Huberman. "Gratitude downshifts the negative and upshifts the positive."

Research has exploded since this early study, providing new evidence that gratitude improves happiness, self-esteem, and resilience; lowers stress, depression, and anxiety; and may provide benefits for individuals who are in recovery for substance abuse and for post-traumatic stress disorder.

What's less understood, however, is the underlying mechanism of gratitude—how is it working in our brains?

"Most of the mechanistic understanding about the brain comes from animal studies—and there's no way you could know if a mouse was in gratitude," Huberman says. There are, however, strong inferences as to why it works: "Gratitude taps into our basic reward systems associated with love and connection. It activates the neurons and hormone systems that produce DHEA, that produce oxytocin," a hormone that plays a role in social bonding. "In other words," Huberman says, "the thoughts and feelings that we call 'gratitude' tap into very powerful, self-generating reward mechanisms."

When Aderhold wrote the gratitude letter to his grandfather, he experienced a strong, internally generated reward via a surge of dopamine, the chemical that tells your brain: This feels good, do it more! Then, when he read the letter to Dadpaw, his actions were reinforced with a blast of oxytocin (what he described as "electricity"), which is one of the fastest ways to promote neuroplasticity (positive brain change), improve brain function, and build a stronger mindset.

"Mental health is multidimensional and supported through a variety of things, such as strong relationships, good sleep, proper nutrition and, if needed, therapy," says Huberman.

"Gratitude is just one piece of achieving mental health—but we know that it's a very powerful one."

Given the extraordinary benefits that gratitude bestows on our brains and bodies, establishing a gratitude practice may be one of the least costly and most accessible forms of natural medicine that every one of us has the ability to tap into.

> **Fig. 1**
> *Gratitude provides exponential
> mental, physical, and social benefits.*

By now, you recognize that creating greater awareness around small physical acts, such as drinking water, connects your brain and body in a positive way. This month, you're going to build on what you've learned by creating greater awareness around small mental acts. **The Gratitude practices you'll engage in for the next 21 days will help you to recognize the good in your own life and honor the goodness in other people.**

The Challenge

Your Gratitude Challenge Exercises:

21 Days of Gratitude:
21 days of Gratitude: For 21 consecutive days, write down at least one thing for which you are thankful for in your Journal.

Silver Lining Essay:
Think about a time in your life when you experienced a major setback and reframe it to see the Silver Lining. Write about it in your Journal.

Gratitude Cards:
Use special postcards to send a note of thanks to three people in your life.

Gratitude Letter and Visit:
Use special stationary to write a letter to someone who has helped you. Visit that person, read the letter, and hand it to them. If you can't visit in person, read it to them in the most intimate way possible (Skype, FaceTime, phone call, recorded message) before mailing the letter.

Before we get to your Challenge, a reminder: Gratitude is not soft stuff. It's a character strength that enhances your wellbeing and benefits society as a whole.

"Some people claim that gratitude is just about thinking nice thoughts and expecting good things," writes psychologist Dr. Robert Emmons. "In fact, gratitude can be very difficult because it requires that you recognize your dependence on others."

As the leading scientific expert on gratitude, Emmons cautions us that "gratitude is not just a nice, warm, fuzzy feeling." It can also stir up such complicated emotions as indebtedness and humbleness. And yet, as with any challenging endeavor, the payoff can be tremendous. As Aderhold discovered, taking 20 minutes to write a letter can enrich your life and uplift your relationships in transformative ways.

The magnitude of your own experience will depend on the effort you expend. So dive in, because you're about to participate in one of the most beneficial mental health practices that science has to offer.

Let's begin with your **21 Days of Gratitude** exercise. Tonight, before bed, open your **Journal** and write down one thing that happened today for which you're grateful: Did a friend do something special for you? Were you pleasantly surprised by an unexpected gift? Did you benefit in any way because of someone else's actions?

For maximum results, write with as much specificity as possible. For example: *My partner left the last splash of milk for my coffee and I felt a small zing of love for her; the dog walker left a funny note about the things my dog did at the park today and it made me laugh; my hands were full when a young man held the door open for me and I'm embarrassed that I forgot to thank him.*

Specificity helps to ensure a strong dopamine release that taps into your brain's attention-reward-reinforcement loop.

"The body doesn't really know the difference between a real and an imagined experience, at the level of your physiology," Huberman says. "So the more vividly you can picture an experience—for example, if you can actually visualize your dog walker writing a note—the greater likelihood that positive hormones will be released and negative hormones will be suppressed."

"Madefor is instilling the importance of journaling in us and it's already becoming easier to practice. I used to view journaling as just writing random stuff in a private diary under lock and key. Now, I understand that it's more about reflecting with intention and that just putting pen to paper is powerful. I am grateful to be getting the hang of this whole journaling thing in my own way."

— Bryan G

You should write in your Journal at whatever time works best for your schedule. However, studies indicate that an evening gratitude practice promotes better and longer sleep. After all, if you're focusing on the people and things you're thankful for, you have less opportunity to ruminate on problems at work, issues with your kids, that thing your mother said—all the usual late-night worries.

Huberman keeps an evening gratitude practice in which he reflects on three questions before going to bed: What's a way in which I served someone today, what's a way in which somebody helped me, and how can I be better tomorrow?

"What's striking to me," he says, "is just how much we can shift our mental states when we start doing these things. It has certainly improved my life."

In fact, Emmons found that study subjects who kept a weekly gratitude journal were 25% happier after ten weeks compared to subjects who were told to list life's hassles.

What does 25% happier look like? Participants in the gratitude study reported higher levels of empathy, alertness, enthusiasm, determination, attentiveness, and energy compared with participants who wrote about a "messy kitchen no one will clean," "doing a favor for a friend who didn't appreciate it," or "stupid people driving." An added bonus: Grateful subjects also had fewer health problems and exercised 1.5 hours more per week.

Conversely, individuals who exist in chronic states of stress and negative emotions are more likely to develop coronary heart disease, immune system depletion, and poor mental health. Gratitude is the antidote. Gratitude blocks the toxic emotions that can wreak havoc on our bodies, minds, and relationships.

When you're journaling, if you find yourself returning to negative emotions like envy, resentment, or regret—put down the pen. As Emmons notes, our brains are comparison-making machines, constantly thinking about the way things are and how they might have gone differently for us—a compulsion that can poison a disposition of gratitude. You can stop the compulsion. It just takes shifting perspective and recognizing the simple gifts—clean clothes, a warm bed, enough food to eat—that you possess in abundance.

When you live in a state of gratitude, it doesn't mean that everything is easier, or that you never feel the pressure and pain of daily living. It just means that you can see the world with a broader frame of reference and refocus on what's important. This is where your Silver Lining Essay comes in.

Your Silver Lining Essay is an evidence-based strategy for training your mind to think differently. Your Essay needn't be formal. You can write a few paragraphs or a few pages directly in your Journal. What's critical is to conjure an event from your past when something didn't go the way you were hoping. Then reframe it to find the good. Maybe it was the worst day of your life when it happened, but now, with time and healing, you can see the positive consequences. Did you grow as a person? Did it open up deeper communication with loved ones? Did it give you perspective about your life's course?

Madefor co-founder Blake Mycoskie trained all his young life to be a tennis player until an Achilles tendon tear at 19 ended his dreams of going pro. Now, when he looks back, he recognizes this trauma as the event that led him to discover his entrepreneurial talents. During his six months on crutches, Mycoskie couldn't carry his laundry down to the basement washing machines, and he couldn't find a laundromat that would pick up and deliver. The dirty clothes piled up until Mycoskie started a door-to-door delivery service that filled a much-needed niche in his college town. Ten years—and several businesses later—he founded the prosocial, global footwear company TOMS Shoes.

"This horrible injury, the end of my tennis career and all that I'd been working for, felt so negative at the time. But now I think: Who knows where I might have been had it not happened?" Mycoskie says. "Maybe I would have just played tennis instead of getting all this experience from age 19 to 29, which allowed me to start TOMS."

The past struggle you choose to reflect on needn't be as life-altering as Mycoskie's was. It just needs to be an episode that feels unresolved—something that still evokes a trace of pain. Maybe it's the time your heart was broken, or you were fired from a good job, or you behaved poorly and hurt a friend. How did the experience open a door for you to meet your current spouse, switch gears to a more meaningful career path, or resolve to change harmful behaviors? Can you see how your current life situation turned out better than you thought it would at the time?

When you sit down to write, give yourself a private space, free of distractions. Think deeply on the past and trace a line from the setback you experienced to the good that ultimately resulted. As Huberman suggests, the more vividly you place yourself in the story, the greater brain rewards you'll reap.

"I think of a gratitude practice like an exercise practice," he says. "In other words, you can do jumping jacks where you're just flopping up and down and probably get some minor benefit. But it's not going to be much. Whereas if you really put your attention on it, and snap those jumping jacks up there, you're going to get a very different effect on your cardiovascular system. It's the same thing with gratitude: Nothing gets results in the brain like specificity."

Your Silver Lining Essay also trains your brain to better respond to future negative events. We all know people who go through the same stressful episodes—holidays with the in-laws, fender benders, dinner-table arguments—yet respond very differently. When you practice finding the silver lining, your brain gets better at something called **cognitive reappraisal**, a strategy for down-shifting your emotional reactions.

You likely engage in cognitive reappraisals all the time. It's when you **take an event that's fraught with negative emotions and choose to respond in a neutral or positive way.** The physician who left you waiting for 20 minutes? Doctor, you must be having a busy day, but I'm happy to finally be able to see you. Your touchy teenager who stares daggers when you ask how her day was? It seems like you're not in the mood to talk. That's okay, I'm here if you change your mind. The crazy soccer dad who's yelling at the referee? He's going through a bad divorce; let's talk to him privately, but cut him some slack.

➤ **Fig. 2**
*Cognitive reappraisal keeps you focused
on the good even in trying situations.*

Cognitive reappraisal isn't about pretending that everything in life is perfect. It's about calmly appraising negative experiences and exerting greater cognitive and emotional control over how you respond to them. These are the traits of good leaders, smart parents, and thoughtful partners.

Your first two Challenge exercises are designed to help you see the good in your life. The next two turn your attention outward to honor the people who've made a difference in your life. Over the next three weeks, send three **Gratitude Cards** to people who deserve your thanks (identify your own cards or postcards with postage for mailing). Identify and use your own special stationery to write a longer **Gratitude Letter** to someone who had a profound impact on you.

It may be tempting to send emails instead of your Gratitude Cards. But think about the last time you received a thank-you email. It probably arrived while you were busy with work or rushing out the door. It's likely that the sender's sentiments were appreciated but quickly forgotten.

Now, imagine the recipient of your Card going to their mailbox and finding your handwritten note among the catalogs and credit card offers. Physical mail conveys a deeper level of respect and intention on your part than simply clicking "send." So choose three people who provided help that changed your life in some small way, then write a few lines of text to properly honor them:

1. Reflect on the gift they gave you.
2. Recognize the goodness of the gift and the giver.
3. Thank them for their help.

It's not enough to say, "Thanks for being there." Instead, tell them what they did that moved you. For example: *When I was sick at home with a cold, you took time out of your busy day to bring me chicken soup. That was awesome. I'm so grateful for your friendship.* Or maybe it's: *Whenever I see you, you ask how I'm doing and make me feel cared for. Thanks for being a good listener—and for always giving me great haircuts.*

Expressing gratitude takes minutes out of your day, but the impact can last a lifetime, spreading ripples of goodwill in your personal and professional relationships. In Aderhold's case, his grandfather showed the Gratitude Letter to everyone who visited him, and he mentioned it multiple times—that was some letter!—to his own son, who in turn told Aderhold how proud he'd made him.

"We're a very close family," he says. "But this resonated among different levels of my family and tied us together." A single act of gratitude had a ripple effect on three generations of men.

- MEMBER MOMENT-

"The Gratitude Challenge was my favorite and also most daunting month. Writing the cards, sending them, and reading the letter outloud to my person was terrifying. But, since then, when I'm having a bad day, I sit down and think about the things in my life that I am grateful for. It definitely helps me get past negative events." - Shelly W

When you're ready to tackle your own **Gratitude Letter and Visit**, think about the individuals from whom you've received guidance or gifts that have changed your life. Are there relatives who took a special interest in your wellbeing? Was there a coach or teacher who always pushed you to be your best? Is there someone special in your life who, if they were gone tomorrow, you'd regret that you hadn't thanked them?

For Arlington, Texas, octogenarian Sharon Clements, the question was more a matter of: Who should I thank for getting me through an illness I almost didn't survive? In 2016, three days before Christmas, Clements contracted a nasty viral infection that sent her to the hospital for 16 days, then a rehab center for another 16 days, then finally home, where she was now dependent on an oxygen tank in order to get enough air into her lungs.

"It just threw me into a tailspin," Clements recalls. "I was really depressed for a while, the deepest valley you ever saw."

Around New Year's 2017, Clements had received the black-and-tan gratitude mailer from a friend but didn't do anything about it right away because she was still recovering. "But I have five children, 15 grandchildren, and eight great-grandchildren," Clement says. "I eventually said to my husband, Walt: 'We need to do this. We have so much to be grateful for.'" She wrote and read letters to each of her children, thanking them for their support and love while she was sick. Then she wrote a letter to her Sunday school class, and to the person who gave her the mailer, and to family members at Thanksgiving, and "it just kind of snowballed from there," Clements says.

She approached the practice with so much **attention** that the feel-good **rewards** she received in her brain **reinforced** the experience to the point where gratitude became an effortless habit—a trait, not just a state. Clements went from being depressed and mired in self-pity to seeing the beauty in life, especially within her own marriage. Some mornings, she says, she'll ask Alexa to "play love music," just so she and her "wonderful, handsome husband" can dance in the kitchen.

> ➤ **Fig. 3A**
> *Gratitude can have*
> *ripple effects...*

> **Fig. 3B**
> *...that touch the lives of people
> you've never even met*

In fact, gratitude is a major factor in marriages that flourish. Dr. John Gottman, a marriage counselor and researcher from the University of Washington, has been studying couples for 40 years, and he's boiled marriage success down to a 5:1 ratio: For every one negative expression (complaints, eye-rolls, frowns, put-downs) couples engage in, there needs to be five positive interactions (compliments, hand-holding, smiles, kind gestures).

What could be easier than thinking of different ways to tell your partner that you appreciate them? You can leave a note of thanks on the kitchen counter when they pull an all-nighter with the baby, help you finish a work project, or bring you hot coffee when yours has gone cold. Or, like Sharon and Walt, you can put on some love music and dance in the kitchen when the spirit of gratitude moves you.

You possess an unlimited capacity to feel and express gratitude. Continue this valuable practice by sharing your joy with others, and the rewards will come back to you tenfold.

Let's Do This

If gratitude ranks as the single most effective indicator of well-being, this month's Challenge has the potential to transform your life and your relationships. The Journal, Essay, Cards, and Letter exercises were designed to draw you into a temporary state of gratitude, again and again, in order to help you establish the trait of gratitude.

For some, gratitude will come easily. For others, it may be a struggle. The truth is, we are hardwired to expend greater neural activity around bad thoughts than good ones. Negativity bias is a survival mechanism, a primitive-brain response that helped our ancestors sniff out danger: Is that a tiger behind those bushes? Is that caveman coming to share his food or steal mine?

But when you engage in gratitude exercises, you're redirecting your modern-day brain to lower the volume of your primitive brain. You're reframing your point of focus to appreciate the good in your life. And you're actively choosing to not get emotionally tethered to the small hassles—bad traffic, messy roommates, and on and on—which aren't a danger at all.

This may feel challenging at times, but when you're struggling to find new ways to say "thanks" or if the Essay feels too painful to write, it means you're making progress.

"Frustration and struggle may actually be the early stages of neuroplasticity," Huberman says. "They're a sign that your brain is trying new strategies."

So lean into that frustration. It's a marker of growth. In fact, the greater your initial feelings of resistance, the greater your development will be. Soon, a grateful outlook comes easily. You can adjust your horizons and weather adversity. You're better equipped to learn from failure and create solutions. All of which points to a healthier, happier mindset.

Today, you are planting new seeds—positive traits and habits—that will grow as you continue to nurture them. The Gratitude exercises you'll take part in over the next 21 days have the potential to ripple out in waves to friends, family, and people you've never even met.

Let's Begin!

Pat's Gratitude Guidance

At the outset of Madefor you set an intention for what you hope to achieve through this program—take a moment to reflect on and record how engaging this challenge might help serve your intention.

It's easy to put this Challenge aside for another day. But the opportunity you have to share your gratitude might not be here tomorrow.

A couple of years ago, a Member chose the most difficult person she could think of for her gratitude letter—her mother-in-law. As soon as she sat down and began to read her letter aloud, bitterness and tension dissipated. For the first time ever, kindness replaced animosity in their relationship. With one act, the Member transformed not only the dynamic with her mother-in-law but also with her husband, children, and other family members. Everything was better. One month later, the mother-in-law passed away unexpectedly.

Put this Challenge aside for another day and your opportunity may pass, forever.

If you struggle to stay on track this month, consider taking this small step—can you write one sentence, find one positive thought, or say two words of gratitude to yourself (and mean it)? If a step is too hard, revisit your intention for inspiration. You got this.

**I recommend <u>listening to the Basecamp</u> I did with Dr. Vanessa Bohns or at least <u>reading the summary</u> (Basecamp Highlights Section of Book). One of her central findings is directly applicable to your Gratitude Challenge: you have more influence than you think. The small acts of kindness you engage in this month have very real and positive effects in the world, reaching not just those you interact with but cascading across all of the lives those people touch as well.

For additional support, check out my <u>Perspectives video</u> for more information around how we designed this Challenge, recommendations on how to approach the daily exercises, and real-life experiences and perspectives from Madefor Members that have completed the journey. Or, listen to this quick <u>Campfire Story</u> for a little inspiration.

*Madefor Videos and Audio recordings can be found on our YouTube page (https://www.youtube.com/@getmadefor)

Fuel up!

Our Challenges are designed to make you pause. You've probably noticed this happening already. Maybe you paused and reached for water instead of aspirin the last time you had a headache. Or you paused to see an opportunity, instead of a hassle, when a problem came your way. These moments reflect the effort and the progress you're making, so keep up the good work.

This month's Challenge introduces a new kind of pause that will fundamentally alter the way you engage with food. We can't wait for you to experience the enhanced energy, greater cognitive function, and powerful sense of agency that comes with developing an acute awareness of how the way you eat affects the way you feel.

Fad diets be gone—it's time to reconnect with the foods that serve you best.

Let's eat!

BLAKE & PAT

The Basics

When Madefor advisor Andrew Huberman was just 19, he vowed to become a successful neuroscientist.

"I approached my scientific career like a professional athlete approaches their sport," he recalls. "I decided: 'I want to be the best-in-class at this thing. I'm going to be a tenured professor at Stanford or Harvard one day, and no one's going to stop me.'"

In college, he studied constantly, ran lab experiments into the night, and rose early to do it all over again. Unlike an athlete, however, he'd failed to consider how his eating habits affected his performance. Huberman's mealtimes were unpredictable, his food choices were erratic, and his energy levels suffered. At one point, he drank so much coffee that he landed in the emergency room with liver toxicity.

"I was 25. The doctor thought I was an alcoholic—but I didn't even drink," he recalls. He quit coffee but started downing Red Bulls, trading one vice for another, and putting his body and mind in a constant battle between fatigue and hyperactivity.

Tired of being tired, Huberman took a hard look at his nutritional habits and decided to eat with **intention**. He also paid close **attention** to his cognitive function after meals; he began to better notice his body's cues of hunger; and he figured out which foods made him feel alert and calm and which ones made him feel sleepy.

For example, he discovered that certain meats, nuts, and vegetables gave him energy and allowed him to skip coffee in the morning. He found that fruit made him feel jittery, so he ate less of it. Starchy foods affected his brain and body in such a way that he enjoyed them mostly in the evenings, unless he had a strenuous morning workout, after which he needed starchy foods to help stabilize his blood sugar.

Soon, Huberman was eating exactly what his mind and body needed, in amounts that felt right for him. As a result, he had a spring in his step, sustained energy all day, and deep, restful sleep at night.

"Under typical conditions, everyone has their mid-morning or mid-afternoon dip. I could avoid that almost entirely. Not every time. But by being able to sleep well at night, I could also be more alert throughout the day," Huberman says of the eating style he still practices today as an award-winning neuroscientist and tenured professor at Stanford.

It's important to point out what Huberman did not do. He didn't go on a trendy diet. He didn't ban whole food groups. He didn't rely on a single "magic" nutrient. He still enjoys ice cream, bread, pasta, chocolate—and eats pretty much whatever he wants. The difference is that he became acutely aware of how food affects his body and mind—and from there he made conscious decisions about what, when, and how much to eat.

"I'm a big believer," he says, "that having a cognitive recognition of what's going on when you encounter food is really important." Unfortunately, what's going on when most of us encounter food is that we tend to go a little unconscious.

From the moment you were born, eating was an instinctive act. You honored your biological hunger, ate as much as you needed, and stopped when you were satisfied.

Best of all, food was pleasurable! Anyone who's ever watched a toddler try his first taste of mashed bananas can attest that humans have a tremendous capacity to derive enjoyment from food. Yet somewhere along the way to adulthood, most of us started to look outside ourselves for answers.

In America, we rely on nutrition-policy recommendations that change from decade to decade (looking at you, Food Guide Pyramid). We make impulse buys at the supermarket, thanks to snack-food makers that pay billions of dollars in slotting fees to ensure attention-getting shelf placement. We swear by the life-changing benefits of a single ingredient, never appreciating the dynamic interplay between ingredients and our individual physiology.

To compensate for our diminishing agency, we adopt rule-bound regimens that promise to cleanse, reboot, and reset our bodies: From no-carb, keto, and paleo regimens that deny our tastes and preferences to cleanses and other fasting fads that ask us to ignore our body's cues to the point where we don't even recognize what hunger feels like anymore.

These short-term solutions might seem effective at first, but they don't create enduring change. Anyone can follow the money to see that quick fixes are failing us. Americans spend $70 billion a year on commercial endeavors that literally promise to teach us how to eat. How did our brains and bodies become so divorced from the most elemental act we were born knowing how to do without any outside help?

"Diet culture is very loud. And when you start listening to the voice of diet culture, you're doing so at the expense of your own biology and unique needs," says noted author, dietitian, and Madefor advisor Evelyn Tribole. **A better plan, she says, is to develop awareness around your unique eating preferences and patterns.**

Around the same time that Huberman was setting out on his dream of becoming a neuroscientist, Tribole and her colleague

Elyse Resch published *Intuitive Eating*, a pioneering book that's given rise to over 200 studies showing benefit and more than 800 certified intuitive eating counselors in 22 countries.

The premise is powerful yet simple:

Listen to your body. It already knows what, when, and how much to eat.

"As you get more and more connected, you not only trust your body better, you also trust other aspects in your life as you're making decisions," Tribole says. "It becomes life-changing."

This isn't hyperbole. Research indicates that individuals who practice intuitive eating have higher "interoceptive awareness," the ability to detect and interpret sensations arising within the body, such as a full bladder, changes in heart rate, muscle contractions, and more.

You developed interoceptive awareness, for example, during your Hydration Challenge when you tuned in to your sensations of thirst and rewarded yourself with a drink of water. (Practitioners of mindful meditation also test higher in interoceptive aware-ness—a benefit we'll explore in future Madefor Challenges.)

Studies show that being able to discern your body's signals (e.g. *I feel full*) and then respond appropriately (*This will be my last bite*) leads to enhanced insight, personal agency, and overall wellbeing.

On the other hand, people with poor interoceptive awareness tend to have higher rates of anxiety, addiction, mood disorders, eating disorders, and other somatic illnesses.

"I really believe it's a superpower," Tribole says, "because if we can start listening to our bodies, we already have all the information we need."

When Huberman started listening to his body, he was rewarded with improved energy, better sleep, and the capacity to operate at his best. But you don't have to be a scientist to generate pleasure and clarity around food. You just need to tune in to your body's innate wisdom.

> ➤ **Fig. 1**
> *Increased interoceptive awareness*
> *leads to greater overall wellbeing.*

The Challenge

For the next 21 days, your Challenge is to become a food anthropologist—a neutral observer who records your experiences without judgment. This month's practice, rooted in the tenets of *Intuitive Eating*, will awaken your natural-born ability to eat in a way that satisfies and respects your body and all the things it can do for you when it is properly nourished.

Before we get to the Challenge exercises, a quick perception check. Imagine for a moment that your bladder is starting to feel full. You're even a little uncomfortable. Soon, your body is sending you urgent signals that you really have to go *now*.

Would you think: *Nope, that's not allowed after 8 p.m.* Or *I just went an hour ago; I can't possibly need to go again.* Would you ignore your aches because nobody else is going to the bathroom right now?

Of course not. But that's how many of us act when we follow rigid food rules (*no eating before noon, no sugar, no carbs*), with little regard for our direct experience of taste, hunger, and satisfaction.

Having a militant approach to food is a sure path toward disap- pointment because you interact with it every day, several times a day. Slip-ups are inevitable. Even if you successfully follow the rules—at what cost? Will you never eat a slice of cake at your child's birthday party or enjoy fresh pasta on that family trip to Italy?

So here goes: The first step to reclaiming your power is to banish the word "diet" from your vocabulary. For some, this is very easy and not a big deal. For others, it will feel counterin- tuitive to everything you believe. In fact, the diet industry has a $70 billion bet that you can't do it. But have no doubt: Diets are short-term fixes with long-term consequences.

Reviews of the scientific literature generally find two things:

1. Calorie-restrictive regimens lead to temporary weight loss.
2. That loss isn't maintained.

This applies to just about every trend that's dominating the headlines right now.

For example, in a famous study at Kansas State University, a nutrition professor lost 27 pounds in ten weeks by subsisting on 1,800 calories a day of Twinkies, Doritos, and Oreos. Even more confounding, his biomarkers of health went in all the right directions: His LDL cholesterol and triglycerides went down while his protective HDL cholesterol went up. To be clear, the professor wasn't extolling the virtues of Twinkies. He was simply disproving the idea that "bad foods" alone cause weight gain, and he wanted to show that all diets work in the short term because they force you to eat fewer calories than you expend.

A yearlong study at Stanford University recently tried to settle the war between low-fat versus low-carb enthusiasts: It's a tie, sort of. Study participants lost an average of 13 pounds on both approaches, yet there was great variability within the groups. Some lost upward of 60 pounds while others gained 15 to 20 pounds, underscoring the fact that one-size-fits-all formulas ignore human nature and physiology.

In fact, a growing number of scientists and academics believe that dieting is harmful. Case in point: a fascinating study of competitors on *The Biggest Loser*, a reality TV show in which contestants endure grueling weight loss and exercise pro-grams. Six years after they debuted their new physiques on the show's finale, 13 out of 14 participants had regained 70% of their lost weight. What's worse, four were even heavier than before the show; all of them were burning an average of 500 fewer calories per day than someone of similar size; and their levels of leptin, a hormone that promotes feelings of satiety, were half their pre-diet levels.

To add insult to injury, their muscle mass had also decreased an average of 10 pounds. It's no wonder that extreme dieting put their chemistry in crisis mode. The human body has finely tuned itself over time for survival. Ignore its cues at your own peril.

Even if you're already in great shape, intentionally going hungry may hurt your body in the long run. Numerous studies show that chronic dieters are more likely to become overweight in their later years.

In a 2006 report, researchers studied 1,838 Finnish male Olympians and professional athletes over 16 years, including 370 athletes who periodically dieted to meet the weight requirements of their sports (e.g., boxing, wrestling, weightlifting). They found that the dieting athletes were three times more likely to be obese by age 60 than their non-dieting peers.

Bottom line: There are thousands of eating styles and trends; they all work; *and* they all don't work.

While there's no single approach for everyone, in communities where people live the longest, researchers have found a few enduring practices:

- Eat in moderation.
- Consume more nutrient-dense foods (fruits, vegetables, nuts, fish) than processed foods.
- Eat for pleasure.

These simple habits are the common denominators of a healthy lifestyle—and a good place to land on the nutrition spectrum. **But before you can even begin to alter your nutritional patterns, you have to change your behavior.** Strict food rules ignore your unique preferences, put you at odds with your own body, and rob you of self-determination. Starting now, you're going to approach food from the inside out—no pills, protein shakes, or special tests needed.

During your Hydration Challenge, you developed greater awareness of how water made you feel. No one has to tell you what kind or how much to drink, because your body already knows. Likewise, with Fuel, you're going to develop greater awareness around food, reconnecting to what your body already knows about what kind and how much to eat.

For 21 days, complete a Food Log (using your Journal) so you can begin to identify your unique patterns. Here's an example of how a Food Log might look:

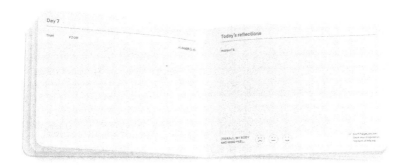

The first step is to get a clear read on your hunger cues. Rate your hunger before each meal on a scale of 1 to 5, with 1 being "not hungry" and 5 being "ravenous." If you've previously been a rules-based eater, your hunger may have been offline for so long that you don't recognize what it feels like anymore.

"Some people experience hunger just in their stomach. Others feel it more in their mood. Maybe you notice difficulty focusing and concentrating," Tribole says. "This is about taking a time-out, paying attention to what hunger feels like for you, and then honoring it before you get into an aversive, unpleasant kind of hunger."

It takes time, but listening to hunger actually helps you better detect *all* of your body's physiological cues (like subtle changes in your heart rate, circadian rhythms, blood pressure, digestive processes, and insulin levels) because you're simultaneously fine-tuning your interoceptive awareness.

You can actually boost this skill by paying close attention to all the physical sensations that arise in your body: a full bowel that feels unpleasant; thirst that originates in your throat and gives you a slight headache; a welcome sleepiness that starts in your lower back and is pleasing. As Tribole notes, picking up on these tiny bodily shifts is like cross-training for body-cue awareness.

As you start to recognize your full spectrum of hunger cues, you'll also get better at assessing satisfaction cues. This can be difficult for those of us who are members of the clean-plate club, ignoring our body's hints at fullness until they become glaring physical signs—distended bellies, indigestion, lethargy.

Next time, at the end of a meal, check in with your body and notice your feelings of fullness. Ask yourself: How would I have felt if I had stopped a few bites sooner? Notice the thoughts that arise, without judgment, and reflect on them in your Journal.

- MEMBER MOMENT -

"My focus has never been on food, it's really amazing what a few weeks of mindful eating can do for you. I am a stress eater, I can feel a shift, I'm finding other ways to deal with stress. I am so thankful for this challenge. It all starts in my mind." - Tara W

When you catch a glimpse of your Challenge Bracelet, Challenge Screen, or Challenge Card, let it be an enduring re-minder to pause and connect with each bite. As you become more attuned to your satiety tipping point, you'll internalize the sensation of fullness and stop naturally, even when there's still food on your plate.

If at the beginning of your Challenge, you notice lots of 1s and 2s in your Food Log, it may indicate that you're eating in the absence of internal hunger cues—a pattern worth reflecting upon. Do you eat because you feel stress, anger, competitiveness? All of us have had the experience of eating when we aren't hungry. Sometimes we're following social cues (*I'm at the movie theater with the kids—time for a large popcorn*); other times it's pure impulse (*how did I get to the bottom of this jar of nuts?*). But when eating in the absence of hunger becomes the norm rather than the exception, it dulls our senses and saps the pleasure out of food.

"Many people go on autopilot when they eat," says Huberman. "You can actually observe yourself doing this and cannot for the world explain why. It tells you that your impulses are actually much stronger than you would like to believe."

A quick trick from Tribole is to eat with your nondominant hand. The challenge forces your brain to pay attention and tends to disrupt mindless eating.

Even if you consider yourself to have a healthy relationship with food, we all maintain subconscious habits around the act of eating. Discovering your patterns can provide invaluable information about your strengths and vulnerabilities. It may unlock answers to questions like: *Why do I feel so tired in the morning? How can my food choices help me to lower stress at work? Am I really in control of my own body if I'm ceding all my food decisions to the latest trends?* Use your Food Log to connect the dots and take stock.

"Anytime you bring the thinking circuitry into a behavior, you're creating top-down control," Huberman says. "You're more conscious of your mental and physical states as you head toward food, interact with it, and after you eat. The result is that you become more deliberate about your choices and less impulse-driven."

Your Food Log is a space to flex that circuitry. You can write about how each meal made you feel, your daily experience in sum, or anything that strikes you as a discoverable moment.

Say, for example, that on Day 3, at 4:30 p.m., you felt level-4 hunger and ate trail mix. Your reflection tells a deeper story: *I was so hungry and trail mix really hit the spot. I ate four handfuls at my desk... mindlessly. Maybe two would have satisfied me?* The next time you feel hungry at 4:30 p.m., your brain pulls up these memories to help you decide what (trail mix) and how much (two handfuls) to eat in order to satisfy your body. Your Journal insights fuel the engine of positive brain change!

As you become aware of your patterns, you may realize that your brain is foggy after certain foods or that your hunger is at level 5 by dinnertime because you're not honoring your body's cues during the day. Like Huberman did, you might try new foods that better meet your needs. When you feel cranky, sleepy, or depressed, your Log can help you analyze trends (*eating vegetables every day makes me feel more satisfied or skipping breakfast makes me tired*) to better nourish and honor your body.

Your second Challenge exercise, Savor Each Meal, is not as easy as it sounds. Very often, we don't connect with our food because we eat while working, reading, watching TV, or checking social media. Instead, be present and savor each bite. Place your phone out of sight to avoid distractions and, at a minimum, **pay close attention to the first, middle, and last bites of each meal.**

Here's an exercise Tribole takes clients through, which you can try at your next meal:

1. First, smell your food and notice the different notes.
2. Put it in your mouth, without biting, and notice the flavor.
3. Chew, without swallowing, and notice the difference in texture.

> **Fig. 2**
> *Connect with each bite and commit*
> *100% awareness to the process of eating.*

As Tribole notes, her clients love this experience, because they haven't paid attention to the act of eating in so long that they're shocked by all the flavors they've been missing.

This month, approach food like a sommelier approaches wine and check in with your body's signals the way a musician listens to and tunes his instrument.

Try to commit 100% awareness to the process.

Then, when you discover certain fruits or vegetables that hit your taste buds just right, take it to the next level: Once a day, eat that new food by itself. Consider the aroma, sweetness, acidity, saltiness. Enjoy how it makes your body and mind feel afterward.

"The whole idea is to make progress," Tribole says. "People think they have to be perfect to be healthy. But that's a trap. You don't have to be perfect in this endeavor. Maybe today is too crazy. Cool. Give yourself permission and start again next time you're able."

Permission granted. Two words that spring so much joy—and something we often deny ourselves. The Madefor method places priority on self-determination: You are the adult, the driver, the shot-caller. You dictate the energy, attention, and outcomes for this Challenge.

It may feel like we're asking a lot from you this month. But learning to eat from the inside-out really *is* a superpower. Give it everything you've got, and you'll gain tremendous mind-body alignment and more pleasure around eating.

Still, there may be days when you just don't have the will to log your food choices or eat three bites with intention. That's okay. Permission granted. On those days, write in your Journal instead.

- MEMBER MOMENT -

"Enjoyed the best blueberries and raspberries this morning. Super flavorful, and amazing what you can start to taste when you focus only on enjoying your food versus reading your email, newspaper, or working. This challenge has been an eye opener on many levels. I'm looking forward to being a food anthropologist this month." - Jennifer S

Everyone begins this Challenge from different starting places. Your Journal can help you unpack the ingrained traits that led you here, take a deeper dive into patterns you're discovering, and examine new ideas about how to move forward.

If you've had rigid thoughts and beliefs about food in the past, this is the time to take a hard look at those experiences and grant yourself permission to reconnect with the joy of eating.

Reflect in your Journal: Prompts to get you started

Do you have strong beliefs or rules around food? How have they impacted your enjoyment of food? Your interactions with family and friends?

Sometimes we eat everything on our plate because it made our parents smile or because our competitive siblings always grabbed more than their share. Are there entrenched food habits from your past that no longer serve you?

How does your body signal that it's hungry? Do you tend to nourish it before hunger becomes ravenous? Can you see how ignoring your body's cues creates mind-body dissonance?

Think of situations in which you've eaten beyond fullness. How did it affect you afterward?

Do you feel like there's a specific number on the scale that you have to achieve in order to be healthy? What pleasures have you sacrificed in pursuit of perfection? How long can you reasonably maintain this number once you've reached it?

Is it important to be productive at all times? Can you see how savoring a meal, with no distractions, is a productive use of your time?

Were you able to enjoy an entire meal (or at least three bites) today without distraction? What did you learn about the food you ate?

Are there foods that make you feel sleepy, give you energy, leave you jittery?

Are there tastes, textures, and aromas that you really enjoy?

What patterns did you notice after one week of keeping a Food Log? Two weeks? Three weeks?

Let's Do This

We want to leave you with one last tip: If you are connecting to what you're eating, there are no "forbidden foods."

This may feel counterintuitive, but when you develop greater awareness around your personal taste preferences, it leads you to make better choices. Snack-food and fast-food companies are going to continue to find clever ways to get us to eat more of their products. That's *never* going to change. What we can change is our behavior around these foods.

For example, if you've consumed ten rice cakes in a row and find yourself looking in the fridge for something else to fill the void, it might be that you're trying to find satisfaction from unsatisfying foods. When you finally allow yourself a piece of chocolate or a slice of pizza, you end up eating more than you actually need. You've deprived yourself for so long, your brain and body react as if you may never get another chance.

But when you become an intuitive eater, you no longer feel deprived. You adjust your choices and portions effortlessly. You ask yourself: *What would hit the spot at this moment? What flavors and textures do I want? How do I want to feel when I finish eating?*

You may have concerns that a "permission to eat" mandate means you're going to wolf down ice cream, potato chips, and cookies. "But that's actually not what happens," Tribole says. "It's the paradox of permission: When you allow yourself to eat what you want, you get to decide, 'Do I really want it right now?'"

Eat mindfully and you will stay in charge.

As you begin this process, if you do experience an urgent desire to tear into an entire bag of Oreos, don't beat yourself up. Go ahead and have the cookies. But be present. Think about the taste and texture: Is it satisfying? Check in after each bite: How does your mind feel? How does your body feel? Do you want more?

"People often end up discovering that the very foods they've been lusting over—they don't even like them," Tribole says. "Sometimes you get stuck in the rush of getting *that* food, and you're not even paying attention to the taste."

Approach all foods equally and let your body tell you exactly what and how much it needs. As you loosen the reins on forbidden foods, you'll focus less on *quantity* and more on *quality*. You'll add more fresh fruits and vegetables to your meals because you enjoy the crunch, texture, and sweetness. You'll better understand the ways that protein-rich and nutrient-dense foods affect your cognitive function and energy levels. And you'll begin to view forbidden foods through a healthier lens.

When you're an intuitive eater, you can enjoy an ice-cream cone with your child or a margarita with friends and welcome the flavors as they hit your tongue and make you smile. You savor the experience. Your mind and body are calm and alert. You naturally stop eating when the delightfulness begins to dull, because you know that this is fun food—not a remedy for true hunger.

And the next time someone tells you that the key to a long life is yak's milk in your coffee, you'll see it for what it really is: a gimmicky trend that dings your wallet and strips you of your agency. *Thanks, you'll say, but I'm pretty sure my body knows better.*

<u>Congratulations, you've mastered the Challenge.</u>

- - -

A reminder: *If you have a medical condition, food allergies, or any circumstances that require professional healthcare guidance, do not begin this Challenge without first consulting your physicians. The Madefor Challenges are designed with an advisory board of experts, and they are safe and effective for the majority of members, but they are not intended to replace the advice and counsel of your doctors.*

➢ **Fig. 3**
*When you understand how the food you
eat makes you feel, better choices follow.*

Pat's Fuel Guidance

At the outset of Madefor you set an intention for what you hope to achieve through this program—take a moment to reflect on and record how engaging this challenge might help serve your intention.

I'd like to offer you another way to think about this Challenge that has nothing to do with what you eat. This month, you're going to strengthen the circuitry of interoceptive awareness, building a better understanding of the signals your body is sending you and how best to respond. We use food as the backdrop for this Challenge for a few reasons.

First, eating is something you do every day, so there is a lot of opportunity to focus, defocus, and refocus your attention on your body's signals.

Second, there isn't one way to eat—there are many healthy dietary patterns, and the trick is to discover what works best for you. This is at the core of Madefor; you will always be your own best guide, but you have to build up your awareness to do so.

Finally, eating affords you a tremendous opportunity to see where inertia has crept into your life. Are you doing something because that's the way you've always done it, it's what was expected of you, it's what you think you should do, or it's simply because you're not paying attention? Whatever the case, when you slow down to understand what your unique needs and desires are, you create an opportunity to reduce inertia.

If you struggle to stay on track this month, consider taking this small step—can you taste the first, middle, and last bite of your next meal? If a step is too hard, revisit your intention for inspiration. You got this.

For additional support, check out my <u>Perspectives video</u> for more information around how we designed this Challenge, recommendations on how to approach the daily exercises, and real-life experiences and perspectives from Madefor Members that have completed the journey. Or, listen to this quick <u>Campfire Story</u> for a little inspiration.

*Madefor Videos and Audio recordings can be found on our YouTube page (https://www.youtube.com/@getmadefor)

Madefor connection

We are all connected

Small steps are no small feat. And you've been taking them with Madefor for three months—longer than a resolution normally lasts.

With Hydration, you achieved some easy wins and learned how paying a little attention to a simple, daily act provides mental and physical benefits.

With Gratitude, you tapped into a powerful mindset that allows you to recognize and share the good in life.

With Fuel, you reconnected with your innate wisdom by listening to your body and trusting it to know what serves you best.

This month, you'll celebrate a fundamental human need: social connection. Your Challenge incorporates the attention, mindset, and powerful wisdom you've developed in the last three months to help you grow closer to the people who play meaningful roles in your life.

Happy connecting,

BLAKE & PAT

The Basics

What matters most in your life? Is the work you do the most important thing to you? Your family? Your friends?

When Madefor co-founder Blake Mycoskie was in his early 30s, he began to contemplate this question pretty seriously. He'd spent all of his 20s putting in 80-hour workweeks as a serial entrepreneur. Now, at 31, he was building TOMS into one of the fastest-growing global shoe brands. Yet something was missing in his life.

One evening, during a visit with his father, Mycoskie asked, "Dad, do you have any regrets? Is there anything in life you wish you'd have done differently?"

Mike Mycoskie had had a long, successful career as an orthopedic surgeon, and three children who were his pride and joy. But he paused and looked at his son, wondering how to answer.

"You know, I actually do have one regret," he said. "I put all my time into building my medical practice, being a good husband, and being a good dad. But I didn't prioritize my friendships. I wish I had. Because now that I'm thinking about retiring, I don't have friends to spend time with."

Mycoskie understood all too well what his father meant, and he could see the same path unfurling before him. "I was so busy, giving everything I had to TOMS, that I could easily see how this could be the beginning of a similar story for me," Mycoskie recently recalled. "And how foolish would it be if it became *my* biggest regret, too?"

Determined to not make the same mistake, Mycoskie went home and sent an email to a half-dozen close male friends he'd known from childhood, college, and work. He thanked them for their friendship and issued a challenge: Let's commit to a group trip over the coming year to catch up and reconnect.

The next summer, everyone he'd emailed met in Colorado for a little fly-fishing and bonding. An annual tradition was born, and along with it, a name—formed only slightly in jest. They called themselves the Rugged Adventure Club, or RAC for short.

In 2018, RAC celebrated its tenth anniversary. "It's been this amazing thing that literally no one misses unless their wife is about to give birth," Mycoskie says. "One of my oldest friends has made every single trip—we call him the Cal Ripken of RAC."

Over the years, RAC has grown to about a dozen guys who meet up once a year to create new stories, relive old ones, and grow closer. The "rugged adventures" usually unfold in the ocean or on mountaintops, but it's what happens at dinnertime that makes the trips special.

"We were always eating together, and one day we said, 'Instead of having all these side conversations, let's use this time to really help each other,'" Mycoskie recalls.

Now, at dinner, someone will pose a question to the group, anything from: *Is there something you wanted to achieve last year and didn't?* to *What's your best memory from childhood?*

"It's not like any of us are experts," Mycoskie says. "But we're all experiencing similar things. So it creates a feeling of support and accountability, because we're also asking, 'How can we, your friends, help you to achieve that thing you're still reaching for?'"

In fact, Madefor was born on a RAC surf trip in Mexico in 2017, when Mycoskie and Pat Dossett discovered during a group question that they shared a deep desire to help people live the best life possible—a conversation that led to the journey you are on right now.

When Mycoskie started RAC, he knew that friends make life better. But he had no idea there were **scientific benefits to connection**. He may have been surprised to learn, for instance, that a 2005 study of more than 1,000 older adults found that those with a strong circle of friends were significantly more likely to **live longer** than those without.

Having close allies **lowers your risk of depression and anxiety**, gives you **greater odds of surviving serious illness**, and even **keeps you mentally sharp**. A 12-year study of 1,100 seniors found that the rate of cognitive decline was 70% less in people who were frequently socially active compared with those who had infrequent contact.

Science tells us that social bonding improves our physical and mental health. But what's happening in our brains when we connect with others is not well understood. Or at least, not yet.

Researchers at the California Institute of Technology recently found that when mice endured just two weeks of isolation, they had a brain-wide increase of a neuropeptide called tachykinin 2, or Tac2, along with greater symptoms of fear, aggression, and hypersensitivity to potential threats. But when scientists injected the mice with a drug that blocked Tac2, the negative symptoms disappeared.

Here's the interesting part: Tac2 is also found in the human brain. We know that oxytocin, a neuropeptide associated with trust and bonding, positively influences our social behavior, making us feel good when we connect. Could Tac2 be oxytocin's inverse, a neuropeptide that makes us feel *bad* when we avoid human contact?

More research is needed, but as lead Madefor advisor and Stanford University neuroscientist Dr. Andrew Huberman notes, "It stands to reason that social isolation is likely causing the secretion of these peptides through your brain and body, making you feel lousy, as a way to motivate you to seek out other people and solve your problem."

We are neurologically wired to connect. It's a survival instinct. Isolation equaled death for our ancestors, who depended on a strong community to hunt, protect one another, and further the species. So it's not a leap to imagine that when we avoid human interaction, our brain releases feel-bad chemicals (perhaps Tac2) that push us toward more social behaviors; and when we engage with others, our brains reward that behavior with feel-good chemicals like dopamine and oxytocin.

Thankfully, it doesn't require much to get the brain rewards of socialization. You don't need to take a trip or buy fly-fishing gear. You simply need to identify and engage with the people in your life with whom you have common ties.

That's what Dossett did when he moved to Los Angeles in 2018 and invited his uncle to join him on a morning swim routine. First it was just the two of them. Then a friend joined. Then *his* buddy showed up.

Now, a group meets in Venice once a week to swim a couple of miles in the ocean, grab coffee, and catch up on each other's lives. "I didn't begin with the intention of starting a swim group," Dossett says. "It's just something I enjoy doing. Now, it's more about the friends than the swim."

RAC and Swim Club members faithfully show up because they enjoy the camaraderie. But on a subconscious level, they're also tapping into the brain boost we all get from:

1. **Seeing familiar faces**
2. **Serving our friendships**
3. **Deepening our relationships**

These simple acts provide the maximum health benefits of social connection—and they make up the three components of your next Madefor Challenge.

> **Fig. 1**
> Making eye contact and greeting the
> people you interact with provides
> scientifically measurable benefits.

 The Challenge

Your Connection Challenge Exercises:

Face the Day:
Every day for one week, make eye contact, smile, and say "good morning" to the first three faces you see upon leaving home. In your Madefor Journal, make a record of whom you greeted and how you are connected.

Teammates Don't Ask; They Do:
Think of two friends who could use your help and come up with a small favor that goes a long way. In your Journal, write down who you helped, what you did, and how it made you feel.

Dinner Party:
Host dinner for four or more people and use your Madefor Connection Cards to get to know one another better. Use your Journal to enhance the experience.

This month's Challenge allows you to connect in ways that are good for **you**, good for **others**, and good for **us**.

Your **Face the Day** exercise, designed primarily to benefit you, begins with eye contact—the smallest act necessary in order to prime your brain for social harmony.

We naturally glean information about people from their eyes. But when we avoid eye contact it can have adverse effects. Research shows that we often (mistakenly) think that people who avert their eyes are less sincere, less conscientious, and less trustworthy. On the other hand, we tend to believe (without proof) that people who look us in the eye have a more sophisticated mind, an ability to act morally, and greater personal agency.

Eye contact also fosters attachment. Marriage therapists know that face-to-face time is invaluable for couples, but studies show that even complete strangers who are made to gaze into one another's eyes for two uninterrupted minutes report greater feelings of affection and interest than subjects who were told to look at one another's hands.

"Faces are very powerful modulators of mood," says Huberman. "Saying 'good morning,' looking someone in the eye—it's good for your mind and the positive effects can persist all day."

Unfortunately, eye contact is becoming a lost social art. Think about the last time you were in an elevator. Were most of the other people (maybe even you) looking down at their phones the entire time? How many times have you seen couples at dinner gazing at screens, instead of one another's eyes? How often have you arose from sleep and reached for your phone instead of reaching for your partner, looking them in the eye, and saying "good morning"?

"It may be that our seemingly endless phone attention and browsing is an attempt to try to get the basic thing we need, which is eye contact," says Huberman. "But that's like eating Styrofoam—we're trying to fill up on something that's empty, so we keep at it."

While it's true that modern technology has allowed us to communicate with friends around the world, as noted social neuroscientist John Cacioppo writes in his book *Loneliness*, increased digital encounters have made us ravenous for real face-to-face encounters—for real connection. When being physically together isn't possible, we try to satisfy our hunger by sending our loved ones texts or gazing at their photograph, a practice Cacioppo calls "social snacking."

"But a snack is not a meal," he writes. "The better move is to work that much harder to reach out to those with whom we share even the most superficial contact in the everyday world."

This bears repeating:

The antidote to our disconnection is to work harder to engage with people we are superficially connected to, our so-called weak-tie" relationships.

Is there a mail carrier, barista, or yoga teacher with whom you interact as you begin your day? **For one week, make eye contact, smile, and greet at least the first three faces you see**. Notice how it changes your interactions. How it lightens your day. How it gives you a sense of wellbeing.

If you're an introvert and these kinds of interactions make you uncomfortable, remember that the discomfort you feel is positive brain-change in action. In fact, there's scientifically measurable value in these encounters.

A 2014 study of more than 300 students and residents in British Columbia found that on days when participants had more social encounters with weak-tie relations, they experienced **greater feelings of happiness, belonging, and wellbeing**.

Cacioppo and other scientists have found that a socially content person transmits signals that are more harmonious and in sync with their environment, and the signals they receive back are also more harmonious. Another way to describe it is **positive emotional contagion**—that experience when you "catch" another person's good mood.

On the flip side, when we feel isolated, our emotional regulation is disrupted and we're less capable of overcoming challenges, less adept at handling day-to-day annoyances, and less able to read others' social cues.

We all know people who get stuck in distorted thought patterns that further alienate themselves from others—the self-fulfilling prophecy of negativity bias. Social connection is the fix. It's impossible to feel lonely when you're chatting with a friendly grocery clerk or sharing vacation photos with your dog walker. These moments remind you that you're an integral part of your community.

- MEMBER MOMENT -

"Besides talking to random strangers and taking the cards everywhere, I have connected to my old, very old high school reunion group, plus signed up to support two charity events and will meet people... I'm a natural hermit, so this is a big deal even leaving my house. Maybe I like people after all!" - Marti F

During this Challenge, if someone ignores your greeting or acts dismissive toward you, try to not fall into negative self-talk. They're probably just having a bad day. Take the opportunity to **write about it in your Journal and reframe the situation** like you did in the Gratitude Challenge when you learned the power of cognitive reappraisal. Have a moment of sympathy for whatever the other person is going through. Then move on. The more you practice seeing situations from another's point of view, the more emotionally in control you will feel.

PRO TIP: *Remember to lean on our Journaling Tips & FAQ at the end of the book if you're feeling stuck.*

"Teammates Don't Ask; They Do" is a valuable lesson that was imprinted on Madefor co-founder Dossett during his time in the military. **In essence, it's about having a bias for action in your relationships.** If a teammate has more gear to carry than anyone else, you don't ask if he needs a hand, you pick up his extra bag and go. If a friend across the country is sick, you don't text her and ask if there's anything you can do, you call her local deli and have chicken soup delivered.

Teammates Don't Ask is your mantra for your next Challenge. This time, you're giving the social benefits to *others* as you find creative ways to serve two strong-tie friendships.

In a recent survey of more than 20,000 Americans, 2 in 5 said they felt like their "relationships aren't meaningful" and that they "are isolated from others." Studies show that chronic isolation has severe health effects, including an increased risk of disease and death that's on par with known risk factors like high blood pressure, diabetes, and smoking. With odds like these, we could all stand to be better teammates.

Can you think of two friends who may be feeling overwhelmed or alone? In the second week of your Challenge, **take 10 minutes to identify two people who are struggling and then come up with meaningful ways to help them.** Your help doesn't have to be life-changing—just a small favor that packs a punch and meets their needs.

A colleague just had a baby? Tell her to choose a night that you can babysit. A sibling lost his job? Offer to spiff up his résumé. A classmate's feeling low? Drop by with her favorite Chinese take-out or just make a daily call and ask, "How are you doing today?"

Teammates Don't Ask is a powerful way to operate in the world because it takes the onus off the other person. Think about the last time you asked someone, "Is there anything I can do to help?" There was likely a pause before they replied, "No, but thanks." Asking for help often makes people feel vulnerable and indebted. So let them off the hook. **Serve the relationship without being asked.**

To be clear, this is not about being a superhero and parachuting into every situation to save the day. It's about being a friend and if the time comes when you are in a jam, have the strength to be vulnerable and allow others to help you.

If a friend is dealing with a complex problem and you're not sure what to do, keep it simple. You can say, "Hey, I recognize you're in a situation, and I'm going to do something. I don't want to waste my time or yours, so what would be most helpful? Can I pick up the kids from school? Drive you to doctor appointments?" If they resist, let them know that it's important to you to serve this friendship.

When you reflect in your **Journal,** write down the names of the two people you helped and what you did for them. How did they respond? How did it make you feel? Use your Journal to consider how your simple acts of compassion further bonded you to them.

A warning: The more you practice a Teammates Don't Ask mindset, the more you'll find yourself, say, helping an elderly woman whose grocery bag just spilled onto the sidewalk or giving a hand to a new dad who's struggling with a car seat. It's not that opportunities to aid strangers didn't exist before. It's that **your brain has shifted from a lens in which helping others takes too much time or diminishes you to one in which it becomes a joyful act that brings meaning to your life.**

> **Fig. 2**
> *Positive emotional contagion is that uplifting moment when you "catch" someone's good mood.*

Your first two Challenge exercises are entry points that move you toward a mindset in which you're actively thinking about who you're connected to and how you can invest in those relationships. Face the Day nudges you into interactions with your weak-tie relations in a "good for me" exercise that brings measurable mental and physical benefits. Teammates Don't Ask shifts your attention outward to your strong-tie friendships with a "good for you" act that gives the benefits to others. Now you're ready to focus on "good for us."

For the final piece of your Challenge, you're going to host a **Dinner Party** for four or more close friends and get to know one another better using your **Madefor Connection Cards** (available in the **Tools & Resources** section).

It's ideal to host your get-together at the end of the Challenge month, when your brain is primed for connection. So send out the invite now and get a date on the calendar that works for everyone.

Remember: There's no pressure to put on a four-course meal or break out the china. This can be a completely casual event. **The goal is bonding.** And your Connection questions are the catalyst, with questions that are inspired by the many friendship-deepening conversations that have taken place at Rugged Adventure Club outings.

As host, start by taking a Card from the top of the deck or picking a question from the list, reading the question aloud, and providing a thoughtful response. The next person can answer the same question or pick a new one.

Above all, model support and encouragement for your guests. For example, if the question is: *What hobbies did you enjoy when you were younger, but now you no longer do them?* and Lucy tells about her family's hiking trips, you might say: "Mike used to hike too—maybe we can do a group hike next weekend?" As Dossett and his swim group can attest, an impromptu meet-up may evolve into a regular get-together.

Ready for a simple social hack to enhance the conversation? **Try active-constructive responding**, or ACR, a communication style that's proven to accelerate the deepening of relationships. ACR is simply about coming alongside another person with enthusiasm and delight as they tell you about a win.

Think of a time that you were brimming with excitement about something you couldn't wait to tell a friend or partner. Maybe you got a promotion at work or you aced a test. How did the other person respond to your news? Did they say, "That's nice, what's for dinner?" (a passive-constructive response); or "Wow, your new job sounds hard, are you sure you can handle it?" (active-destructive); or did they change the subject and tell you about their own day (passive-destructive)? These would *not* be examples of active-constructive responding.

With ACR, you enthusiastically walk through the other person's experience with them as they retell it. If a guest is answering a question about a life achievement they're proud of, **practice ACR by making eye contact, smiling, and listening intently**.

When there are big moments in their story, **offer encouraging interjections**, like: "That must have felt amazing"; "I can totally picture you saying that"; and "Then what happened?" Ask for details that **let them relive the experience as if you were by their side**: "How did you learn you'd won?"; "Who was there?"; "When did you realize the significance?"

When they finish their story, help them imagine how this achievement compels even more wins: "What a great accomplishment. I have to imagine that an experience like that really paves the way for more success."

> **Fig. 3**
> *When you engage in ACR, you come alongside the other person's journey with enthusiasm and delight.*

ACR isn't about being nice; it's about active listening. It's not about faking interest; it's about picturing the other person's experience in your mind. It may take some practice. And it may even feel strange at first. But soon, you'll find it's one of the most satisfying and effective ways to strengthen a relationship.

In a fascinating study at the University of California, Los Angeles, researchers videotaped 79 dating couples as they discussed positive and negative events. They found that participants who interacted in an active-constructive style felt more understood, validated, and cared for—and were less likely to have broken up two months later.

Practice ACR at your dinner party, at home, at work, and any time you want to really connect with someone. As you draw out more energy and happiness in the other person, *you* feel more energy and happiness in the relationship.

To keep the good feelings flowing, write down what you said, how the other person reacted, and how it made you feel in your Journal. Committing your memories to the page with vivid details will intensify the effects and generate the feel-good chemicals that tell your brain: *This behavior is pleasurable; do it again.*

Let's Do This

You began this Challenge with a question: What matters most in your life? While there's no single answer for everyone, science confirms what you likely already knew to be true:

We are meant to connect.

Follow this month's Challenge as directed, and you'll gain an even deeper appreciation for the people you're connected to and the benefits of investing in those relationships.

Your Face the Day exercise gives you a small, daily act that anchors you in the sensory experience of social connection. Teammates Don't Ask provides an opportunity to serve two people in your life who need your help. Your Dinner Party and Connection questions offer a fun way to bring friends together for deeper dialogue.

Celebrate your wins this month by continuing the practice after your Challenge is done. For example, the next time a friend is facing a problem, if you catch yourself saying, "Can I help?" shift gears and say: "You know what—never mind. Here's what I'm going to do... Would that help?"

You don't need to host a party every month to bond with friends. You can meet up for a weekly coffee, a monthly hike, or a yearly trip. And while your Connection questions are a great conversation starter, any question that's posed with intent will suffice.

For example, when Dossett turned 39, he asked this question at his birthday dinner: *What was the most valuable lesson that your father taught you?* The responses from his friends were compelling and informative for Dossett, who was about to be the father of twin girls.

For Mycoskie, nothing beats the benefits of face-to-face hang-outs with his buddies in RAC. But between trips, the group relies on a text message chain to stay close and supportive of one another.

Often, the texts are as simple as: "Hey, check out this photo of my kid eating it on the half pipe... I feel old." But sometimes, it's a member dealing with a problem in their marriage or a personal health crisis. Within seconds, RAC friends are calling, writing, and showing up.

In a way, "showing up" is what this month is all about. By shifting from a passive role to actively fostering deeper con-nections, you're giving your brain what it's wired for: a sense of purpose and community. Savor the moments of unexpected joy that come when you direct your attention toward others and they engage back.

You are connected.

Pat's Connection Guidance

At the outset of Madefor you set an intention for what you hope to achieve through this program—take a moment to reflect on and record how engaging this challenge might help serve your intention.

By now you understand that the value of Madefor isn't in anything we tell you, it's in the actions you take once you set the book down and step out into the real world.

In this Challenge you continue to cultivate a bias for action, taking advantage of even the briefest of opportunities to change the trajectory of someone else's day through eye contact and a smile. This isn't just a few random acts of kindness or a thoughtful dialogue, this is a different way of moving through the world—one that builds you and those around you up at the same time. I hope you enjoy this Challenge as much as I do, and I hope you complete it feeling more connected.

If you struggle to stay on track this month, consider taking this small step—can you engage one person, in one brief moment, from a place of curiosity and compassion? Allow yourself to see and feel what happens when you do so, and if it feels good, do it again, and again, and again. If one step is too hard, revisit your intention for inspiration. You got this.

**I recommend <u>listening to the Basecamp</u> I did with Dr. Lisa Feldman Barrett or at least <u>reading the summary</u> (Basecamp Highlights Section of Book). One of her central findings is directly applicable to your Connection Challenge: You require the participation of others to effectively regulate your nervous system. Said another way, connection is a biological imperative, and you are at your best when you invest in connection.

For additional support, check out my <u>Perspectives video</u> for more information around how we designed this Challenge, recommendations on how to approach the daily exercises, and real-life experiences and perspectives from Madefor Members that have completed the journey. Or, listen to this quick <u>Campfire Story</u> for a little inspiration.

*Madefor Videos and Audio recordings can be found on our YouTube page (https://www.youtube.com/@getmadefor)

Just breathe

If Madefor were a mountain, you would be standing on the summit, your adventure halfway complete. Most people think the mountaintop is the goal. But the real growth is in the journey and the obstacles you overcome along the way to return home a better version of yourself.

Over the last four months, we've helped guide your steps, but you determined the path—from the number of bottles of water consumed and to whom you expressed your gratitude, to what food fuels you best. In fact, it was you who set your destination at the outset by writing an intention in your Journal.

Take a moment now to check in on your intention. Are you moving closer to it? Farther away? Or has your intention changed?

Understand where you are now and where you're headed. Keep your intention in mind as you carve out time this month to connect with one of your most powerful internal tools—your breath.

Just breathe,

BLAKE & PAT

The Basics

Get ready. You're about to embark on what may be the most challenging leg of your Madefor journey—daily breathwork.

Decades of scientific research tells us that a consistent, intentional breathing practice can lead to greater resilience, enhanced cognition, and better control over our physical, mental, and emotional states. So why don't more of us engage in breathwork?

Maybe it's because meditation apps, yoga retreats, breathing "experts," and trendy breathing styles ask you to commit time and energy to practices that are hard to sustain.

We're going to take a different approach: focus on the smallest practice to deliver real benefits in 21 days.

This month, you're going to use your breath to:

- Positively alter your brain and body for greater focus and resilience.
- Change the way you respond to stressful situations in real time.

Breathwork can be a game-changer. That's why professional athletes, entrepreneurs, and military leaders use it to achieve optimal performance—people like six-time Paralympic medalist Dan Cnossen, a biathlete and cross-country skier who inspires global audiences with his strength and fortitude.

Cnossen was 33 when he first joined Team USA in the 2014 Winter Paralympics in Sochi, Russia. "I did not perform well," he recently recalled. He couldn't seem to break higher than a sixth place-showing. "I'd over-trained. My life was out of balance. It was a big lesson learned the hard way."

Cnossen took those big lessons and spun them into gold.

Four years later, he rejoined Team USA in Pyeongchang, South Korea. But this time would be different. This time, he'd rested and recovered in between trainings; he'd started graduate studies at Harvard to develop his mind alongside his body; and he'd vowed, above all, to be present.

"In Sochi, I kept looking at the Jumbotron during races," he said. "My new game plan was: *Do not look. If the announcer's voice comes into your brain, let it go and refocus.*"

His biggest test was biathlon, a timed competition combining fast-paced skiing and precision shooting. Sit-skiers like Cnossen, whose legs are amputated above the knee, use specially designed chairs fitted onto a pair of skis. Racers launch from the start line at staggered intervals. Come in too hot and your aim suffers; too slow and you fall behind. So Cnossen learned to control his breathing: *inhale... exhale; inhale... exhale; hold it—then shoot.*

His mind-body training paid off. In his first race, a 7.5km biathlon, Cnossen was so focused, he didn't even realize he was in the lead. Cnossen and teammate Kendall Gretsch made history as the first Americans to win biathlon gold in the Paralympic or Olympic Games. And Cnossen went on to medal in every race he entered, bringing home an additional four silvers and a bronze.

"Everyone talks about the gold-medal race," he says, "but it's not even the one I'm most proud of." In *that* race, a 15km cross-country event, Cnossen was flying downhill on his second lap when he lost control and tumbled down the hill, face-first, poles askew, and arms bloodied. His steely focus was gone.

"I started thinking about how many people were ahead of me, how I could never make up that much time," he says. With about 35 minutes left, he decided to quit and save his energy for the next race. But then he heard his coach's voice: "You're still in it! Let's go!"

A switch went off in his brain, shifting his perspective to: *Wait... I've got 35 minutes to work my way back to the lead.* He took a deep breath and pushed harder. By his last lap, he was exhausted, overheating, muscles burning—and yet somehow, he fought his way back to a silver medal.

"A medal, when you get down to it, is really just a representation," Cnossen says. "This one represents not quitting despite the doubt in my mind that tried to take over."

It also represents Dan Cnossen's unbreakable growth mindset. And not just in competition—in life. Like in his 20s, when he entered the military with a palpable fear of the water. He got in the pool every day to face his fears and eventually became a Navy SEAL. Or on that terrible day in 2009, during a night-time mission in Afghanistan, when a blinding white light and explosion could only mean that he'd stepped on an IED, and Cnossen told himself: Breathe, ignore the searing pain, make it to the rescue helicopter.

Or when he woke up in a Maryland hospital eight days later, and doctors told him that his legs had been amputated, that he'd broken his pelvis and some fingers, and other awful news that's hard to recall because he was on heavy pain meds. Even then, all Cnossen could think was: *I need to get back to my team.*

Many months and surgeries later, after discovering that his new prosthetic legs weren't going to carry him through the sand and rugged terrain of Afghanistan, Cnossen accepted the crushing reality that he was never going back to his team.

Except somehow, it wasn't crushing for Cnossen. It was a setback, it was depressing—it was many things. But the Cnossen way is to "let it go and refocus." So the guy who was afraid of water and became a SEAL is now the guy who'd never skied before his injury and became a six-time Paralympic medalist in Nordic skiing. How does he do it?

Cnossen says that when he races, he's constantly in conversation with himself. "It goes something like this," he says. "'Come on, dig deeper, breathe, focus on technique. Can I go harder? Should I go harder? Go harder. Push over the top of this hill. Don't let up.'"

Don't let up.

His determination is extraordinary. But he's not a superhero. He's simply honed a number of inside-out tools—like breathwork, gratitude, positive self-talk—that help him push past doubt, fear, and discomfort to achieve whatever he sets his mind to. And inside-out tools, as you already know, are far superior to outside-in tools.

"Outside-in tools like caffeine or extreme diets can get you fired up," says Madefor advisor and Stanford neuroscientist Dr. Andrew Huberman. "But if that's all you've got, it's not enough. Individuals like Dan, who've developed their inside-out tools, are more powerful because they don't need anything else. They can self-reward by setting intentions, expressing gratitude, elevating their baselines with proper hydration and nutrition. That is true power, true confidence." Inside-out tools are what you've honed along your Madefor journey.

And now, you're going to complement your arsenal with one of the most effective tools that Cnossen relies on and practices daily: **breathwork**.

By the end of your Challenge, you'll be able to direct your breath at will, just like Cnossen does, to let go of doubt, be present, refocus on the big picture, and never let up.

> **Fig. 1**
> *Inside-out tools give you greater
> power over how you feel.*

The Challenge

> ### Your Breath Challenge Exercises:
>
> #### 21 Days of Attention:
> Every day, set a timer for at least ten minutes, focus on your breath and direct your attention to a loving-kindness or mindfulness practice. See below for your practices.
>
> #### 21 Days of Intention:
> Every day, find one opportunity to shift your mental and physical state using at least three energizing or calming breaths. See below for your practices.
>
> #### Reflect in your Journal:
> Each night, write a few sentences in your Journal reflecting on your exercises and how they affected your day. Connect the act of breathwork to how it made you feel.

Have you noticed that all of your monthly Challenges include both **attention and intention exercises?** These brain-building practices are designed to help you unlock the best version of you—your inner Dan Cnossen, so to speak.

Your Hydration Challenge, for example, wasn't about getting you to drink a specific amount of water each day, it was about getting you to *intentionally* engage in a new behavior consistently. When you wrote in your Journal and tracked your intake, you cultivated *attention* around the act of drinking water, creating self-generated rewards.

This month, you're going to practice attentional breathwork that's proven to cultivate resilience, enhance cognition, and prevent stress; and you'll also engage in intentional breathwork to feel more relaxed or energetic, depending on what serves you best in the moment.

Breathwork will not endow you with superhuman endurance, heal cancer, or bestow Buddha-like patience. What it can do, according to established research, is reduce symptoms associated with anxiety, insomnia, and depression. It can confer greater immunity, recovery from injury, and relief from chronic pain. Best of all, you can access the mental benefits of breathwork any time.

Try it right now:

1. Close your eyes and take a deep inhale to a silent count of four.
2. Hold it for two seconds.
3. Exhale to a silent count of eight

You just practiced intentional breathing. Do you feel more calm? More energized? **In general, a long inhale and short exhale achieve an energizing effect; while a short inhale and long exhale has a calming effect.**

Before we dig into your Challenge, a quick primer on form: If you've ever watched a baby breathe, they do it naturally, from the diaphragm, belly rising with each inhale. But over time, stress and changes in our bodies cause us to engage in more shallow, chest breathing. If this sounds like you, then let babies' belly breaths be your model. And inhale primarily through your nose, if you can, as there's strong evidence that nasal breathing is far superior to mouth breathing. For example, your nasal passageways filter allergens and germs, and humidify the air you take in.

All of which helps keep bacteria and viruses from entering your lungs, so you can avoid common colds and flu.

Nasal breathing is also more effective during exercise because it releases more nitric oxide, a gas that increases carbon dioxide in the blood, which in turn releases oxygen. When you mouth-breathe during physical exertion, your cells don't get as much oxygen, causing you to fatigue sooner.

The bottom line is diaphragmatic breaths and nasal respiration are highly recommended. But do what works best for you.

Don't let form be a barrier to practice. Just breathe.

Let's start with 21 Days of Attention. Each day, carve out at least 10 minutes as part of your daily routine. Mornings are an ideal time because it helps to anchor your day. Upon rising, start a timer and **direct your attention toward loving-kindness or mindfulness** (see below for guidance), two practices drawn from the evidence-based techniques of **mindfulness-based stress reduction, or MBSR.**

Developed in 1979 at the University of Massachusetts Medical School by Dr. Jon Kabat-Zinn, MBSR began as a training program designed to help patients reduce stress and pain from chronic illness. It worked so well, healthcare providers began practicing MBSR to stave off their own burnout and exhaustion.

MBSR is so effective, it's used by entrepreneurs and professional athletes to reduce anxiety, increase stress tolerance, and optimize performance. In fact, among the 200 "billionaires, icons, and world-class performers" author Tim Ferriss interviewed for his book *Tools of Titans*, about 80% say they engage in some form of mindfulness practice.

According to its creator Kabat-Zinn, mindfulness is: "The awareness that emerges through paying attention, on purpose, in the present moment, and nonjudgmentally to the unfolding of experience moment by moment." For you, this means that during your breathwork time, you want to be completely attuned to the sound of your inhales and exhales, the movement of your belly, the air filling your lungs. If your mind wanders, notice it without judgment, then return your focus to your breath.

A mindfulness practice won't prevent or cure disease, but if done daily, it can set you up for a lifetime that's relatively free of pain, according to Dr. Daniel Goleman and Dr. Richard Davidson, whose best-selling book *Altered Traits* dispels common myths about breathing and meditation, while providing new evidence on the benefits of prolonged practice.

For example, just three days of mindfulness training produces a short-term decrease in certain cytokines, which are the molecules in our bodies responsible for inflammation. Just 30 hours of practice leads to lower levels of the stress hormone cortisol and improved overall mental health.

Mindfulness can also help sharpen your attention skills and improve your working memory. In a study at the University of California, Santa Barbara, students who engaged in two weeks of mindfulness practice improved their GRE (graduate school assessment exam) scores by more than 16%.

To be clear, ten minutes of mindfulness will not result in lifelong health and wisdom. You have to continue the practice to reap the rewards. But a ten-minute practice will help you achieve your goals that day.

That's what Cnossen aims for with his mindfulness practice. "Being able to refocus is really helpful in working toward a goal," Cnossen says. "When you're distracted, you know how to come back to the task at hand."

Sometimes, he'll begin with a silent intention and a reminder to trust in the process. "Mindfulness is good for you and for others in your life because having calm, steady people around benefits everyone," Cnossen says. "You can be that calm, steady person."

For your 21 Days of Attention exercise, **you have a choice of mindfulness or loving-kindness breathwork,** which is an equally powerful exercise that draws on MBSR as well as concepts from your Gratitude and Bonding Challenges. We provide you with guided sessions of each on our YouTube (https://www.youtube.com/@getmadefor), also linked in your Tools & Resources section.

21 Days of Attention:
Each day, do at least 10 mins of mindfulness or loving-kindness

Mindfulness: Dan Cnossen's Breathwork Routine

1. Find a comfortable position and take four deep breaths.

2. Resume natural breathing and focus on the sound of your breath.

3. When thoughts enter your mind, notice them without judgment. Then let them go and refocus on your breath.

4. When ambient noises distract you, notice where they're coming from. Then let them go. Let your breath be your anchor.

5. After you've settled into your practice, do a body scan. Start at the top of your head, slowly go down to your neck, shoulders, arms, and chest, checking in with each part of your body.

6. If itches, muscle tightness, or other sensations come up, notice them. Then let them go and refocus. If feelings come up for you, acknowledge and honor them without judgment. Then let them go.

Loving-Kindness:

1. Find a comfortable position. Close your eyes and take a deep belly breath.

2. Slowly exhale while releasing the tension in your head, neck, and shoulders.

3. Check in with yourself. You can't provide loving-kindness to others if you don't give it to yourself. How are you feeling? Are emotions coming up? Honor them. Then let them go.

4. Next, check in with your body. Any areas of stress or pain? Notice them. Let them go.

5. When you're ready, turn your attention toward either loving-kindness to close-tie relationships or a loving-kindness mantra.

Loving-kindness to close-tie relationships:

Imagine a person from your past or present whom you love deeply. See them standing on your right, sending you their love. Feel the warmth coming from them. Now imagine another important person in your life, standing on your left side, sending you their love. Next, picture your closest friends, relatives, and mentors encircling you, sending you wishes of health, happiness, and wellbeing. Accept their love, kindness, and compassion, and then send it back to all of them. Wish them health, happiness, and wellbeing. Stay with this circle of loved ones for some time. Breathe in their loving kindness and exhale it back to them.

Loving-kindness mantra:

Silently repeat to yourself: "May I be safe; may I be healthy; may my life unfold with ease." Wish these compassionate states for yourself first. Then repeat the phrases, inserting the names of loved ones. Then repeat them for weak-tie relations in your life. Finally, wish them for all beings in your world, even those who may have brought you harm.

> ➤ **Fig. 2**
> *Attentional breathwork builds your*
> *capacity to refocus and stay present.*

Daily loving-kindness practice is proven to induce greater feelings of compassion and connectedness. And it can help you to stay mentally strong and proactive during difficult times.

In a 2008 Stanford study, researchers asked subjects to close their eyes and send thoughts of kindness and compassion to two people they loved. A control group was told to imagine two acquaintances and focus on their appearance. Afterward, both groups were shown a picture of a stranger. After just seven minutes of practice, the loving-kindness group felt more connected and positive toward the stranger than control subjects did.

Researchers at the Max Planck Institute in Leipzig, Germany, wanted to see if longer trainings had stronger results. First, they hooked up subjects to functional MRI machines that scanned their brain activity as they watched videos of people in distress. Not surprisingly, the upsetting videos elicited neural activity in regions of the brain associated with pain perception and unpleasantness.

Next, subjects attended a six-hour loving-kindness training, where they expressed feelings of warmth and care to themselves and others. Then they watched the distressing videos again—but this time, their neural activity shifted toward regions of the brain associated with love and affiliation. The training had actually *altered* the way their brains responded to stress.

The study's lead author, psychologist and neuroscientist Olga Klimecki, noted that this remarkable change shows that instead of just feeling bad about another's suffering, we can stay calm, feel compassion, and *act*. This is a major distinction.

As Klimecki explains, people who work in helping fields (e.g., nurses, police, humanitarian-aid workers) often experience high levels of burnout, fatigue, and depression—a state known as empathic distress. When we experience empathic distress, we *literally* feel another's pain, which can actually lead us to become aggressive and *less* inclined to help.

But loving-kindness training fires up a different, self-protective circuitry in our brains than empathy does—it's a circuitry that allows us to feel concern *without* bombarding our own brains with pain. We can see another's suffering as separate from ourselves and react with prosocial helping behaviors, rather than withdrawal.

It can even reverse the effects of excessive empathic distress, as researcher Klimecki notes, "by actively strengthening neural activity related to reward and social connection." In other words, loving-kindness practice creates neuroplastic changes that make your brain better.

- MEMBER MOMENT -

"The Madefor breath challenge has helped me collect myself in stressful times with my kids, so much so that I shared the tactics with my book club. Everyone in the group is a mom of kids under 10, so we all can use some redirection of our internal states. The conversation ended up opening up a wonderfully vulnerable conversation about mental health, struggles we are facing, and our collective gratitude for each other. Who knew three breaths could do so much?"

- Brie O

Try loving-kindness for yourself and see how it affects your life in beneficial ways. Then reflect on your experience in your Journal to amplify the rewards.

Your 21 Days of Attention practice gives you two very different ways to enhance your brain and behavior in an enduring way. **Now, we turn to 21 Days of Intention**, an exercise that provides an *immediate* mental and physical payoff for better results in any situation.

For this part of your Challenge, you're going to intentionally direct your breathing to one of two states: **calm focus or energy**.

This practice is so effective and instant, that you can use it any time you want to stay in control during a potentially stressful situation. But for the purpose of your Challenge, you should practice intentional breathing at least once a day.

Having a difficult conversation that's making your heart beat faster? Try a calming breath to steady your adrenaline and emotions. Studying late into the night? Try a series of energizing breaths that replace a cup of coffee.

As Madefor advisor Huberman reminds us, we are the only species that has the ability to direct our internal states. "A dog doesn't wake up and say, 'I'm sleepy, but I'm going to try to feel more energetic.' Only humans can do this," he says. "Yet we often forget to deploy breathing to upshift or downshift our energy levels."

It's crucial to do intentional breathwork at least once a day, because it primes your brain to recognize moments when breathing is helpful. When you're present to the opportunities, you're more likely to use this powerful inside-out tool.

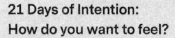

21 Days of Intention:
How do you want to feel?

For calm focus: short inhale, long exhale

1. Slowly inhale from your diaphragm (your belly rises more than your chest) and through your nose.

2. Silently count to four as you inhale.

3. Pause at the top of your breath for a count of two.

4. Slowly exhale through your nose to a count of eight.

For energy: long inhale, short exhale

1. Take a strong, long inhale through your nose to a silent count of six.

2. Exhale quickly to a count of two. Just let it go; allow your breath to gush out through your nose and mouth, releasing all the air from your lungs.

Try calming breaths (short inhale, long exhale) when:

You wake up feeling anxious

You're stuck in traffic

You're late for an appointment

You receive a confrontational email that needs a response

You're dealing with someone who's angry or irrational

You had a rough day and you're about to walk into your house

Try energizing breaths (long inhale, short exhale) when:

You wake up feeling sluggish

You're about to give a speech or presentation

You want to be on point for an interview

You're walking into a party and need a boost of confidence

You're experiencing a late-afternoon energy crash

You're burning the midnight oil on a project

You're craving a coffee or soda

➢ **Fig. 3**
Intentional breathing helps you to
better navigate life.

For example, in your Gratitude Challenge, you learned that we are wired to dwell on negative thoughts as a survival mechanism. But when we're feeling low, these thoughts can wander and spiral into a default-mode cycle of sadness, doubt, and shame. Studies show that practices like intentional breathwork can help to tame a wandering mind, so you can "let go and refocus."

"The real power in breathwork is realizing that you have control over your inner landscape and can regulate how you feel anytime you want," says Huberman.

So how do you want to feel? More excited? More relaxed? Or do you want to stay right where you are?

Intentional breathing gives you control of internal levers. You drive. You decide if you're going to accelerate, brake, or go on cruise control.

Cnossen, for example, uses daily breathwork to keep himself in steady cruise control. "Some days," he says, "when I'm stuck in line at the airport or waiting for an appointment, those are golden opportunities to take a couple of deep breaths and refocus. It resets me."

As Huberman notes, when you control your internal states, "You stand a lower chance of getting triggered under stress, and a higher chance of being more effective at all the things you do— which means you can really show up for the people in your life."

Attentional breathwork provides you with greater resilience and focus; while intentional breathwork lets you change the way you respond to stressful situations in real time. Commit to your two new breathing practices and soon you'll begin to internalize and rely on these powerful inside-out tools.

Let's Do This

Stress will always be with us. It's a survival mechanism that nature uses to nudge us to find a mate, hunt for food, and protect our tribes. Our ancestors needed it to live, but in our modern-day world, stress often keeps us from accomplishing our goals and being present for others in the way we want to be. It doesn't have to be that way for you.

The next time you feel anxious, glance at your **Challenge Bracelet or visual cue** and remember that you possess an inside-out tool that you can deploy at will. At the end of this Challenge, stay the course at a pace that works best for you. Maybe that's doing loving-kindness breathwork every other day for 10 minutes. Maybe one night this week, take three deep breaths before you walk into your home so you can clear your mind, let go of tension, and be present for the people you care about.

It may feel difficult at times to incorporate breathwork into your daily routine. If you miss a practice, don't beat yourself up. Just get back in the driver's seat the next day. And the next. Commit to this month's Challenge. It's one of the simplest yet most powerful inside-out tools you possess. Which is why so many successful people—from physicians and business titans to Paralympians—rely on it to achieve their dreams.

It's time to take your Metrics of Change Survey!

Track key areas of change throughout the Madefor Program by completing the short five-question survey provided in the back of the book - *it will only take 5 minutes to complete!* For the most accurate results, we recommend completing the survey before your Month 1: Hydration Challenge, Month 5: Breath Challenge, and Month 10: Vision Challenge (3 times total).

Complete the survey (Tools and Resource Section).

Pat's Breath Guidance

At the outset of Madefor you set an intention for what you hope to achieve through this program—take a moment to reflect on and record how engaging this challenge might help serve your intention.

Each Madefor Challenge is meant to serve as an entry point, not a destination, helping you to feel and better understand the benefits of your actions, so that over time, you can discover how best to be you.

By removing the destination this month, you take away the pressure of trying to arrive at some mythic place of enlightenment and instead you learn to appreciate how your breath can be engaged to drive your body and mind in a way that suits you best.

If you struggle to stay on track this month, consider taking this small step—can you direct one intentional breath? Allow yourself to feel what happens when you do so. Recognize that this tool, your breath, is always with you and always elicits a response—you have control, no matter what is happening around you. If one step is too hard, revisit your intention for inspiration. You got this.

For additional support, check out my <u>Perspectives video</u> for more information around how we designed this Challenge, recommendations on how to approach the daily exercises, and real-life experiences and perspectives from Madefor Members that have completed the journey. Or, listen to this quick <u>Campfire Story</u> for a little inspiration.

*Madefor Videos and Audio recordings can be found on our YouTube page (https://www.youtube.com/@getmadefor)

Shift into motion

 You're a mover. You've been moving your whole life, although your relationship with movement has changed over time.

At first, it was a natural part of your day: You explored, took risks, and found joy in motion. But then something changed and the focus narrowed to results: a better body, a faster time, a perfect score.

At Madefor, we believe that movement is the path and the reward. We've studied and worked alongside some of the best experts in the field to pressure-test your Movement Challenge. All agree that wherever you fall on the fitness spectrum, the practices you're about to engage in bring real and attainable mental and physical benefits.

This month, join us in a new and counterintuitive approach to movement. This Challenge has the potential to shift the way you think about fitness as you power your brain and body for life.

Keep moving,

BLAKE & PAT

The Basics

"Let's play!"

When we were young, these two words were an invitation to move our bodies with joy. To chase a friend in a game of tag, jump into a pile of leaves, or roll down a grassy hill until we fell into heaps of laughter.

But somewhere along the way to adulthood, we lost touch with how much fun it can be to move. We started calling it "exercise" or "working out." Maybe that's when movement transitioned from being a regular part of life into, essentially, a chore.

For some of us, exercise is a highly regimented, results-oriented activity, which, we've convinced ourselves, requires the right cross-training shoes, gym membership, and digital devices in order to measure, record, and track our actions with precision.

Maybe for a short time, we actually got better at running, swimming, cycling, or lifting weights. **But our bodies are capable of a much greater range of motion—and play is where that full variety shows up.** When we stopped playing, and started focusing on reps in the gym and data on a device, we set down a path toward limited range of motion and a decline in all the benefits that physical activity can bring to our bodies, hearts, and minds.

Not anymore. This month, you are going to reconnect with the simple joy of movement. You'll bounce, bend, roll, and balance to a special **Movements video series** created by Madefor advisor Rory Cordial, a physical therapist and strength-and-conditioning specialist (available in your Tools

& Resources section). Cordial's clients include elite athletes and world-renowned entertainers, who rely on his custom designed movement programs to help them perform at their very best. Now he's designed one for you that specifically aligns with your Madefor journey.

As part of your Challenge this month, you'll also add a brain-boosting activity into your life with a daily **Attention Walk**—ten minutes of unstructured forward motion that's proven to build mental and physical muscle.

To be clear: Madefor Movement is not an exercise program or workout routine. It's a new way of appreciating your body and all it can do for you. This small perception shift makes flexing your muscles and getting your heart rate up a more natural, fun, and sustainable practice you can do for a lifetime. You still get the health benefits of exercise, but the difference is that you'll begin to incorporate more activity into your life as an integral part of how you operate in the world. Movement becomes its own reward.

If you're already athletic, you may think you've got this Challenge covered or that it's not grueling enough. But very often, active adults engage in repetitive habits that don't honor their body's full range of motion.

For example, if you do an exercise-bike routine every morning, your legs will get stronger and you'll have more power within that specific plane of motion. But the same stooped position that serves you well on the bike doesn't serve you well when you're bending over to pick up a child or loading luggage in the car or dancing with your partner. **Life requires a wide variety of biomechanical movements.** Hyper-specialization comes at a cost, including repetitive stress injuries and an inability to do other activities you enjoy.

In fact, professional athletes are especially prone to injury, inflammation, and decreased range of motion as they age, according to Cordial, because they engage in repetitive motor operations, like throwing baseballs 95 mph or bracing for impact from a 250 lb linebacker.

"Elite performers can push their bodies beyond what normal people are comfortable with," Cordial says. "Even when their muscles are screaming and their body says 'stop,' they can keep going. But they won't be able to keep moving like that for long if they don't learn how to counteract the damage from repetitive stress."

Wherever you fall on the activity spectrum—from sedentary to super-active—chances are you've picked up habits over the years that can lead to decreased mobility and increased pain. That's what happened to Cordial's client Laura Gordon, a former professional tennis player and coach who, at 34, woke up in unbearable pain one morning.

"My neck was tight; my upper back and shoulders were locked up," Gordon recalls. "If you've ever slept on your neck wrong and you can't really move it—it was like that but 50 times worse."

A natural athlete, Gordon worked out several times a week, trained for marathons, and was constantly in motion. But her muscles were so stiff she could barely move, except to type an urgent text: *Rory, 911. Please come see me.*

Right away, Cordial could see that her body was "glaringly out of whack." He put his hands on her neck and shoulders and said, "*Oh.* This is not good. What did you do?"

Gordon had spent the previous weekend traversing the Santa Monica Mountains with a 35 lb pack on her back, training for a 25-mile Grand Canyon hike she and her sister were planning to do as a fundraiser for her favorite charity.

That hike, she explained to Cordial, was just eight weeks away. She had to get better soon. She couldn't let the charity or her sister down.

Cordial went to work, loosening up Gordon's muscles. After a week of conditioning, he got to the important next step of helping Gordon retrain her brain: She needed to self-correct the sport-specific habits that had led to her injury.

She learned, for example, that the way she'd held a tennis racket for the last 20 years—shoulders tense and hunched forward as she waited for a returned ball—had likely caused her neck problems. In fact, her posture was not all that different from how many of us sit in front of a computer: shoulders hunched, neck tense, chin down.

"I hold a lot of stress in my neck and shoulders," Gordon says. "So when I hiked for 25 miles with a heavy backpack, I was tensed up for 11 hours. I didn't even realize I was holding tension until everything locked up."

After incorporating Cordial's custom movements into her life, some of the same ones you'll learn in this month's Challenge, her posture improved, her shoulders relaxed, and her head and neck kept in healthy alignment.

Two months later, Gordon and her sister geared up at the South Rim of the Grand Canyon. It was the first time she'd worn the heavy pack since her injury, and she was nervous about hurting herself again.

Over two long days of backpacking from the South Rim, down to base camp, and then up to the North Rim, Gordon occasionally checked in with her body, listened for pain points, and recalibrated her posture.

"Any time I felt a little bit of tension, I'd remind myself, 'Keep your head back, release your shoulders. Just relax,'" she says.

When they reached the North Rim, the finish line, a heavy blanket of snow covered the red ground. For Gordon, it was a beautiful reward for a successful journey. In the end, they'd raised more than $90,000 for charity—and she did it completely pain-free.

"It was amazing," she says. "As athletes, we don't listen to our bodies very much. When you're 21, you just move however you want and don't think about repercussions. But movement gives me light and joy. So I want to be able to do it well for the rest of my life. That's what Rory has given me."

And that's what this Challenge is going to give you: Easy ways to engage in intelligent, natural movements for life, so that your body is loose, strong, and capable of its full range of motion—the kind of motion you were born knowing how to do.

"The power is in its simplicity," Cordial says. "It's just about bringing greater awareness to how we move."

Whether you're someone who sits at a desk all day or an athlete who's constantly pushing your body, **this Challenge meets you where you are.** So get ready to reclaim the joy of movement for a lifetime.

The Challenge

Your Movement Challenge Exercises:

Attention Walk:
For 21 consecutive days, take a ten-minute daily walk to give your body, heart, and brain a big lift. Put your phone in your Madefor Pouch (or leave it at home) and be present to your environment. Give yourself permission to enjoy the simple act of forward motion.

Madefor Movements:
Once a day, for 21 days, set your timer and spend at least ten minutes following the patterns in your Madefor Movements video series in your Challenge Motivation section.

Reflect in your Journal:
Each night of your Challenge, write a few sentences about your experiences. What thoughts or feelings came up during your Walk? Did your Movements give you greater physical control? Reflect on how motion made your mind and body feel.

We all know that movement is good for us. But exercise often feels like something we have to do instead of something we *can't wait* to do.

"The best workout I had this year wasn't a workout at all, it was a soccer game with a friend and his kid," says Madefor advisor and Stanford neuroscientist Dr. Andrew Huberman. "It was just us kicking that ball around in the same way we did when he and I were kids, back when we'd go out and skateboard for an entire day, or go hiking in the hills and then find a lake to swim in."

"Real wellness is about doing the things that are good for you, not because you've talked yourself into it," he says, "but because you actually *really* enjoy it."

During your Fuel Challenge, you discovered that eating is more pleasurable when you listen to what your body truly wants, rather than listening to the latest diet guru. It wasn't about a number on a scale. It was about reclaiming your innate wisdom around food—which ultimately led you to eat more of the vitamin and mineral-rich nutrients your body needs to perform at its best.

Likewise, with Movement, your goal this month isn't about hitting a specific number on a fitness tracker. It's about reclaiming your ability to move with ease and joy.

As you break through old patterns and explore new ways to move, you'll begin to have a greater sense of what your body needs to feel strong, limber, and ready to go. You'll be reminded of how easy it is to play any time you want, no gym membership or special equipment necessary.

- MEMBER MOMENT -

"I've loved this. As a former yoga instructor that was sidelined due to repetitive stress injury and surgery, this has allowed me to reconnect to the love of movement. 10 minutes first thing in the day is blissful!"

- Courtney W

There are two components to this month's Challenge: Your **Attention Walks** tap into the mental and physical benefits that a daily walk provides, encouraging more motion in your life as you internalize the rewards; while **Madefor Movements** give you greater control of your body using Rory Cordial's specially designed patterns, inspired by the movements of our youth.

Let's start with your Attention Walks. Once a day, stop whatever you're doing, set your phone aside, and take a walk outside for at least ten minutes. Make time for your Walk that's distinct from any other physical activity you engage in each day.

As you interact with your environment, be present to your body. How do your leg muscles feel as you walk up a slight hill? Notice the tension in your neck and shoulders, then inhale deeply and release it. As you breathe, take in the scenery. Enjoy the aromas from your neighborhood café, the sound of birdsong, the feel of the ground underneath your feet. Be grateful for your body's ability to sense all these things as it propels you forward.

If you're an athlete and hyper-focused on performance, you may have disconnected with the pleasure of walking. This is a great time to take deep belly breaths and just be present. You don't need to complete a certain number of laps, just go at a pace that feels comfortable. Say hello to the people you pass by. Kick a rock down the sidewalk for fun. Or better yet, bring a **Movement Ball*** (identify your own) and bounce it as you walk. See how you can change the velocity and trajectory of its journey with subtle changes in the way you throw it. Check in with your muscles and joints, notice how they feel, and honor all the hard work they do for you. *(*Your Movement Ball can be any ball that serves the same purpose - lacrosse, tennis, rubber, etc.)*

"Just walking once a day will make you feel more invested in the world around you. Before long, you'll want to get out there even more," says Madefor advisor and Harvard Medical School psychiatry professor Dr. John Ratey, whose best-selling book

Spark investigates the transformative effect movement has on our brains.

When you walk, Ratey says, you're bathing your brain in feel-good chemicals. He ticks them off like a recipe for happiness: "We have dopamine, norepinephrine, serotonin, oxytocin, endorphins, endocannabinoids," he says. "All are elevated when we move—and this list just gets us started."

Add to that list: proteins that play pivotal roles in our thought processes, like brain-derived neurotrophic factor, or BDNF, which nourishes our brains like fertilizer does a garden; and vascular endothelial growth factor, or VEGF, which stimulates the formation of blood vessels to bring more oxygen and blood flow to our brains.

A daily **Attention Walk** can be a game-changer at work. Whenever you feel mentally stuck on a project or just need to get the creative juices flowing, a short walk is proven to super-boost your creativity. In a 2014 study at Stanford University, researchers asked 176 adults to complete creative-thinking tasks after walking or sitting for 5 to 16 minutes. **They found that the walkers' creative output increased by 60% compared to the sitters.**

"Even just a ten-minute walk can bring about greater arousal, creativity, and motivation," Ratey notes, citing inventive thinkers from Aristotle to Richard Branson, who are known for favoring walking meetings over sit-downs because they generate more novel ideas and solutions.

> **Fig. 1**
> *Movement is like Miracle-Gro
> for the brain.*

In fact, Ratey calls movement "Miracle-Gro for the brain" because it can even spur neurogenesis, the formation of new brain cells. And if you're among the 1 in 8 American adults who take antidepressants, **just 30 minutes a day of movement can be more effective than medication**, according to research from Duke University.

"It's simply one of the best treatments we have," Ratey says. He's seen the benefits up close. As a clinical psychiatrist and author of 11 books that have been translated into 17 languages, he's helped people around the world to alleviate symptoms from ADHD, ADD, depression, addiction, and other mental disorders simply by incorporating more movement into their lives.

If your job involves hours of sitting, a daily **Attention Walk** might even save your life. In a 2016 study of 8,100 adults over age 45, researchers found that **people who frequently sat for more than 90 minutes at a stretch had a 200% greater risk of early death** by any cause than those who almost always sat for less than 90 minutes at a stretch.

<u>Think about this when you look at your Movement Ball. Promise yourself that you will move your body more.</u>

Countless studies show that people who engage in regular activity have better odds of preventing or managing high blood pressure, cholesterol, and diabetes. It can also reduce your risk of heart disease, breast cancer, stroke, arthritis, and a host of other chronic illnesses. Your daily ten-minute **Attention Walk** is an easy entry-point for getting more movement into your life—and it doesn't have to be a knee-buckling, collapse-at-the-finish-line kind of effort. If you can feel your heart beating or if carrying on a conversation makes you catch your breath a little, then you've reached a good threshold for enhanced overall wellbeing.

Movement is dose-dependent: the more you move, the greater your rewards. **But just 150 minutes a week (about 20 minutes a day) is the minimum dose for achieving maximum benefits**, according to the latest evidence-based guidelines from the U.S. Department of Health and Human Services. **And here's the twist: That number includes *any* dose of activity**. Just four minutes of pacing during a phone call or six minutes walking to your car is beneficial and counts toward a 150-minute goal.

Keep your **Movement Ball** in a place where you spend the majority of your day, and let it serve as a reminder to get up and move. Take it with you on a walk and invite a friend or co-worker along. Soon, you'll naturally incorporate more movement into your day. The next time someone asks to meet for coffee, suggest a walking meeting instead. When you get home from work, grab a leash and go play with your dog. Or take an after-dinner stroll with your roommate, partner, or kids and enjoy the night air. You don't need an excuse. Just move.

➤ **Fig. 2**
Your Movement Ball is a reminder to get up, walk, play, and reconnect with the joy of motion.

The second part of your Challenge prepares you for a lifetime of better movement. To begin, set a **Timer** and find a comfortable space that's big enough so you can lay down with your arms outstretched. Then access your **Madefor Movements video series** (available in your Tools & Resources section).

The end goal is that you learn the patterns so well, they become muscle memory and you can do them any time you wish, no screens needed.

Before you start, close your eyes and do a brief body scan. How do your head and neck feel? Are you experiencing any tension? Any pain points? Just as you did in your Breath Challenge, build your interoceptive awareness by noticing and honoring your body's signs and signals. Breathe into these points of constriction and let the tension go. Express gratitude for all your body does for you. Then begin moving.

When Laura Gordon injured her neck, she discovered that years of playing competitive tennis caused debilitating postural habits. "Even just picking up weights or lifting a suitcase, I never did it right," she says. After working with Rory, she knew she was headed toward a dim future unless she changed her habits. But Gordon's sport-specific habits aren't all that different from the physical maladjustments non-athletes pick up.

"Text neck" refers to the epidemic of stiffness, headaches, and muscle weakness among smartphone users who hold their heads forward and down to look at their phones. "Mom posture" (the slumped-and-rounded-shoulders look that results from carrying babies on your hips) can lead to early wear and tear on the spine, but it also strikes dads and anyone else who sits in a forward-flexed posture all day looking at a computer screen.

Given our poor habits, imagine a world in which you can no longer get up and down from the couch with ease. How would you feel if you had to pass up camping trips, bike rides, and hiking with friends? Picture not being able to get down on the floor to play with a child because it's too painful. That's the kind of future we all face when we neglect to listen to our bodies and recalibrate to healthier, more natural alignment.

Gordon had a world-class physical therapist and performance coach to help her repair her body and prevent future injuries. But the majority of individuals don't have the access or re-sources to bring someone like Cordial into their lives. That's why we asked him to create an effective routine that you can do in less time than it takes to enjoy a morning cup of coffee.

Cordial has traveled the world caring for clients, but he grew up in Missoula, Montana, with a physical therapist father, two younger brothers who became chiropractors, and a sister who's a massage therapist. You can imagine the dinner-table conversations the Cordial family had about the tight quadri-ceps or misaligned spines they'd seen that day.

What makes Cordial unique is that he has encyclopedic knowl-edge of physical therapy, biomechanics, physiology, anatomy, and kinesiology, but he also knows what it takes for an athlete to reach optimal performance.

Cordial goes on tour with Grammy Award–winning singers to keep them in top shape, is routinely flown out to work with professional athletes who want to stay healthy during their season, and is the trusted go-to when they want to gain an advantage during the off-season. Because **he understands both the body's current capacity and its wider potential**, he can show a Major League Baseball player how to add speed to his fastball with less injury, or teach a world-class entertainer how to be her best night after night.

For your **Movements Challenge**, you'll spend 10 minutes a day with Cordial, following his lead as he guides you through a practice that incorporates his years of training and experience. Cordial's techniques are inspired by the scientific principles of developmental kinesiology (how we develop movement), arthrokinematics (the movement of joint surfaces), and motor control (how we regulate and enact movement).

<u>In essence, you're going to reconnect to the motor functions you developed and perfected as a baby.</u>

"Babies engage in movement patterns and positions that are hardwired into their nervous systems," he says. "No one shows a baby how to roll over or sit up. They have perfect alignment as they transition to a half-kneel to standing to squat to crawl. Those patterns are the blueprint for normal adult movement."

Research indicates that after 30, men and women begin to naturally develop bone loss. Sedentary behaviors lead to further bone loss and restriction of movement, putting you at greater risk of a bad back, broken hips, weak ankles and knees, and torn rotator cuffs—all of which reduces your ability to remain independent as you grow old. But Rory's patterns can help you achieve a fuller range of motion and mobility for a lifetime. You can reverse the effects of bone loss, and reduce the risk of falls and injuries, simply by moving your body with greater control and more frequency. As you integrate rolls, crawls, moving on hands and knees, and other playful motions into your daily movements, you'll gain enduring stability.

"These movement patterns build the literacy of the body," Cordial says. "You're reconnecting with what you were made to do: To interact with the environment around you; to be able to get up and down from the floor with ease; to maintain good form and posture; and ultimately to engage in life's activities with freedom and confidence."

"Once you're comfortable with the positions, then you can start to explore your strength: 'Can I lift this leg? Can I reach that? Can I move even faster?' That's when it's time to *play*," Cordial says.

In fact, the last portion of your series is *all* about play. When most people think of getting fit, they think of going to spin class, yoga, lifting weights. Cordial's goal is to get you to think about playing.

"As kids, we learn by touching things, and climbing, and gathering spacial awareness. As adults, we lose touch with exploration," he says. "The longer you live your life being out of touch with how you were designed to move, the more you lose access to early movements, to exploration, to engaging with your environment."

That doesn't have to be your reality. Just ten minutes a day with Cordial puts you back in touch with foundational biomechanics.

It's a little like learning to ride a bike or drive a car: Once the motions are wired into your brain—you can steer, brake, and accelerate with control and ease—you begin to see the world a little differently. You start to venture out, enjoy your new freedom, and move more. As Huberman puts it, "There's a whole other channel of new experiences available to us when we drop in to our ability to find joy in movement."

For some, that might look like greater confidence as you hit a hiking trail, join a game of pickup soccer, or finally construct that fort your kids have been dreaming about. For others, it might mean incorporating better mechanics into your motions, like automatically squatting like a baby to pick up a pencil, or getting on one knee as you reach across your garden to pick a tomato.

Your **Madefor Movements video series** (available in your Tools & Resources section) is designed to meet you at your current

163

fitness level. If you're already physically active, you'll engage in some of the same operations that Cordial puts top athletes and entertainers through to help them achieve optimal performance and mind-body control. If the patterns come easily to you, then concentrate on your form, be present to the sensations in your body, and focus on releasing tension.

Alternately, if just rolling from your back to your stomach feels really difficult, that's okay too. Spend ten minutes working only on that. Take your time practicing each pattern until you're ready to try the next one.

A bad back or knees shouldn't prohibit you from doing your Challenge, but if you have serious disabilities, then practice the spirit of the Movements using modifications that meet your needs.

> **Fig. 3**
> *A baby's natural movement patterns are your blueprint for better movement for life.*

21 Days of Movement: Journaling prompts

What ways did you move today?

Were there any areas of tension or stress in your body?

What did moving your body allow you to do today that you enjoyed?

How or where would you like to move your body tomorrow?

Did moving provide any positive outcomes or additional benefits throughout your day?

What sights, sounds, and smells did you notice on your Attention Walk?

How did you feel after your Walk?

Did you notice yourself moving differently after your first week of Madefor Movements? Second week? Third week?

Did you have any aha moments about repetitive patterns that may be causing tension in your body?

What were your favorite ways to move and play as a child?

What types of movement now bring you the greatest joy?

Write about a time you moved alongside friends.

What activities and movements do you want to be able to do in old age?

Write about a time this week in which you found yourself moving just for fun. How did it make you feel?

A quick word on journaling: If you've been a little lax with it, now is the time to commit to a daily practice. Refer to the provided journal prompts to get you started. Just taking a few minutes before bedtime to reflect on the Challenge will keep you on track and reinforce your new habits.

In a study at New Hampshire University, researchers found that subjects who recalled a positive memory about physical activity were significantly more likely to engage in that activity again compared to students who did not reflect on their experience. But even when they recalled a negative memory, they were *still* more apt to engage compared to the control group.

So just write. If you don't enjoy moving at first, that's fine. Put your thoughts on the page and keep at your practice. The neural focus that writing creates builds internal rewards.

<u>Soon, movement becomes its own reward.</u>

Let's Do This

Results are important. But results are about a destination, an end-point. Your Madefor journey is about process. The goal of your Movement Challenge isn't to develop rock-hard abs or be the fastest mom in the Labor Day 10K.

Your goals are to:

1. Acknowledge any mental barriers to physical activity you may have developed, let them go, and reconnect with the simple joy of movement.
2. Listen to your body. Pay attention to where you're accumulating stress. And begin to let go of that stress in ways that serve your body best.
3. Learn a few subtle biomechanical corrections that will help you move with control and ease for a lifetime.

Instead of obsessing over how many reps you completed or how many miles you ran, **give yourself permission to slow down and be present to what your body is feeling**, to how it moves, to how you may be stressing it in ways that can cause damage.

At the end of the month, you want to be able to say: "I learned to listen to my body and discover where and when I hold tension. I know how to recalibrate the way I move so as to better serve my body. I'm grateful for all it does for me, and I'm going to honor it by giving it what it needs to stay strong for life."

That's true mind-body integration.

For the next three weeks, as you go through your Challenge, commit to nurturing your body with healthy, joyful movement.

And when you put on your Challenge Bracelet or glance at your Challenge screen, or notice your Movement Ball sitting on your desk, let them be reminders that you deserve more playtime in your life.

You don't need to wait for an invitation from anyone. Just move!

- - -

A reminder: *The Madefor Challenges are designed with an advisory board of experts, and they are safe and effective for the majority of members, but they are not intended to replace the advice of your doctors. If you have a medical condition, do not begin this Challenge without first consulting your physicians.*

Pat's Movement Guidance

At the outset of Madefor you set an intention for what you hope to achieve through this program—take a moment to reflect on and record how engaging this challenge might help serve your intention.

This month is not about fitness. It's not about losing weight. And it's certainly not about performance. It is about rediscovering the joy of movement and the ways in which you can serve your body with movement. I understand how that may come across as too soft (especially if you're an athlete or someone with a dedicated fitness regimen); however, after having served thousands of Members from every background imaginable, I can tell you that everyone benefits when they take time to listen to and serve the body with movement.

Last year, I received a note from a Member, explaining that she was dismissive of this Challenge at first. At 64 years of age, she "knew" what she could do with the limitations of her body and didn't see any value in trying something new. During the Challenge, she had a breakthrough—a realization that at some point in her life, she had unknowingly internalized the belief that her best days were behind her. Through this Challenge, she was able to identify and set that limiting belief aside and embrace a new reality—her best days are ahead.

I hope you have some fun with this Challenge as you discover new ways to tune in and serve your body with movement.

If you struggle to stay on track this month, consider taking this small step—can you close your eyes for a few breaths, listen to what your body says, and move accordingly? Feel what happens when you do—remember, movement at any dose is good for you, and movement begets movement. If one step is too hard, revisit your intention for inspiration. You got this.

**I recommend listening to the Basecamp I did with Dr. Kelly McGonigal or at least reading the summary (Basecamp Summary Section of Book). One of her central findings is directly applicable to your Movement Challenge. The more you move, the better life is. Movement expands your capacity for pleasure. How cool is that?

For additional support, check out my Perspectives video for more information around how we designed this Challenge, recommendations on how to approach the daily exercises, and real-life experiences and perspectives from Madefor Members that have completed the journey. Or, listen to this quick Campfire Story for a little inspiration.

*Madefor Videos and Audio recordings can be found on our YouTube page (https://www.youtube.com/@getmadefor)

A walk in the park

Every Madefor Challenge you've completed so far has involved a dialogue. You've been building your awareness of the call-and-response conversation that takes place between your body and the small habits you engage in. When your body tells you that it's hungry, thirsty, or ready to move, for example, you respond in kind.

This month, we ask you to build on your progress as you engage with a familiar environment in an unfamiliar way: We want you to have a dialogue with nature.

We promise, it's not as silly as it sounds. When you become more aware of the signals your brain and body are sending and receiving within your environment—whether you're walking through a busy city or a peaceful park—you begin to better understand how this daily conversation affects your mental and physical wellbeing.

The steps you take this month will prove that a dialogue with nature is a conversation worthy of your time.

Enjoy your better nature,

BLAKE & PAT

The Basics

Imagine you lived in Tokyo, one of the most densely populated cities in the world. Every day, you'd be one of the 13.6 million people who squeeze into 846 square miles of glass-and-steel skyrises, roaring bullet trains, and concrete expressways. Maybe you'd be among the millions who go to fluorescent-lit offices each morning to stare at computer screens, breathe recycled air, and leave at nightfall, when the city buzzes with neon signage so bright it practically vibrates the bones.

This electric urban capital probably doesn't make you think of lush green landscapes. However, in 2005, Tokyo is where scientists began to make new discoveries about the protective effect that nature has on our bodies and brains.

Most of us intuitively know that it feels good to walk in the park. But at Tokyo's Nippon Medical School, immunologist Dr. Qing Li wanted to know if there was evidence behind these feelings. What he discovered was groundbreaking: **Spending time in natural settings not only lowers our stress and elevates our mood, it's also a super-charged battery boost to our immune system.**

Nature makes us happier and healthier. It replenishes our attention reserves. And the positive effects are long lasting.

As Li and other scientists around the world have discovered, nature is an effective balance point to the stress of modern life.

This month, you're going to unplug, recharge, and experience the benefits of nature with three Challenge exercises proven to raise your mental and physical baselines and give you a greater sense of wellbeing.

It was 1982 when the Japanese government first invented the phrase *shinrin yoku*, or forest bathing, as a way to entice people to bathe in the healing effects of its many forests and, hopefully, feel more invested in protecting them. But by the early '90s, Japan had entered a long period of recession that brought alarming levels of stress and depression among its hardworking citizens. Since talk therapy was not widely culturally accepted, *shinrin yoku* became a public imperative, an easily accessible way to lift the mood of a nation.

By 2004, the government began funding research to investigate *shinrin yoku* from a scientific perspective and Dr. Li led the charge, taking groups of men and women with hectic careers on day trips into the mountains of Iiyama in northwest Japan. They hiked muddy trails, touched the cool red bark of Japanese cypress trees, breathed in fresh mountain air, and provided the scientist with blood, saliva, and urine samples before and after their journeys.

Previous research had established that spending time in nature correlated with positive changes to our heart rate, blood pressure, and stress hormones (cortisol and adrenaline). Even just a view makes us feel better, as healthcare-design expert Roger Ulrich discovered in 1984 when he found that hospital patients with windows that faced trees recovered quicker and asked for less pain medication than patients who had a view of a brick wall.

But as an immunologist, Dr. Li wanted to know: *How does spending time in nature influence our natural killer cells?*

Natural killer (NK) cells, a vital part of our immune defense system, actively seek and destroy virally infected cells. They do this surveillance work with the help of cancer-fighting proteins perforin, granulysin, and granzymes. (Researchers are racing to create NK-cell therapies for prostate cancer, leukemia, lymphoma, and other diseases.)

Li found that after just two days in nature, his stressed-out hikers were more relaxed *and* they got a remarkable immune system boost: **Their NK-cell activity increased by 53% and the number of NK cells in their blood rose by 50%.** Their granulysin, perforin, and granzyme proteins also rose significantly. Best of all, **the changes were long-lasting: 30 days later they still had 15% greater levels of NK cells than before their nature trip.**

"I was happy, but not so surprised," Li recently recalled. In fact, he wondered if the spike in health was simply the result of exercise. So he conducted more studies: He took one group on forest walks and another on city walks, then compared their results. The forest walkers still had higher NK cell numbers— and their immune boost lasted longer than the city walkers'. Nature, not just walking, was causing these remarkable results.

Li had a hunch that it had something to do with the chemistry of the forest, or more specifically, the protective chemicals in the Japanese cypress or hinoki (*Chamaecyparis obtusa*) tree.

If you've ever walked through the woods and noticed the Christmas-y smell of pine or the pungent menthol of eucalyptus, you're actually breathing in chemicals that the trees release to communicate with their environment. In simple terms, these aromatic chemicals warn hungry insects, birds, and bacteria to stay away. But the trees also use chemicals to exchange information, like the time when Sitka willows in Washington sounded the alarm on a devastating caterpillar infestation.

> **Fig. 1**
> *Unplug and join the conversation.*

As geobiologist Hope Jahren describes in her book *Lab Girl*, the ravaged, dying willows flooded the air with distress chemicals that traveled over a mile to another group of Sitka willows. The second group picked up the airborne alerts and began to emit chemicals that made its leaves unpalatable to the fast-approaching insects. When the caterpillars reached the second grove, they died of malnourishment. The trees survived thanks to the protective language of the forest—the same kind of invisible language that seemed to be having an immune system boost on Dr. Li's test subjects.

Japanese hinoki trees also emit "phytoncides," or protective chemicals, which are lemony and woodsy to the human nose. Li wondered if simply breathing them could have an effect. So he had study participants go about their normal day, but for three nights they slept in a Tokyo hotel room in which he'd filled a normal household diffuser with hinoki essential oils.

The results were astounding: Significant increases in the numbers and activity of NK cells, decreased levels of stress hormones, better sleep, and improved overall mood.

Think of it this way: When we commune with nature, we are drawn into a conversation. We take in the protective chemistry of the forest whether or not we even realize it. Li's research proved that you can bring the forest home with you. **He found that just by breathing the hinoki essential oils, test subjects received about 50% of the positive effects they received from taking walks in the woods.**

Since the publication of his work, the amiable, bespectacled professor has become a celebrity among nature enthusiasts and the bestselling author of *Forest Bathing*, a book that's been translated into 26 languages. Thanks to Li and other researchers, there are now 62 "forest therapy bases" across

Japan and a new field, forest medicine, that's sparked global scientific inquiry.

In South Korea, for example, the government has spent $14 million establishing 34 "healing forests" as national research centers. The UK-based Forest Bathing Institute is working with governments and universities to bring people into the woods for research. In Scotland, the largest national hospital system lets doctors prescribe time outdoors as part of a patient's treatment plan. And the United States has its own 150-park-strong "ParkRx" initiative that encourages physicians to write nature scripts for better health.

And yet, all the science and worldwide interest simply affirms what we innately know to be true: We are better when we spend time in nature.

And now you're going to experience the language of the forest, with Challenge exercises that bring the great outdoors into your life in ways big and small. So get ready to recharge, because you were made for nature.

The Challenge

Your Nature Challenge Exercises:

Find a Moment (small doses):
Once a day for 21 days, Find a Moment to bring the forest home. Spray your Hinoki Air Mister or grab your small object from nature (like a flower, pine needles, mint, etc.), close your eyes, and take ten deep breaths. Be present to the positive effects. Find additional ways to bring nature into your day and write one or two sentences in your Journal about how it made you feel.

Find a View (medium dose):
Once a week over the next three weeks, take a 20-minute break and Find a View. You can lie down and stare at the sky or find a vantage point where you can see the horizon. Let your attention wander. Write about the experience in your Journal.

Find a Connection (large dose):
At least once over the next three weeks, spend an entire hour in nature and Find a Connection. Go to a large park, a natural reserve, or a coastal trail and tune in to the conversation happening all around you, paying attention to the visual fractals. Bring your Journal and write about the different ways you connected with nature and how it made you feel.

Evolutionary biology tells us that we were made to move in the wild. It's where trees, plants, and streams gave our ancestors nourishment, shade, and cover from predators. It's where we hunted and raised our families for millions of years. So maybe it is not so surprising, as Li notes, that we are measurably healthier after spending time in nature.

And yet, we are slowly disconnecting from our evolutionary home. In 2008, the World Health Organization reported that more people lived in cities than rural settings for the first time in human history. By 2050, two-thirds of the world's population is expected to move to cities.

Humans have lived in nature for more than 2 million years, a symbiotic relationship that is hardwired in our brains. We've only been living in cities for about 3% of our existence on the planet. We don't know if this nature-deprivation experiment is going to work out for us, but we do know that our brains are paying the price.

Cities are bastions of efficiency and culture. But they also stress us out in ways we may not even notice. That buzzy feeling people get when they visit a place like New York or London? It's partly a result of the **anthrophone**, or man-made noise, that we pick up: the clinking of silverware, lively conversations, music pouring from cafés. Just as we engage in a sensory conversation in the forest, we are constantly sending and receiving signals in urban environments. This constant, wide-ranging conversation excites the senses, but it frazzles the brain.

Research shows that a wide variety of wildlife is responding to our ever-rising anthrophone (airplanes, traffic, motorcycles, motorboats) with stressful behaviors and a decrease in population. So it follows that humans are also a little burned out from increasing exposure to honking horns on our way to work, leaf blowers beyond our bedroom windows, and increased airplane traffic at all hours of the day.

If the brain were a computer, it could consciously process about 120 bits per second, which is about the bandwidth needed to listen to two people talking at the same time—and you know how hard that can be. Now add the anthrophone. In fact, take a moment to close your eyes and listen to the man-made sounds that surround you. Do you hear the low hum of kitchen appliances, the drone of construction work, someone having a very loud phone conversation?

We may think we are tuning out the anthrophone, but this exercise makes us aware of the myriad sounds our brains are processing and making decisions about. A screeching tire, for example, may startle you into action (*look outside*), but the distant whirring of a power saw is registered and filed away.

"We have evolved the ability to pay attention to multiple things at once. It's called covert attention," says Madefor advisor and Stanford neuroscientist Dr. Andrew Huberman. "But the problem is that covert attention is very energetically costly to our brains."

And it gets even more costly when you add technology to the bill. The anthrophone demands attention through our auditory channels, but screens demand our attention through vision, touch, and sound. That's a massive conversation for the brain.

Countless studies tell us that excessive screen time (phones, computers, tablets, and TVs) leads to depression, anxiety, low self-esteem, and poor sleep. **Still, we spend nearly 12 hours a day in front of screens.** One in ten people even admit to checking their phones during sex. We spend five years and four months scrolling through our social media feeds in the span of a lifetime. (In comparison, we spend about three years and five months eating and drinking.)

"We are paying a price for it," says Harvard psychiatrist and Madefor advisor Dr. John Ratey, whose book *Go Wild* tells us how to find our better selves in nature. Ratey cites the increased rates of ADD, ADHD, and other mental disorders that seem to be directly connected to our nature-deprived and digitally distracted lives.

"We fail to appreciate the value of green space," Ratey says. "But we should take a cue from the Japanese, who began prescribing nature as an antidote to the 24/7 lifestyle."

Urban life and modern technology have made our lives simpler. There's no going back. But when we recognize the attentional toll that they take on our brains, we can begin to strike a better balance.

Let's start your first challenge: Find a Moment. This exercise is a nod to the powerful effects of small doses of nature. Just as Japanese scientists distilled hinoki oils to lower stress and raise the health baselines of test subjects, you're going to use a nature object of your choosing (like a flower, pine needles, mint, etc.) to the same effect.

Once a day, **Find a Moment** to bring the forest home:

1. **Close your eyes and hold your nature object in front of you.**
2. **Take ten full belly breaths, and be present to the calming effects.**
3. **Find additional ways to connect with nature today, and write briefly in your Journal about what you did and how it affected you.**

This Challenge seems simple, but it's an essential entry point for getting microdoses of nature into your day. Refer to the "21 Days of Nature" Challenge description below or in your Tools & Resources section. We recognize that modern life can make it hard to get time outdoors. And if you live in a colder climate, winters can feel endless. That's when small moments become your go-to remedy, a restart button that keeps you balanced.

In fact, even brief exposures have strong benefits, according to a study in *Scientific Reports*, which found that 120 minutes a week in untamed environments conveys better health, mood, and feelings of wellbeing. And the time you spend is cumulative, according to the study authors.

This means you can take your morning coffee and go barefoot in the backyard; breathe in the scent of your nature object and do your breathing practice at your desk; walk back from lunch on the tree-lined side of the street; and eat dinner with a view of trees. Soon, you've surpassed a weekly two-hour dose.

Your second Challenge, Find a View, restores your brain's attention reserves using "deliberate disengagement."

"Deliberate disengagement is when you try to relax and disengage your mechanisms of attention. You're letting your attention drift," Huberman says. "And being in nature is a readily accessible way to achieve deliberate disengagement."

Once a week over the next three weeks, take a 20-minute break and find a place where you can lie down and stare at the sky. Or seek out a vantage point that allows you to look out across a vast horizon.

Once you've found your view, breathe deeply, let your focus go soft, and allow your attention to wander. Maybe you'll lose yourself in thoughts about other people, or work, or what you want for dinner. **Give yourself permission to think about anything or nothing at all. This is how you give your brain the break it needs from a media-heavy environment.**

"From the moment you get up in the morning until you go to sleep at night, your life is a series of screens. It's crazy," Huberman says. "But deliberate disengagement is a way of replenishing these stores of attention, allowing you to focus and be more present when you need to be."

➢ **Fig. 2**
Connect with nature daily.
Even small doses provide big benefits.

We often think of "Netflix and chill" as a relaxing way to re-charge. But TV actually requires more cognitive bandwidth and may not be as restorative as, say, watching a sunrise.

Attention Restoration Theory, according to environmental psy-chologists Rachel and Stephen Kaplan, posits that when we're in nature, our attention is lightly occupied, leaving room for our brains to do "mental housekeeping." But watching TV grabs all of our attention. It's difficult to resist. As such, there's no room for tidying up lingering thoughts or resolving problems that have been in our mental periphery.

Finding a View is a way to positively leverage your default mode network, a mental process we've discussed in past Madefor Challenges. When your mind defaults to negative thinking, it puts you at higher risk for stress, depression, and mental illness. But being in nature seems to flip the default mode switch. **As you stare at a horizon and let your attention drift, your mind has the space and time to reflect on life, plan for the future, and recover from stressful situations.**

To test whether time in nature really protects us from our spi-raling negative thoughts, researchers at Stanford sent 38 test subjects on a 90-minute walk in a natural grassland area with oak trees *or* in a heavily trafficked thoroughfare. After their walk, participants self-reported their levels of rumination and were given brain scans. The nature walkers all reported less broody thinking—and their brain scans confirmed it with less neural activity in the subgenual prefrontal cortex, an area of the brain linked to negative emotions. The participants who walked along the busy streets didn't show any reduction in their rumination or corresponding brain activity.

The Find a View Challenge is an easy way to restore your brain's attention and reset its capacity for a positive growth mindset. And it only takes 20 minutes a week. To boost the mental rewards and reinforce this new habit, write about your view and how it made you feel in your Journal.

For your third Challenge, spend at least an hour in a local park, a wooded trail, a nature reserve, or anywhere you can **Find a Connection** in the wild. This time, you're going to immerse yourself in the smells, sounds, textures, and sights of your environment, paying special attention to nature's calming visual signals, or fractals.

Fractals are the complex natural patterns that replicate in similar ways at all levels of scale, from tiny to huge: the geometric spirals of a succulent, the repeated markings across a bird's wingspan, the up-close intricacies of a snowflake. Scientists believe that just gazing at fractals—nature's mathematic language—can bring positive shifts to our mood and stress levels.

- MEMBER MOMENT -

"I live in the country and really thought I was "in nature". But this past couple of weeks I realized I simply passed through it, trying to reach my destination. Now it is my destination." - Tara W

Physicist Richard Taylor, a professor at the University of Oregon and an expert on the relationship between art and science, has led a tremendous amount of research on fractals' ability to soothe and inspire us.

In 1999, Taylor studied the patterns of Jackson Pollock's famous drip paintings to find that the artist composed his layers of paint in a dense web of fractals similar to the fractals found in trees, clouds, and coastlines. No wonder so many find Pollock's paintings mesmerizing: He was innately recreating nature's hypnotic patterns before scientists even knew they existed.

More recently, Taylor has studied how fractals affect our stress levels. Using eye-tracking technology, functional MRIs, and skin conductance to measure nervous activity, he found that gazing at fractals can reduce stress by up to 60% and that it even lights up the parahippocampus, a part of the brain that helps to regulate emotions.

One theory for this calming effect is that fractals are a simpler image for our brain's visual systems to process than, say, the sharp lines, bright lights, and chaotic architecture of a Times Square or a Tokyo.

"About 40% of the volume of the human brain is used for visual processing in some way or another," says Huberman. "So your visual system is the dominant mode by which you spend your attention or recover your attention."

Looking at your phone while waiting in line at the bank may seem relaxing, but as Huberman notes, "you're actually adding more stress to your day, you just don't realize it. It's like taking pennies from the penny jar all day long. It doesn't seem very expensive, but it can become costly over time." Gazing at nature's fractals, on the other hand, is a simple way to make deposits in your mental bank account.

Your three Challenge exercises help you carve out opportunities to reconnect with nature. As your brain picks up the soothing signals of your environment, you get:

1. A boost to your immune system
2. A replenishment of your attention reserves.
3. A more positive mindset

> **Fig. 3**
> *Nature's fractals can*
> *soothe and inspire us.*

When you go to Find a Connection, receive nature's signals however it feels right for you. You can touch the bark of trees and notice the smooth and rough textures. Take a deep whiff of the fragrant smells—and beneficial phytoncides—that the plants and trees are emitting. Listen to the birds chatter as they alert other animals to your presence. And let yourself be mesmerized by the symmetrical patterns all around you. Those fractals are proven to lower stress, and they may even inspire your creative side.

Remember to bring your Journal so you can jot down a few sentences about what you see, smell, touch, and hear—and how it makes you feel. Connect the dots between the science and your experience. How do your brain and body respond to walking through the woods? Do you want to spend more time among plants and trees? Less time? Reflect on the exercise and the rewards that it brings you.

21 Days of Nature:

Small Doses:

Spray your Air Mister or grab your object any time you need a dose of the forest.

Add plants to your home and workspace.

Get a small aquarium with live fish.

Listen to birdsong, one of the most calming sounds of nature. When you can't go to the real thing, Wild Sanctuary is an online archive of authentic nature sounds from around the world.

Once an hour, gaze at nature through a window or in a photo.

Medium Doses:

Walk on the tree-lined side of a street.

Take the longer, more scenic route to work.

Have a meal outside at a park, beach, or green space.

Walk barefoot with your feet directly on the grass, soil, or sand.

Spend time gardening; plant seeds and watch them grow.

Large Doses:

Spend at least an hour in the woods, mountains, or desert.

Go swimming, snorkeling, or fishing in a natural body of water.

Visit your local state park or closest national park.

Go camping and spend the night in nature.

Plan a backpacking trip to an eco-destination.

Let's Do This

Every Challenge you've undertaken on your Madefor journey includes an element of awareness and connection. This month, you're raising your awareness of how you are connected to your environment and how it communicates with you in ways you may not even notice.

Some people say they feel more alive when they are surrounded by the frenetic conversation of urban life, or that the great outdoors makes them feel lonely because the volume is so much lower than what they're used to. If this describes you, that's totally fine. Engage in the Challenge exercises as well as you can, striking a balance that feels right for you.

The conversation of the city is loud, electric, and constant. But because it's going on in the periphery, we often fail to notice how it contributes to our feelings of depletion. Once you become more aware of how time in natural settings gives your brain a much-needed rest, you may begin to crave it more.

Soon, you develop a greater sense of your connection to nature, and you interact with it in a sustainable, meaningful way.

After all, it's our original home. So unplug and tune in to the conversation. **You were made for nature.**

- - -

*A **reminder:** Nature is good for us! But use caution when exploring any environment. From poison oak to strong ocean currents, nature's wild side can be unforgiving. Let common sense be your guide.*

Pat's Nature Guidance

At the outset of Madefor you set an intention for what you hope to achieve through this program—take a moment to reflect on and record how engaging this challenge might help serve your intention.

What I find special about this Challenge is that once you experience nature on a deeper level, you can't unsee it. Nature surrounds us, and when we pay attention to the dialogue between our body and our natural environment, good things happen.

If you struggle to stay on track this month, consider taking this small step—can you step outside and spot a tree, a flower, a plant, or a bird, and appreciate the sounds, sights, and textures of nature? Remember, your body is always in dialogue with the environment that surrounds you. If one step is too hard, revisit your intention for inspiration. You got this.

**I recommend <u>listening to the Basecamp</u> I did with Dr. Lisa Miller. One of her central findings is directly applicable to your Nature Challenge: The science of spirituality shows that you have an innate hardwired capacity to always feel loved, guided, and never alone. Time in nature expands this capacity.

For additional support, check out my <u>Perspectives video</u> for more information around how we designed this Challenge, recommendations on how to approach the daily exercises, and real-life experiences and perspectives from Madefor Members that have completed the journey. Or, listen to this quick Campfire Story for a little inspiration.

*Madefor Videos and Audio recordings can be found on our YouTube page (https://www.youtube.com/@getmadefor)

Madefor clarity

What's the story?

The things you own tell a story—the story of you.

Ideally, as you move through life, your narrative and your possessions stay in sync—your stuff perfectly captures the story you tell yourself and others about who you are.

But sometimes our lives change and our possessions do not. Without time to think through life's transitions, we end up holding on to objects that no longer serve us or tell our story.

This month, you're going to make the time.

As you go through the Challenge, you may decide to make adjustments to your belongings, your story, or both. But there's no pressure to give everything away or reorder anything. Simply stay connected to your story and your stuff will sort itself.

Turn the page,

BLAKE & PAT

The Basics

In 1995, tech designer Graham Hill started his first website-building business with a cousin, and then sold it three years later for the kind of money that would significantly change his life.

Before he became a dot-com success story, Hill grew up the eldest of six siblings on a small farm in Quebec to "fairly conservation-minded parents," he says. They shared hand-me-down clothes that were patched and repaired; they'd wash and reuse plastic bags to carry their lunches to school every day; and his parents drove an old, reliable Suburban until it rusted to pieces. In other words, they used everything they owned.

But when Hill found himself suddenly wealthy at 28, he did what many of us would do: He went on a shopping spree. "I bought a four-story, 3,600-square-foot, turn-of-the-century house in Seattle; a brand-new sectional couch; a pair of $300 sunglasses; and, of course, a black turbocharged Volvo with a remote starter," he says.

Hill felt compelled to fill up his big, empty house, so he bought bedroom sets, stereo equipment, kitchen appliances, and "weird little gadgets that I would not have time to set up, so I forgot I even owned them," he recalls.

When work led him to New York, Hill rented a 1,900-square-foot loft in SoHo, which also needed to be furnished. "It started to feel really wrong, like I was just filling up space," he says. "At some point, I thought to myself: 'Who have I become?'"

In fairness, he had become a typical American consumer, albeit one with considerable means. Americans spent $240 billion in 2017 on things like jewelry, watches, luggage, and smartphones—twice as much as we'd spent in 2002. We're going for larger houses, too. The size of a single-family home in 2017 was 2,426 square feet, a 23% increase in size from two decades earlier. And when our stuff outpaces our space, we rent more space: The number of self-storage units in the United States is double what it was 20 years ago.

Why do we collect so much stuff? One explanation is that it's part of a hardwired survival instinct, a behavior that drove our Stone Age ancestors to hoard food and animal skins as protection during periods of scarcity. "It's why we get a rush of dopamine to the brain just clicking that 'buy now' button on Amazon," says evolutionary biologist and author Dr. Rebecca Heiss. "But today, we have an abundance of choice—in mates, food, clothes, objects to decorate our caves—and this instinct leads us to over-consume."

"It's not fundamentally bad or good that we are wired to acquire objects," adds Madefor advisor and Stanford neuroscientist Dr. Andrew Huberman. "It's just the way our brains get us to move toward goal-directed behavior." As Huberman notes, even animals exhibit this instinct: birds collect possessions for their nests; squirrels cache nuts; dogs bury bones.

But for humans, the instinct becomes more complex because **our possessions also stand as symbols of our identity**. A flag hanging in the neighbor's front yard isn't just a decoration, it symbolizes her connection to her country; a bike rack on a friend's car isn't just a convenient way to transport his bike, it symbolizes his love of the outdoors.

Our belongings are not just *things* to us—they are us, says York University professor Russell Belk, an expert on cultural habits around physical objects. According to Belk's "extended self" theory, we begin to see things outside our physical body—a bath toy, a pet cat, a blanket—as parts of our "self" as young as the age of two. Anything labeled "mine" can also be perceived as "me."

But as we age and our self-concept evolves, our connection to our belongings evolves too, and we shed the objects that no longer serve us in their functionality or as symbols of our identity. That's when, for example, a child abandons a security blanket, a new dad trades in the sports car for an SUV, and a grandmother passes on her jewelry to her grandchildren. After an initial feeling of loss, Belk says, there's often newfound energy and freedom. Or, as Hill would soon discover, a burst of creativity. When we let go of things that no longer serve us, we discover new ways to restore our feelings of wholeness.

And that's what your Challenge is this month. Over the next three weeks, you're going to take a closer look at your relationship with your belongings and how they are bound up in your sense of self. As you go through the exercises, you'll take inventory of a single space in your home, reflect on why you might be holding on to items that no longer serve you, then redeploy them to the greater service of someone else. In the process, you're going to flip the primal switch that drives us all to collect things, and create new, internally generated rewards by redeploying those items.

According to Belk, there are natural times of transition—a graduation, new job, marriage, or a big move—when we feel more ready to shed possessions. But often, the momentum of these periods causes us to miss the opportunity to check in on our belongings, so we continue to hold on to them long after their usefulness to us has expired. If you've moved around a lot, like Hill has, you may discover you've been carting boxes of possessions that you never use (*hello, fondue pot!*), or that you've lost interest in (*looking at you, Thighmaster*), or that no longer match your sense of self (*sorry,* Star Wars *action figures*).

In his early thirties, Hill took a long, hard look at his possessions and asked himself, "Do I own these things or do they own me?" He didn't like the answer: His stuff had become a burden. Nothing he owned represented how he saw himself—as someone who cared about conservation, the environment, and being free to go whenever adventure called. So Hill made a big decision to change his life again. He shed the homes, the car, the furniture, and all the gadgets, and moved to Spain to be with a girlfriend. Holed up in her modest Barcelona apartment, he had a major perception shift: *I can be happy with less.* In a burst of creative energy, he started an environmental news website and then hit the road with his girlfriend.

"We lived out of our backpacks and spent time in Bangkok, India, Morocco..." Hill says. "It was terrific. We were working hard and saving money. We had very full lives."

In fact, Hill determined that everything he really needed could fit in two bags: "In one solar backpack was my office, which included my laptop and whatever else I needed to work; the other bag held my clothing."

Eventually, Hill returned to New York, where he moved into a 350-square-foot apartment—about 10% of the space he had in Seattle. He started a consulting firm that helps people design space-conscious homes with foldable and stackable furniture, walls that move, and beds that double as dinner tables. He also became a vocal advocate for essentialism, the art of living and doing more with less so you can engage with just the things, experiences, and people most essential to you.

Shedding possessions helped Hill get back to his roots and remain true to his identity. But his minimalist lifestyle would probably feel extreme for most. So let's be really clear:

The point of this Madefor Challenge isn't about quantity; it's about quality.

We're not going to ask you to give away things you treasure. And we're certainly not guilting you for having a large home, a garage full of sports equipment, or an office with the latest and greatest technology.

We're simply asking you to tune in to your relationship with your stuff—to develop greater awareness around how your concept of self goes beyond skin and bones. It also extends to things you surround yourself with. This month, take time to recognize the belongings in your possession that no longer serve you or your sense of self. When Hill paused to assess his possessions, he realized they bore no resemblance to how he saw himself—and it was freeing.

That's also how evolutionary biologist Dr. Heiss felt when she left her academic teaching position to run a risky start-up company. Heiss shaved off a major possession—her hair!—in a symbolic act of liberation from an identity that no longer served her.

"My entire life, I'd been told that you go to college, get a stable job, and stay there forever. But at 31, I looked around and thought, 'I am going to die in this job.' I could actually see myself fitting into somebody else's mold of what my life should be like," Heiss recalls of the moment that led her to cut her hair and change her life.

"For me, this act said: 'My hair doesn't define me. I've let other people dictate what I should do and how I should look. But now I'm going to create the person I want to be. This is *my* story that I get to tell."

What stories do your possessions tell about who you are? This month, take a closer look at how your stuff defines you. Then redeploy the items that no longer fit your needs or your story.

As with all Madefor challenges, you decide the right balance. You are in the driver's seat. As you begin to develop a greater awareness around your relationships with your belongings, that clarity becomes an entry point for insights into all of your relationships.

The Challenge

Your Clarity Challenge Exercises:

Week 1: Reflect

In the space of a week, you're going to choose three items that you have very strong feelings about: One that you use frequently (**keep**); one that no longer serves you but you're not ready to part with (**clarity**); and one that you're ready to put into better service elsewhere (**give**). Write about these items in your Madefor Journal, using the prompts provided.

Week 2: Sort

Pick one space in your home—a drawer, closet, garage, or any area you can tackle in a week—and sort through all the items in that space. Stuff you're ready to redeploy goes in your **Giving Bag**. Things you're not ready to part with go in your **Clarity Bag**. Write a few sentences in your Journal, connecting the objects you sorted to the roles they once played (or still play) in your sense of self.

Week 3: Redeploy

Execute your giving plan: Find a person or place where at least one of the items in your **Giving Bag** can be put into better service. Write about the experience in your Journal. How does it feel knowing someone else will be able to use something that no longer serves you.

Let's dive right into your Challenge. **On Day 1** of your Reflect exercise, spend time thinking about the items you use every day. Choose an item you feel strongly about—a desert-island belonging that you can't do without. Maybe it's a pair of perfectly worn-in running shoes, or your dad's wristwatch, or the kitchen knives that you faithfully sharpen after every use.

Think about how this item serves you in its functionality (*it helps me to: stay fit; be on time; cook dinner*) and in how you see yourself (*I'm a runner; I'm a CEO; I'm a chef*).

Ultimately, this Challenge helps you connect the dots: *Here's how I see myself, and here are the objects that tell my story.* Write a couple of sentences in your Journal about what you learned about yourself from your reflections. Then, gather two bags of your choice, to prepare for Days 2 & 3.

On Day 2, identify at least one item among your possessions that you're not ready to let go of even though it no longer serves you. Again, think of objects that elicit the strongest emotional response—something that is no longer of use to you, and yet the thought of parting with it brings you anxiety. Put this item in one of your bags, we'll name it your **Clarity Bag,** and write a few sentences in your Journal about the item, how it once served you, and why you're not ready to part with it. See the "Week 1: Reflect" sidebar for Journaling prompts below to get you started.

Often, as Belk says, we hold on to things that we no longer use because they stand as "memory markers" of our identity, values, and heritage. That busted typewriter in your friend's closet, for example, signals that she values literature. And that torn concert T-shirt you can't bear to toss marks a happy time in your life. Other times, we imbue objects with another person's identity. Which explains why you might hold on to your aunt's gaudy jewelry that you'll never wear or an ex- girlfriend's college sweatshirt that was left behind.

"Attaching meaning and importance to objects is fundamental to our culture," says Huberman. "We give gifts on holidays. We exchange marriage rings as a token of our investment in another person. This is deeply embedded in how we operate, with a very clear reward system associated. But there's also a zone where, if an object no longer serves you and it's collecting dust—maybe you can find new rewards around the act of giving those objects away."

Which brings us to the final Reflection point. **On Day 3**, choose one item that you are ready to give away and imagine who might really want this item. Put it in your second bag, which we'll refer to as your **Giving Bag**, and then write a few sentences in your Journal about how this item once served you, why it no longer does, and who might be able to put it to better use.

This exercise is set up so that you Reflect deeply on one item— keep, clarity, give—per day. But we want you to feel free to take the entire week to complete this task. The important point is to choose items that have deep meaning for you, then reflect on those feelings in your Journal.

To be clear: There are no right or wrong reflections. Your goal is simply to start developing greater awareness about your relationship with stuff. How do (or did) these objects play a role in your sense of self? What stories do these possessions tell about you? Are you comfortable with these stories? Or are you ready to shed these objects and begin a new story?

Week 1: Reflect

Write in your Journal about three objects (keep, clarity, give) that hold deep meaning to you. These examples are simply to help you get thinking.

Stuff I'm keeping:

What is the item?
My cast iron skillet; my laptop.

How does it serve me?
It reminds me to cook at home; it allows me to work from anywhere.

How does it play a role in my extended sense of self?
It shows that I care about my family mealtimes; it signals that I'm someone on the go, who works for myself.

Stuff I need clarity on:

What is the item?
My golf clubs; a baby blanket.

How did this item serve me?
Playing golf bonded me and my dad; the blanket kept my baby warm when I brought her home from the hospital.

What role did it play in my extended sense of self?
When I look at these golf clubs, it reminds me that I was a good son; this blanket feels like a part of my child and reminds me of how much I cherished being a new mom.

Why is it no longer serving me?
I haven't played since Dad died; my child is too big for this blanket.

Is there someone or something that this object could better serve?
The local high school golf club; a women's shelter.

Stuff I'm going to redeploy:

What is the item?
My record player and vinyl collection; college textbooks.

What did it serve me?
It was cool to play records when my friends came over; I studied these books constantly to get my degree.

Why does it no longer serve me?
The novelty wore off and the records are collecting dust; I haven't opened these books since I graduated.

How did it play a role in my extended sense of self?
It symbolizes my taste in music and reverence for older ways of doing things; these books signal that I am smart and hardworking.

Is there someone or something that this object could better serve?
The senior citizen recreation center or the neighbor kid who's into vinyl; the public library.

Now that you've reflected, you're ready for **Week 2: Sort**. Here, you're going to carry out the same process in one entire space in your home. It can be as small as a kitchen drawer or as big as a bedroom closet—or even an entire garage. Just choose an area that you can go through within a week's time. For this exercise, you're essentially putting stuff in one of three places:

1. **Keep**: You use these items, they serve you well, and you're keeping them.
2. **Clarity**: These items no longer serve you, but you don't feel ready to let go of them. Put them in your Clarity Bag.
3. **Give**: These things no longer serve you. You don't use them, or they represent an identity that no longer fits, or you just want to give them to someone who would appreciate them. Put them in your Giving Bag. If something is too big for the bag, write down the item on a piece of paper and put that in the bag.

Try not to feel overwhelmed by the task ahead of you. Just start in one spot and slowly work your way toward completion. Spend as much time as you need to consider: *Do I use this object? How does it play a role in my identity? Could it serve someone else better?*

"For example, when I assess my space," says Madefor co-founder Pat Dossett, "I see two surfboards that I've used once in the last two years. I hold on to them because I have this aspiration that I'm going to have the time to surf one day. And they signal my identity: *I am a surfer.*"

Yet when Dossett reflects on how long those boards have sat untouched (his cat has built a nesting spot on them), he recognizes that when he does find time to go to the beach, he actually swims. He's a swimmer.

"The truth is, I'm probably not going to find the time to surf," he says. "And they could be in the hands of a kid who maybe really wants to surf, but can't because he doesn't have a board."

Give yourself the time and space necessary to reflect on items for which you feel a strong emotional attachment. There's no judgment here. You are the authority. You decide what to keep, give, or set aside until you find clarity.

If you are sorting items with sentimental value, like books and baby clothes, taking digital photographs of these possessions before putting them in your Clarity or Giving Bag may help you preserve the memories and lessen feelings of loss.

A tip from Hill: Write down the date you filled your Clarity Bag, and then come back in six months and ask yourself: *Do I remember what's in this bag? Have I actually used anything from this bag since I filled it?*

> **Fig. 2**
> *A clear space fosters a clear mind.*

- MEMBER MOMENT-

"My BIGGEST breakthrough is that I've given myself permission to heal the aspects of me that formed my identity through my stuff. I purchased many "kitchen toys" when working as a chef. Since I've stopped, the toys have sat on my counter, reminding me of how much I've lost by not working as a chef anymore. This challenge helped me see the guilt I was holding deep inside myself. I decided to donate the items to a soup kitchen and freed myself of that misinformed identity. Just because I'm not currently working as a chef, doesn't mean I'm not a chef. This is hugely transformative for me."

- Johnathan H

"If you don't remember what's in there or you didn't use anything, that should provide the answer: You could probably let it go," Hill says.

If this Challenge feels hard at first, here's some inspiration: When you clear a space, you're not just learning how your stuff defines you, you're also receiving proven brain benefits, like better cognition, lower stress, a sense of agency, and relief from decision fatigue. Put simply, a clear space fosters a clear mind.

Researchers at Princeton University found that a hectic visual environment distracts our attention and decreases our performance results on simple tasks. In a study of 32 families, UC

Los Angeles scientists found that people who lived in messy, clutter-filled homes had higher cortisol levels and reported more stress than those who lived in tidy homes. An orderly home can even reduce the out-of-control feelings that lead to snack attacks! A study out of Cornell and Syracuse universities found that undergraduate students who were placed in a chaotic, messy environment consumed three times as many cookies as participants who were in a calm, controlled environment.

Just making decisions, one after another, on whether to Keep, Give, or seek Clarity on an object provides greater top-down control because you're practicing swift problem-solving. It's the same feeling you get when you cross items off a to-do list: You're in charge. You're getting it done. You have agency.

Finally, clearing the decks gives your brain a break from decision fatigue. Remember, your brain is making thousands of decisions a day, from simple choices (picking a pair of shoes that go with your pants) to complex operations (selecting dinner from a ten-page menu). All this decision- making is tiring. But when you clear a space, it gives your brain a much-needed rest as well as a shot of dopamine every time you interact with that space.

Don't believe it? Just imagine a messy, disorganized spice cabinet, with expired ingredients, bottles falling out, packets of soy sauce stuck to the shelf. Every time you open it, you have to search for that *one thing* you need. Now picture opening the same cabinet and seeing clean, orderly shelves, with everything visible at a glance. Feels pretty good, doesn't it?

After you've chosen and cleared out your space, write a few sentences in your Journal about your connection to the possessions you sorted. How did it feel to go through them? Did you gain any insights by looking at the stuff you keep? Try to connect your possessions (*surfboard, skateboard, chalkboard, self-help books*) to how you view yourself (*surfer, skateboarder, teacher, seeker*). Does that identity still hold true for you? If not, why? Did you feel gratitude after seeing all the items you own but don't use or need? Let it be a reminder of your abundance and how good it feels to share your bounty with others.

Which brings us to **Week 3: Redeploy**. Now you're going to execute a giveaway plan that rewrites the primitive script we all have in our brains that tells us more is better. You're going to make *giving* feel as pleasurable as acquiring.

Start by reviewing the objects in your Giving Bag: Are there items that could be put back into service elsewhere? That piano keyboard collecting dust in the family room: Is there an orchestra class at the nearest public school that could use it? The expensive chess set that nobody has ever used: Is there a chess club in your city that might like to have it? Is one of your weak-tie relations pregnant and in need of the crib in your garage?

You may be tempted to load up the trunk and drop everything off at the nearest charity collection box, but that's not the Challenge. **Your Challenge is to intentionally think about a person or place that might benefit from the possessions you no longer need.** Just apply that extra level of curiosity. Even if all you do this month is match one item to the perfect home, you're making tremendous strides toward reinforcing the positive brain benefits.

"Our reward system drives a lot of our behavior, so once a possession loses its joy for you, redeploying that object becomes its own form of reward," says Huberman. The extra attention you put on your Redeploy exercise makes it more likely that the next time you feel disconnected to something you own, you'll shed it sooner and give it a new home.

Imagine, for instance, how good it will feel to give the neighbor's kid a bike to ride. Think of the leg up you'd be providing a student who needs a scientific calculator for her chemistry class. Or the comfort you're providing to the dogs at the animal shelter with your old blankets and towels.

As you hand over your items, try to give without expectations. "This is key," Huberman says. "Because if you're emotionally attached to someone else's use of the item, what if they don't use it? You've put your pleasure in someone else's hands."

Instead, let the act of giving be your joy so that you control the reward mechanism and you reinforce your own positive behavior. Be sure to write about your Redeployment plan in your Journal so you can superboost the giving experience.

Week 3: Redeploy

Not sure where to rehome your belongings?
Here are some ideas to get you started.

- Senior recreation centers
- Libraries
- Public schools
- Women's Shelters
- Local clubs
- Animal shelters
- Homeless shelters
- Prisons
- Soup kitchens/Food banks
- Children's hospitals
- Daycares
- Places of worship

➢ **Fig. 3**
How can someone else benefit from
possessions that no longer serve you?

Let's Do This

Think back to your first Madefor Challenge, when you developed awareness around the act of drinking water. You tracked how much water you drank, logged your progress, and reflected in your Journal. These self-generated rewards helped you create and reinforce a "keystone habit" of better hydration. Keystone habits are practices that spur even more positive behaviors. For example, the keystone habit of better hydration drives behaviors like eating with intention, setting aside time for self-care, and moving your body more.

This month, you're developing the keystone habit of clarity. As you develop greater clarity around your possessions, it drives positive behaviors in other areas of your life. And you may even begin to consider, like Hill did, whether the activities you're pursuing enrich you or burden you. Or you may decide, like Heiss did, that the story your possessions tell about you no longer holds true.

This month, create the person you want to be. This is your story. <u>You were made for clarity.</u>

Pat's Clarity Guidance

At the outset of Madefor you set an intention for what you hope to achieve through this program—take a moment to reflect on and record how engaging this challenge might help serve your intention.

This Challenge uses your physical possessions to explore a more fundamental question: What are you carrying around that no longer serves you? This Challenge may be the one that gets revisited most often by Members, as there's a lot to unpack (no pun intended). So don't feel pressure to tackle everything on the first pass, but do continue to lean into a state of curiosity for what comes up as you navigate this month. I find that putting pen to paper, even if I don't know what I want to say, is extremely helpful in this Challenge.

If you struggle to stay on track this month, consider taking this small step—identify and reflect on one object that best tells your story, so that you can embrace and savor how your story makes you feel. If one step is too hard, revisit your intention for inspiration. You got this.

**I recommend listening to the Basecamp I did with Dr. Everett Worthington or at least reading the summary (Basecamp Highlights Section of Book). One of his central findings is directly applicable to your Clarity Challenge: When you carry the burden of unforgiveness it does not serve you well. But you have the ability to forgive, to replace negative emotions with positive emotions, and in doing so to free yourself to live a happier healthier life.

For additional support, check out my Perspectives video for more information around how we designed this Challenge, recommendations on how to approach the daily exercises, and real-life experiences and perspectives from Madefor Members that have completed the journey. Or, listen to this quick Campfire Story for a little inspiration.

*Madefor Videos and Audio recordings can be found on our YouTube page (https://www.youtube.com/@getmadefor)

Here comes the sun...

🌙 Can you believe it's been almost 300 days since you first started Madefor? Each day marked by one complete rotation of the earth, one sunrise, one sunset and, hopefully, a lot of small, baseline-elevating steps along the way.

But one critical baseline remains: Rest. Your entry point to better rest involves a dance of sorts. As with all dances, rhythm is everything.

Photons, the particles that comprise light, dance from the sun to your eyes to a very small region in your brain that syncs your body to the rhythm of your environment. When you are in step with the sun, you rest and recover with ease. But when your timing is off, your rhythm suffers and dysfunction ensues.

This month, you're going to tune in to the rhythm of your environment. After all, you were designed to rise and rest with the sun.

Let's dance,

BLAKE & PAT

The Basics

We've all suffered through periods when a lack of sleep affected our ability to think, from the student who studies so late into the night that she can't even comprehend the exam questions the next morning, to the exhausted new parent who dials a phone number then promptly forgets whom they're calling.

But when Madefor co-founder Pat Dossett was in the military, he endured a period of poor sleep that lasted nearly a decade. Dossett and his teammates deployed across the globe, trading day for night, relying on sleeping pills to get shut-eye, and catching catnaps whenever and wherever they could. Chronic sleep deprivation, Dossett told himself, just came with the job of being a SEAL. And yet he knew that it also had the potential to threaten their performance and safety.

"When you're on an operation," he says, "even a small cognitive-performance deficit can mean the difference between life and death."

That's exactly what investigators of the 2017 collisions of the USS *John S. McCain* and the USS *Fitzgerald* found when they reported that "fatigue or ineffective fatigue/rest management" was a factor in the deadly accidents. One study found that two-thirds of troops who served in Afghanistan and Iraq had insomnia after returning home, with sleep problems being the primary reason veterans seek medical treatment.

Military leadership began taking a serious look at the overall health and wellbeing of the force during Dossett's time as a SEAL, and one of the first areas they focused on was sleep. Soon, Dossett and his teammates were getting memory foam mattresses and pillows they could take on deployments, and eye masks to help block out light. Prescriptions for sleeping pills were replaced with natural supplements like melatonin. And educating soldiers about the benefits of sleep became a priority.

"The focus on sleep and the new tools certainly helped," Dossett says, "but even though I had all the information, it didn't change one very important underlying issue."

Proper sleep recharges our bodies, sharpens our brains, and raises our baselines so we can begin each day with vitality. In your first Madefor Challenge, you learned that operating in a state of chronic dehydration can add up to potentially dire mental and physiological consequences. The same is true with chronic sleep deprivation.

For Dossett, the underlying issue was that his circadian rhythms were chronically out of sync. **Circadian rhythms are those internal cyclical processes that have a pivotal impact on sleepiness, wakefulness, temperature, digestion, hormonal fluctuations, and more.** Our sleep patterns ebb and flow depending on personal circumstances and physiological changes and experiences at different phases of our life. But at the most basic level, the urge to sleep is primarily driven by two things: a prolonged state of wakefulness, which results in a daily buildup of sleep pressure; and 24-hour circadian rhythms. Animals, plants, and even bacteria possess circadian rhythms, which are regulated by the rise and fall of the sun.

Dossett could never get his circadian rhythms—and therefore his internal biological processes—in alignment because of his erratic exposure to light. In fact, well-timed light exposure is so central to rest and recovery that we've made it the focus of your Challenge.

"Light is the most potent stimulus for entraining circadian rhythms," says Madefor advisor and UC Irvine School of Medicine professor and psychiatrist Dr. Ruth Benca, an expert on the relationship between sleep and brain health. "Light is like a drug in a way, because it has potent effects on our brain and behavior. And when we're subjected to regular, natural light cycles, we have more regular sleep patterns."

And it's not just sleep. Every biological process in your body is influenced by light.

"Every cell in your body has a clock that runs on a schedule," says Madefor advisor and Stanford neuroscientist Dr. Andrew Huberman. "And there's a clock in one brain region, the suprachiasmatic nucleus, or SCN, that acts as the master clock. When your SCN is set properly, it helps all your clocks run together and your digestion, your heart health, your mood, and your sleep are all better synchronized."

The SCN is like the conductor of an orchestra, directing all the other clocks to tick in perfect rhythm. But for many years, it was a mystery how the SCN worked and how it synchronized to the light-dark environment. After all, it sits above the roof of your mouth and deep inside your skull, with no access to external stimuli—no clue as to when the sun rises or sets. Thanks to recent discoveries, we now know that clock-setting process actually begins in our eyes.

Our eyes contain what are called intrinsically photosensitive retinal ganglion cells, or ipRGCs, which have little to do with vision. Instead, when ipRGCs detect light through your retina, they send a signal directly to your SCN master clock that, essentially, says: *It's morning; wake up and be active.* Or when they are quiet, the signal is: *It's getting dark; be still and rest now.*

Your body's circadian rhythms actually follow a slightly-longer-than-24-hour period. This means that if you lived in constant dim light conditions for a few days, you'd find yourself going to bed later and later. So your brain depends on sunlight entering the eye to trigger your ipRGCs to tell your SCN what time it is in order to keep your internal circadian rhythms aligned, or "entrained," to the solar day-night cycle. This explains why you feel jet lag when traveling abroad: Your master clock is set to the light cycle from where you took off rather than where you landed, and you need time to entrain to your new environment's light-dark cycle.

For Dossett, his internal clocks were constantly at odds with his environment, leaving him chronically jet-lagged, sleep-deprived, and prone to poor performance he wasn't even aware of.

In a 2011 Stanford study, researchers examined the performance of basketball players before and after they added one to four hours of extra sleep to their routines. After just two weeks of extended sleep, the players ran faster sprints (15.5 seconds versus 16.2 seconds) and their free-throw percentages increased by 9%—a significant improvement. What would a 9% performance increase look like in your life?

When Dossett turned 31, he left the military feeling mentally and physically depleted. Disconnecting from the world seemed like the best way to recharge, so he bought a ticket to the remote Mentawai Islands in West Sumatra. To get to the island chain, he flew from Texas to Los Angeles, to Tokyo, to Jakarta, to Padang, and then he took a five-hour boat ride. By the time he set foot on the beach, he felt as if he'd traveled to the moon. First, he took off his shoes. Then his watch. Then he tossed his phone in a drawer.

Within a few days of island life, Dossett's internal physiological cues began to align with nature: He awoke at sunrise, ate when he was hungry, drank when he was thirsty, moved his body all day, and fell asleep shortly after sunset. His mind was sharper than it had been in years. His body felt relaxed and strong, like a well-tuned instrument.

"I had returned to the natural rhythms of life," Dossett recalls. And he didn't need special pillows or pills to get there.

"I discovered that the tools I had been using in the Teams weren't really necessary, and in some ways, they'd held me back," he says. "I was able to reconnect to my internal tools, which actually made me more resilient, more rested."

Granted, it took some time and space in a stress-free environment for him to make this connection. But you certainly don't have to fly across the world and live like a native to achieve better rest and recovery. One of the simplest ways to achieve more regular sleep patterns is to be more intentional about your exposure to sunlight.

"Sunlight is the most beautiful light—it's perfect," says Madefor advisor Dr. Samer Hattar, chief of the Section on Light and Circadian Rhythms at the National Institute of Mental Health. Hattar was among a small team of scientists who first discovered ipRGCs. His research has helped people to better understand the interplay between light and our biological processes so we can sleep better, avoid jet lag, and hopefully prevent and treat conditions like depression, obesity, and chronic illness.

As a chronobiologist (someone who studies biological rhythms), Hattar views Dossett's experience as a prime example of the immediate benefits to our minds and bodies when we sync our internal clocks to our external environment.

"His system was relaxed. Everything was aligned. Everything was synchronized," he says.

Relaxed. Aligned. Synchronized. This kind of robust health is within reach for all of us. Over the next 21 days, you're going to develop greater awareness around the ways that light exposure affects your biological clocks. Each morning, you'll get a daily dose of natural light to kickstart your SCN and set your internal clocks to the rhythms of your environment. Each night, you'll wean yourself from light sources like phones, tablets, and other devices that interfere with your circadian rhythms. And, of course, you'll spend time reflecting on your new intentional behaviors and how they're changing the way you think about rest.

The recommended tools to help you achieve these goals are an analog **Alarm Clock** and **Sleep Mask** (identify your own). But think of these tools as bridges: They aren't your destination; they're leading you to a place where, soon, you can rely on your internal tools.

As with all Madefor Challenges, the power lies within you. How well you commit to the practice determines the benefits you'll receive. We believe that you'll soon find, just as Dossett did, that synchronicity can be a life-changing experience.

The Challenge

Your Rest Challenge Exercises:

21 Mornings of Sunlight:
Each morning for 21 days, go outside and get at least 15 minutes of sunlight to trigger your SCN master clock and promote better rest in the evening.

21 Nights of Rest:
Each night, leave your phone and other digital devices where you can't see them or reach for them. If you need an alarm to wake up, use your analog Alarm Clock. Use your Sleep Mask to help block out light while you sleep.

21 Days of Reflection:
Each day, record in your Journal how many minutes of sunlight you got in the morning, as well as any reflections on your Rest Challenge or past Challenges that affect your experience this month. See "21 Days of Reflection" writing prompts below.

For thousands of years, human physiology was tightly tied to the sun. Our internal biological processes evolved and aligned to the natural 24-hour light-dark cycle of our environment, which helps us achieve optimal metabolism, greater physical wellbeing, and improved brain function during the day, as well as better sleep at night.

But in the last century, the advent of electricity has caused a major shift in our exposure to natural light. The power grid has made it possible to work and play longer than we ever imagined. But it's altered the timing of our circadian clocks and affected our biological processes and sleep patterns.

In studies at the University of Colorado, Boulder, researchers found that participants who spent six summer days camping in the Rocky Mountains, with no phones, flashlights, or other artificial light sources, began to fall asleep four hours earlier than before the trip. If you normally go to bed at 11 p.m., imagine how it would feel to suddenly be sleepy at 7 p.m. and then awake by sunrise. This is what Dossett experienced as well.

We were designed to align to the 24-hour solar cycle. Research shows that late circadian and sleep timing are associated with poor cognitive performance, fatigue, mood disorders, obesity, and many other chronic conditions. Just as you discovered in your Nature Challenge, we are drawn to the great outdoors because it was our environmental home for thousands of years. Part of that allure is natural light.

"Light exposure to the eyes is the fundamental way in which our brain and body know what's going on in the world," says Huberman. "That alignment is our set point of when we're going to feel alert, when we're going to fall asleep, when we're going to feel like exercising, when we're going to feel friendly, and when we're going to feel grumpy—it's all determined by light exposure."

Let's start your first Challenge exercise, 21 Mornings of Sunlight. Each morning, within a few hours of waking up, spend at least 15 minutes in natural sunlight. You can sit outside, walk your neighborhood, go for a run and move your body—whatever you prefer. Just create an intentional morning practice dedicated to this simple act, which rewards your brain and kicks off your SCN master clock.

For the purpose of your Challenge, we set the time to 15 minutes to ensure you're getting a meaningful dose of clock-setting morning sunlight. If you have the opportunity to spend more time outside, that's great. But the actual number of minutes you need depends on a variety of factors, including the intensity of sunlight in your environment. "If you're in California, and there's really bright light and no clouds, then it's less. But if you're in England on an overcast day, it's probably more," says Huberman, who also warns that you should never look directly at the sun, which can cause serious eye damage.

If you're at all concerned about skin damage, you needn't receive direct sunlight, says NIH chronobiologist Hattar. "If you're outside, in the shade, but in a sunny environment, you'll still get several magnitudes more light stimulation than you'd get indoors," he says.

Morning light is optimal, because it's the time when your system is most responsive. "Put it this way," says Huberman. "The longer you've been in the dark, the more available your body and brain are for resetting." In other words, after an extended period of darkness, light in the eyes tells your master clock: *Time to wake up!*

We all have the occasional crazy-busy morning, when it's impossible to find 15 minutes for a quick sunbathe. If you miss your daily dose, try to make up for it at noon. "It's not going to be as effective for your clock as morning light," Hattar says.

"But you'll still get some benefits." Those benefits, according to Hattar and other researchers, include:

1. Sharper cognition and alertness
2. Stronger immune system response
3. Better mood
4. Easier ability to fall asleep at night, because you're entraining to the solar day

> **Fig. 1**
> *The SCN directs all your clocks
> to tick in perfect rhythm.*

Hattar's research has had a profound effect on his own habits around sunlight. "I don't have curtains in my house and I wake up really early—the sun rises with me," he says. "In the morning, I drink my coffee outside. When I walk or drive to work I never wear dark sunglasses. At my office, I have huge windows and I never pull the curtains down. I always eat my lunch outdoors, even when it's hot, just to expose myself to light. Light is an obsession."

Huberman's morning sunlight routine, coupled with bedtime practices like breathing and gratitude, have also made a difference in his life. "I actually prioritize these as much as exercise," he says, "but they're probably more powerful because you're anchoring yourself in the morning and you're anchoring yourself at night."

Which brings us to your evening practice, 21 Nights of Rest. You've anchored your morning with light, now you're going to close the loop by giving yourself dark, natural conditions for rest.

For the next 21 nights, decrease light exposure as much as possible in the hours leading to sleep. At bedtime, make sure that all phones, tablets, and eReaders are out of sight and out of reach. (If you like to read in bed, a paper book is best.) And when you're ready to go to sleep, use your **Sleep Mask**, if necessary, to block out any light. Use an **analog Alarm Clock** if waking up on time is a concern.

If you're among the 71% of people who go to bed with their phones, this Challenge is going to require tremendous willpower. But consider the benefits of waking up with more energy and moving through your day with focus and enhanced performance. Devices in bed make this harder to achieve because they delay the onset of sleep in a couple of ways:

1. **The light from your devices, which is intense and close to your eyes, suppresses melatonin release in your brain, delaying sleep onset.**

2. **Your mind needs to be relaxed. Scrolling through social media, catching up on emails, and scanning the day's headlines engage your brain in activities that have an alerting, rather than calming, effect.**

Some people take melatonin supplements to help with sleep, but as Huberman notes, it's a powerful hormone that can suppress puberty and reproduction. "I don't recommend it, except on occasion, and at very low doses," he says. Natural melatonin doesn't put you to sleep. Rather, it tells your brain: *It's dark now, time to get ready to sleep*. But if your eyes are still detecting light, the release of this sleep-alerting chemical is delayed.

A study at Brigham and Women's Hospital found that when test subjects went to bed with an iPad instead of a printed book, they produced 55% less melatonin and needed an extra 10 minutes to fall asleep. That might not sound like a lot, but it's a sleep deficit that adds up over time.

- MEMBER MOMENT -

"As a self-described night owl, turning off devices at a set time each evening has made a huge difference. I realized that getting on my phone or tablet before going to bed caused me to override my body's sleepy signals. As a reformed morning grouch, opening the curtains or stepping outside and getting a dose of sun in the morning helps me get energized to tackle the day." -Valerie A

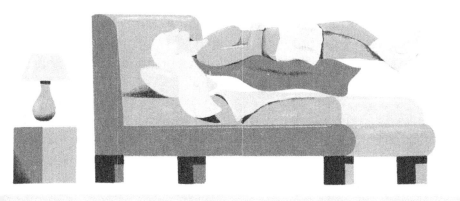

> **Fig. 2**
> *Better sleep brings better cognitive,*
> *emotional, and physical power.*

"Of course, there are plenty of people who are on their devices or watching TV before they go to bed, and they still get to bed at a regular time, fall asleep okay, and wake up at the right time in the morning," says Benca. "But you do have to wind down before you can sleep. And we know that the more gadgets you have in the bedroom—the more that you're engaging with these very stimulating devices—the longer you're going to stay up."

Bottom line: Devices are light sources and stimuli that can interfere with your sleep—and not just at the onset of bedtime. If you've ever woken up in the middle of the night, checked your phone, and started stressing out because it's 3 a.m. and you're worried about falling back to sleep—guess what? You've just compounded your problem. Looking at your phone after an extended period of darkness tells your brain: *Light detected! Stop releasing melatonin. Wake up!*

"You're essentially jet-lagging yourself," says Huberman. "Even if you fall back asleep, your system was jolted. You're not going to feel it that day. But the next day and the one after that, you're going to have sleep issues."

Some people apply blue-light filters on their devices because they know that the light-detecting cells in our eyes are maximally triggered by blue. That's certainly a helpful option. But as Hattar points out, "Blue light is only one component. The *intensity* of light is much more important."

Dim, red light, says Hattar, does not trigger the waking process, and is the best color-intensity combination if you need light in the middle of the night.

The optimal solution, of course, is to avoid interacting with your devices. Commit to the Challenge for 21 consecutive nights and see how it feels for you. Believe it or not, "no devices at bedtime" *also* includes sleep-tracking tools.

21 Nights of Rest:

Ten more ways to get better sleep

1. Dim all the lights in your home and cease use of screens to prepare your brain for sleep. Benca recommends doing this two hours before bedtime, when possible.

2. Make your bedroom as dark, cool, and relaxing as possible.

3. Journal each night to clear your head.

4. Avoid caffeine six to eight hours before bedtime as it interferes with adenosine, one of the brain chemicals that causes sleep pressure.

5. Avoid excessive fluid intake in the evening if it causes you to wake up in the middle of the night to urinate.

6. Alcohol is a major sleep disrupter, so avoid it if you can.

7. If you wake up during the night, avoid bright light. Dim, red light is best, if needed.

8. Try to schedule sufficient time for sleep (at least seven hours is ideal), and go to bed at about the same time every night, when possible.

9. When traveling, eat and sleep aligned to your new environment to help with jet lag.

10. Stay connected to all your Madefor practices because they keep your baselines raised and give you greater top-down control.

About 15% of Americans use wearable sleep-trackers to learn more about their patterns. Yet research finds that these tools are unreliable indicators of sleep quality and can actually lead to such poor habits as staying in bed too long in order to meet an arbitrary number of hours, checking the device in the middle of the night, and creating a sense of anxiety and perfectionism around sleep. Researchers at Rush University Medical School report that patients who get plenty of rest and exhibit no signs of a disorder often still insist they have a problem—simply because their Fitbit says they do.

"I don't track my sleep because I feel like that's taking me in a direction I don't want to go," says Huberman. "These things can make you increasingly paranoid about sleep. But it's important to remember that your system is resilient. You can adapt and get back on track. The goal here is to create a system of averages that keep your baselines high."

In fact, every baseline-raising Challenge you've completed on your Madefor journey lays a strong foundation for success this month. That's why you're going to return to them in your **21 Days of Reflection** exercise.

For the next three weeks, take a few minutes each day to jot down in your Journal:

1. **The number of minutes of sunlight you got in the morning.**
2. **Any insights on how your morning and evening practices are affecting you. Or any reflections on how past Challenges are helping you with Rest.**

21 Days of Reflection:

Prompts to help get you started

Connect how it feels to get sunlight in the morning with the knowledge that you are intentionally directing your internal processes.

Are you noticing any changes in your sleeping and waking patterns?

Do you find that you're feeling more ready for bed or falling asleep earlier?

Do you enjoy writing or reading in bed, instead of using digital devices?

Have you woken in the middle of the night and reached for your phone? How long did it take for that habit to phase out?

How have you used cognitive reappraisal and **Gratitude** to shift your perspective when negative thoughts kept you awake?

Has the new way you approach **Fuel** helped you fall asleep easier because you ate what your body needed—not too much or too little?

How has a deeper sense of social **Connection** anchored your day? Do you greet the people you see during your 21 Mornings of Sunlight exercise?

Have you used your **Breath** practice to jump into action each morning and feel calmer each evening?

Has **Clarity** around your possessions led you to create a more relaxing home environment?

For example, in your **Fuel** Challenge you tuned in to your internal sensations of hunger and satisfaction, making it less likely that you'll go to bed with a full stomach, which can interfere with sleep. You also now see the value of **Moving** your body every day, of being **Connected** to your weak-tie relationships, and of taking relaxing **Breaths** and practicing **Gratitude** in the evening to help you wind down. All of these habits help you get better sleep.

"The quality of your sleep is in large part dependent on the quality of your waking life," says Benca. "And then sleep also impacts how you feel during the day—they all fit together."

They all fit together. When you align your internal physiological processes—whether it's thirst, hunger, nature, rest, or any other basic human need—with the external signals of your environment, you are living in synchronicity.

"And in life," says Hattar, "synchronicity underlies everything. Synchronization with your environment is essential."

As Dossett learned, it's all just "information" until you make the connection. So take the time each day to write a few sentences about your experience. Make the connection and reward yourself for doing the work.

One final thought: You should do your journaling exercise at whatever time is best for you, but we suggest an evening practice. As you learned with Gratitude, nighttime journaling clears the mental decks so you can avoid a spiral of negative, default-mode thinking. Evening journaling helps you get the most leverage out of sleep. Because in addition to being a powerful recharging process, **sleep is when the positive brain changes happen.**

Whether you're studying to be a London cabbie or trying to develop new behaviors, sleep is when that neural transformation takes place.

"Learning events trigger neuroplasticity, but the actual *changes* are during sleep. That's when the reordering of your brain circuitry occurs," says Huberman. "If you're a jogger, you don't get better at running during your run. You have to have a period of rest for adaptation. It's the same thing with your brain."

Rest gives you mental sharpness, emotional balance, enhanced performance, and a healthier brain and body. Rest is when the key fits into the lock and opens the door to a whole new way of thinking and being. So prioritize this month's Challenge, and give yourself the gift of rest and recovery.

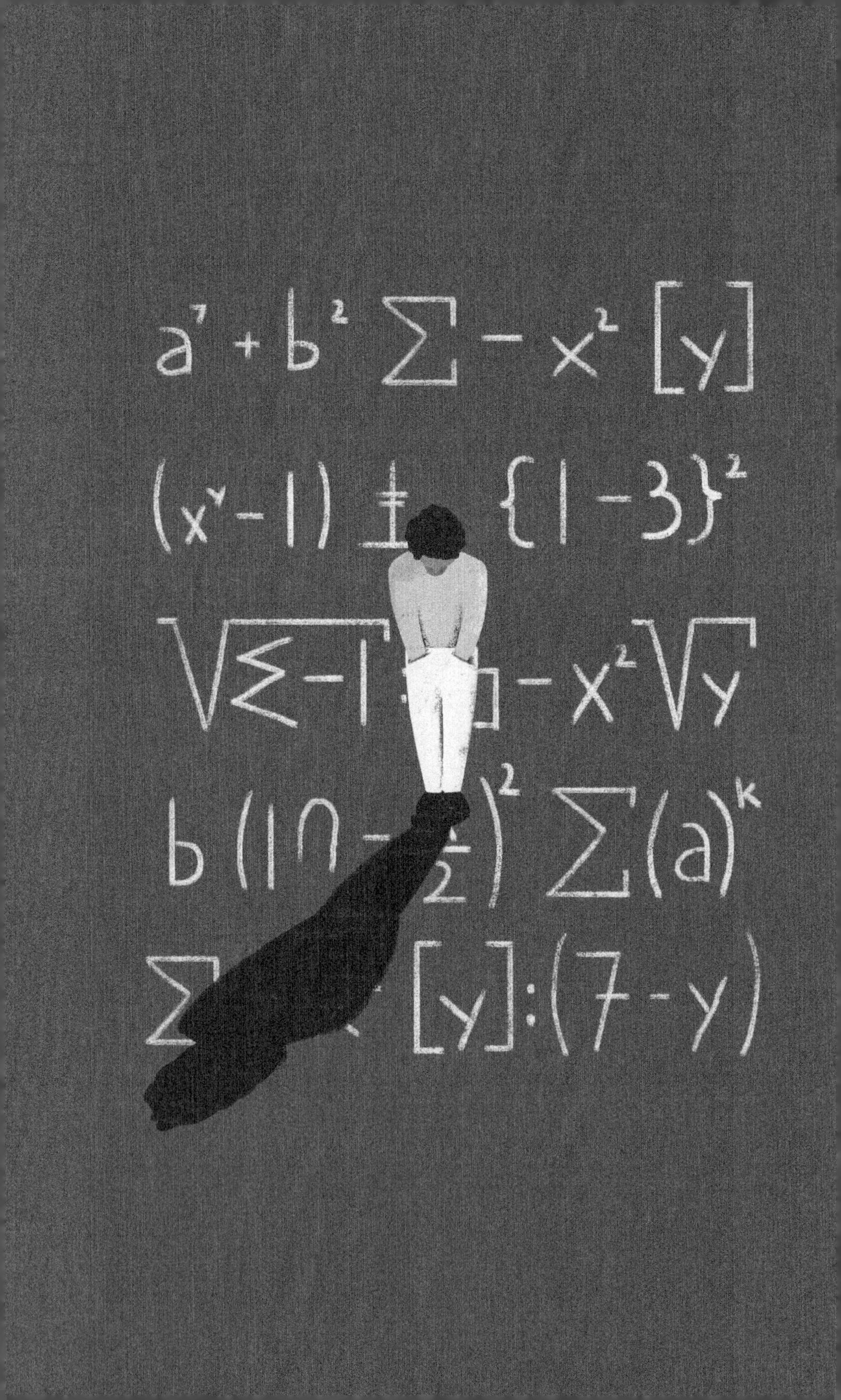

> ➤ **Fig. 3**
> *Sleep is when neural*
> *transformation happens.*

Let's Do This

Here's what success looks like by the end of your Challenge: Your morning ritual makes you feel alert and ready to go; you move through your day able to tackle whatever comes your way; your evening journaling relaxes you so you fall asleep easily. Congratulations! You're in sync with your environment and, as Hattar says, synchronicity is everything.

When you feel ready, see if you can put your analog Alarm Clock in a drawer, just like Dossett put away his watch and phone when he reset his natural rhythms. "I learned that I didn't need an alarm," he says. "It was just a safety net."

You already know when and what to eat, how best to move, what time to sleep, and when to rise. And if you're someone who already wakes up minutes before your alarm goes off, then you know you've got this.

Your Madefor journey has been a slow, steady road of progress—not a sprint toward perfection. So if you suffer setbacks or feel like you've lost the thread, try to remember that you possess a set of practices and habits that can make you feel better again.

"I know what it means to be in sync and I know what the rewards are," says Dossett. "So that affects my behaviors in positive directions in an enduring way. Whether it's Hydration or Movement or Gratitude or Rest—you don't check the box when you finish each Challenge and now you're fixed. But you connect with the benefits. Soon, your perception shifts, nudging you in directions that allow you to bring your best self to the world."

- - -

A reminder: Madefor Challenges are designed with an advisory board of experts, and they are safe and effective for the majority of members, but they are not intended to replace the advice and counsel of your doctors.

Pat's Rest Guidance

At the outset of Madefor you set an intention for what you hope to achieve through this program—take a moment to reflect on and record how engaging this challenge might help serve your intention.

You already know how important rest is, and that, without it, you quickly devolve into the worst version of yourself. So it might seem strange that for such an important behavior, Madefor isn't challenging you to do more. But, our goal isn't to try to get you to do everything; it's to get you to do the one thing that makes everything else better.

When you get in sync with the natural light cycles of your environment, you give your body a chance to function the way it was designed. Members are always surprised by how impactful this month is. I hope you are as well.

If you struggle to stay on track this month, consider taking this small step—find the sun's light and feel its warmth on your skin. Savor how the light makes you feel. If one step is too hard, revisit your intention for inspiration. You got this.

For additional support, check out my <u>Perspectives video</u> for more information around how we designed this Challenge, recommendations on how to approach the daily exercises, and real-life experiences and perspectives from Madefor Members that have completed the journey. Or, listen to this quick <u>Campfire Story</u> for a little inspiration.

*Madefor Videos and Audio recordings can be found on our YouTube page (https://www.youtube.com/@getmadefor)

You've changed!

Over the last nine months, you've been in action, raising your baselines and building an incredible arsenal of inside-out tools that will continue to serve you well in life.

Although the steps you took were small, your effort was heroic—well done. Now all that's left to decide is where you want to go next.

Even though your Madefor journey is coming to an end, your vision for what's next is just beginning. We can't wait to see what you will achieve. After all, a better world begins with the best you.

Adventure awaits,

BLAKE & PAT

The Basics

This month, we begin with the story of you. A wise man once said that to find out what you are made for, you first have to figure out what you're made of, and for the last nine months, you've been doing just that.

You've discovered, for example, that your body knows exactly what, when, and how much to eat and drink when you listen to its cues. You've experienced gratitude and social connection in a meaningful way, and recognize that they are *essential* to mental, emotional, and physical health. You've found that you can shift your state of mind and be more resilient with the simple power of your breath. And you've reacquainted yourself with how good it feels to move your body with ease, to spend time communing with nature, to have clarity around the objects you possess, and to rise and rest with the sun.

Congratulations! This is a tremendous accomplishment. The inside-out tools you've internalized are not passing fads; they're enduring practices that will *always* benefit you. In fact, you're not the same person you were when you began your Madefor journey. You've changed.

Think back to your **Onboarding Guidebook**, when you learned about the London cab drivers who memorize maps, drive every street, and study every landmark in order to obtain "the Knowledge." If you've ever taken a ride in an official black cab, you've seen it: The drivers navigate efficiently and effectively without GPS because they already know exactly where and how to go. They've internalized the Knowledge using attention and intention, which created neuroplastic changes in their brains.

Attention and intention are also what you used to change your brain for the better. Just like the cabbies, you can trust your brain and body to tell you what they need and how to operate as you move forward in the world. The learning you gained wasn't from a tool we recommended you to use or anything we've told you in a Guidebook. Your wisdom is a direct result of the internal rewards *you* created when you engaged in the monthly Challenges—and you'll never lose it.

- MEMBER MOMENT-

"The biggest internal shift for me has been that I'm not "reacting" to the world around me anymore, I'm much more present. I'm moving through my day with intention and when a stressful situation comes up I stop and use my breathing and think how can I be my best in dealing with this situation? Stress is unavoidable but I see now by moving through the day with gratitude and honoring connections, that my whole lens through which I move through life has changed." - Melissa P

Of course, we all go through periods when life sends us veering off track. Sometimes it's because we're dealing with big, stressful transitions like a new job, the arrival of a baby, or the end of a relationship. Other times the accumulation of small, daily stressors—traffic, noisy environments, a lack of sunlight and fresh air—can lead us off course. But now that you've got the Madefor knowledge, you'll always be able to get back on track. If it helps, you can revisit the Guidebooks, put a bracelet back on, or re-engage with the Challenges. But no matter where you are in life, you will always have the knowledge—you can see a light shining up ahead and you know how to navigate there.

So, now that you've discovered what you are made of—and you recognize that you alone hold the answers—it's finally time to figure out what you are made for. Where do you want to direct all the capacity for good that you've unlocked?

This month, you're going to tackle the big questions: What's most important to you in life? What kind of legacy do you want to leave behind? And what's your vision for the future? When you began this program, you wrote an intention inside your Journal—an idea about what you hoped to accomplish by doing Madefor. Maybe you achieved that intention. Maybe you didn't. Or perhaps it changed. But if you feel like you've fallen short in this program, take a few minutes right now to reflect on why: Did you complete every Challenge? Did you skip any? Did you rush through one, giving it less attention than it deserves?

It's fine if life threw a curveball at your plans. But if you've got unfinished work here, we strongly suggest you pause and go back to complete any Challenges you missed. Re-read the Guidebooks and re-familiarize yourself with the exercises. In other words: Invest time in you. It's your growth. Your life. Don't do it halfway.

On the other hand, if you've completed all the Challenges and feel excited and ready to move on, then let's use your original intention as a point of departure for a bigger vision:

How do you want to show up in the world?

After all the knowledge you've gathered, now it's time to find out what you are made for.

> **Fig. 1**
> *When life sends you off course, you know how to get back on track and move forward.*

∞ The Challenge

"Socrates said it best: 'The unexamined life is not worth living,'" says Madefor advisor and leadership mentor Dave Phillips. "If you're not focused on the things that are most important, you're certainly not living to your potential in a way that's going to be truly satisfying to you."

Madefor co-founder Blake Mycoskie first met Phillips, an executive mentor for high-performance CEOs and business leaders, in 2009. At the time, TOMS was flourishing and expanding, but Mycoskie felt like his personal growth was stunted. Phillips helped Mycoskie identify the values and vision that now define his life and influence every decision he makes.

"I help high-performing leaders find greater meaning for their organizations all the time," Phillips says, "but it's incredible what can happen when you do the work for yourself—it's transformational."

"He really cuts through the noise and helps me to identify what matters most in life," Mycoskie says of his longtime coach and mentor. For this month's Challenge, we've drawn on Phillips' work and the lessons from his book, *Three Big Questions*, to help you think through what matters most in your life as you complete your Madefor journey.

You'll start by identifying your Top 3 Values. Just as the practices you've engaged in over the last nine months have given you greater top-down control, affirming your values is another inside-out tool that gives you greater strength, resilience, and capacity to thrive.

Values are scientifically defined as "the fundamental attitudes guiding our mental processes and behavior." To put it simply: Values give life meaning and strengthen your sense of integrity, because they define who you are and dictate everything that you do.

Psychological research finds that affirming your values can make you feel less defensive and more calm, decisive, and connected to others. When you have well-defined values, you can better see opportunities to act in a way that aligns with them. But if you don't know your values, as Phillips cautions, you are more likely to prioritize *actions*—to define yourself by what you do.

"We've created this message in our culture that a great life comes from the activities that we do. But it's actually the other way around," says Phillips. "Our values should dictate what we do."

Think about it this way: A parent may say that he wants his child to get good grades, go to a good college, find a successful career, and have a big family. But deep down, the thing that's most important is that his child lives out her core values. If she's deeply unhappy because she sacrificed social connection, joy, integrity, and other core values, then all her success doesn't hold much meaning.

"To be someone has more to do with how we describe ourselves than the activities we do. This is the starting place of a life well lived. This is knowing yourself," says Phillips. "I'm talking about character—who you are when no one is looking."

Let's begin your first Challenge exercise. During Week 1, give yourself about 30 minutes with no distractions and turn to your Madefor Values Inventory (below or in your Tools & Resources section). Underline all the values that feel most relevant for you and write in any additional ones you identify with that are not on the list. Don't worry about narrowing down the list right now; just go with your gut.

Your Challenge is to identify the values that have served you well in life. What values do you want to live by? Who do you want to be when no one is looking? There's no judgment in this exercise. Only you can decide your values. They may be a natural extension of what you believe in (such as honesty or discipline) or what comes naturally to you (humor or hard work).

Sometimes we're too close to see the traits that others readily identify in us. So it can be tremendously helpful (and even fun!) to ask a trusted friend or family member to weigh in: *You've known me for many years—what would you say are my personal values? Don't hold back.*

After you've underlined your chosen values, let them percolate in your mind for a few days. Notice the small moments in the course of a day that speak to your values. **See if you can link your actions back to your values**. This is the **attention** piece of the exercise, and it's crucial to determining your Top 3.

For example, did you spend time alone this week because you value independence or solitude? Did you get lost in a poem or a sculpture because you value creativity or truth? Did you stay late at the office because you value hard work or wealth? Make the connection.

Notice, too, the times when your values are disconnected from your actions. Maybe you recognized that you're going through the motions at work or in a relationship, even though authenticity is important to you. Have you lost touch with friends since starting a family, and you'd like to place a greater emphasis on friendship? Is fun a value you lived by when you were younger but aren't getting much of anymore?

When you're ready, come back to your Values Inventory and review the choices you underlined. Do they still feel right? Did you notice that your actions point to different values you hadn't thought of? Are there others that, upon reflection, also apply?

➢ **Fig. 2**
Values are the traits and principles
that have served you well in life.

Week 1: Identify Your Top 3 Values

**Use this Values Inventory as described in your Challenge exercise.
Write in any additional values that are meaningful to you.**

Humility	Wisdom	Fun
Inspiration	Discipline	Love
Justice	Honesty	Faith
Passion	Victory	Peace
Security	Authenticity	Moderation
Self-reliance	Grace	Control
Being realistic	Joy	Nature
Respect	Playfulness	Power
Hard work	Friendship	Learning
Wealth	Endurance	Experience
Optimism	Touch	Gratitude
Family	Service	Risk
Energy	Comfort	Honor
Generosity	Fortitude	Integrity
Happiness	Curiosity	Balance
Courage	Goodness	Hope
Kindness	Simplicity	Creativity
Fame	Growth	Being present
Loyalty	Charity	Intelligence
Beauty	Patience	Sensitivity
Truth	Logic	Independence
Laughter	Poise	Stimulating change

Now, narrow your list by circling just your Top 3 Values. Given your reflections over the last few days, which three are primary to you? Write them down in your Journal and reflect on your choices: Why are they important? How have they shown up in your past? In your present? What actions in your life align with these values? In what ways have you acted out of alignment with them but now you see how important they are?

By choosing your Top 3 Values and writing about them in your Journal, you're reaffirming the traits that have made a difference in your life and signaling to your brain: *These values are important; recognize opportunities to bring them into action.* Soon, this will create small shifts in your behavior. You'll linger at the park a little longer, for instance, because you cherish nature, or you'll open a savings account for a grandchild because you care about security.

Affirming your Top 3 Values also fosters more goodness in your life. For example, if you chose honesty, then you're going to feel a sense of excitement and responsibility when someone asks for your feedback. If curiosity is important, you'll feel more empowered to ask questions and learn about a problem until you have an informed opinion. Sometimes your values will conflict, and you'll have to decide what's most important to you. Phillips notes, for example, that a value of adventure can be great. But if it means that you are leaving home every weekend to pursue the next experience, then that value loses its goodness and conflicts with your value of family.

"Knowing your core values gives you something to go back to when you make decisions," says Mycoskie. "If you're thinking about leaving a job, taking a job, being with this partner, dealing with your kids in a certain way—you've already got your objectives to turn back to. You know what to do."

When Mycoskie and Pat Dossett became friends, they quickly discovered they had a shared value of service. Doing work that brings about a greater collective good brings them both a sense of fulfillment—which is why they teamed up to create Madefor. But affirming your values can bring anyone, at any stage of life, greater clarity at work. For example, a grocery bagger who values empathy will feel more rewarded when she makes a customer smile or helps someone to their car, because she has a clear sense that achieving moments of empathy gives her work deeper meaning.

As you become more grounded in your values, you'll recognize the importance of modeling them to your partner, your family, and your communities. After all, these traits indicate to the world how you operate and how you expect others to behave with you.

Phillips cites the experience of a client who had a very successful business in Chicago, fancy cars and mansions, and all that comes with great wealth. But after thinking through his values, he stood up at Thanksgiving, in front of two dozen family members, and made an announcement. "He said to them, 'I never want you to guess what your grandfather is about and what it means to carry this family name,'" Phillips recalls. "He told them, 'We are people who are contributors and givers in culture. We are people of love and grace and courage. And this is what it means to carry the last name that you all carry. Now, let's eat.'"

One last bit of advice: You may be tempted to enumerate a dozen values that you want to abide by. But it's important to focus on just your Top 3. Life is complicated and busy. By reducing this aspect of your Challenge to an accessible list, something your brain can actually grab hold of and aim for, you're setting yourself up for success. Having just three distinct values you want to embody means you're more likely to notice moments when opportunities arise to square your actions with your values. Seize those moments.

For Week 2, you're going to Imagine Your 90th Birthday Party.
Now that you've looked back over your life to determine the
values that have shaped you and given you strength, it's time
to look to the future and find out where they lead.

Mental imagery, like the kind you'll use in your 90th Birthday
Party exercise, has a powerful effect on our bodies and minds.
In a fascinating report from Ohio University, researchers found
that simply *imagining* exercise made subjects stronger. In the
study, 29 volunteers had their wrists wrapped in surgical casts
for a month. For 11 minutes a day, 5 days a week, half of the
volunteers sat still and imagined that they were flexing the
muscles in their immobilized wrists. When the casts were re-
moved, the subjects who'd simply thought about exercise had
wrist muscles that were two times stronger than participants
who had done nothing at all.

Imagery practice is so effective, professional athletes (notably,
legendary golfer Tiger Woods, tennis star Billie Jean King, and
the late boxing champ Muhammad Ali) use it to improve their
competitive edge.

When Team USA Winter Olympians practice it, they don't just
imagine a successful performance; they also picture the views
from the bus windows as they make their way to the venue and
the questions asked at the news conference afterward. That's
because the more specific you can be, the better your brain can
detect and seize opportunities to achieve success.

For this part of your Challenge, spend about an hour in a quiet,
private space where you can close your eyes and imagine that
you have just arrived at your own 90th birthday celebration. Get
a picture of what the room is like. Are you in a retirement home,
your current home, a vacation home? Are you dancing at your
party or are you in a wheelchair? Are you with grandchildren
and great-grandchildren? Who else is there with you? When

you're ready, open your Journal and use the writing prompts below to create a vivid scene (also available in your Tools & Resources section).

"These prompts are the same questions I ask clients when we talk through this exercise," Phillips says. "They help to create word pictures that plant an idea, a feeling, a sense of connection to your future. The clearer you can see your future, the more your subconscious mind goes to work trying to build a bridge to that imagery."

As you look around your party, picturing loved ones and listening to people toasting you, reflect on how you've lived out your Top 3 Values. Are there aspects of your life at 90 that you are proud of?

Week 2: Imagine Your 90th Birthday Party

Journaling prompts

1   Who's at your party?

2   What's the quality of these relationships?

3   What's your health like? Do you travel, are you independent?

4   What will your daily activities be when you are 90?

5   Are you living out your values?

6   At the end of the party, someone will stand up and say, "I know you as well as anyone at this party, and I want to tell you what I think was your most important contribution, because it best describes who you have been throughout your life." Who is that person and what would they say?

Are there areas where you see potential for greater growth and progress now?

As Phillips notes, this is not always an easy exercise to complete. It can bring up difficult emotions about past expectations for our lives, which may not have come to fruition. But the value here is taking the opportunity to refocus. Given your present circumstances, what's the best way that life can unfold for you going forward?

Which brings us to Week 3. So far, you've drawn from your past to identify the values that give greater meaning to your life, and you've looked to the future to imagine how those traits might play out in your life. Now, it's time to **Create Your Vision Statement**—the bridge that connects your past to your future.

A strong Vision Statement will push you further than you thought possible, addressing your unique strengths and skills in order to live the life you were made for. So use this time to remove any mental constraints and have fun just *imagining* who you could become.

Imagine bouncing out of bed excited for the life you are creating. What would that look like for you? When you were younger, did you have a different vision than the life you are living now? Does that vision still hold meaning for you?

"Don't give up on it. It belongs to you," Phillips says. "Set aside the voices that tell you to settle for second best, that tell you to compromise, that tell you you're not good enough."

Phillips suggests imagining your most exciting dreams. "Why not? And if not now, then when?" he says. "After all, if you merely think about things as they are, you can expect more of the same. But if you think of the way things could be, you are more likely to create that future."

➤ **Fig. 3**
*When you envision your biggest
dreams, you create that future.*

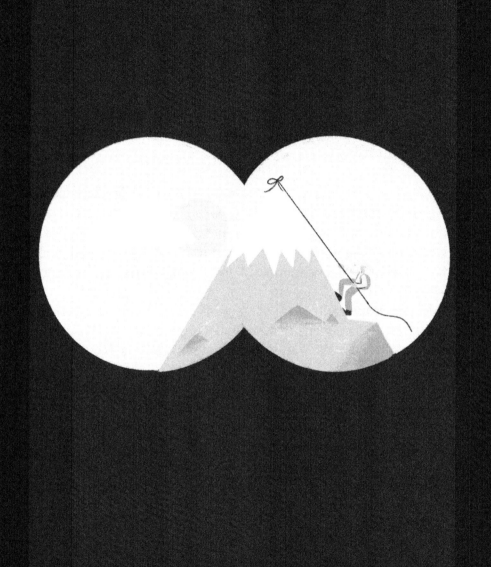

Maybe you want to write a best-selling book that shines a light on an issue you care about. Perhaps your vision is to start a business and be your own boss. Or maybe you long to travel the world and make new friends. Whatever your vision is, honor it. People often avoid imagining bold visions because of a fear of failure or false humility. But your life is a gift. So dream big.

There's no judgment, but keep in mind that vision is rarely about getting the bigger house, the fastest car, the top sales award. It's more about how you will show up in the world for yourself *and* for others. In fact, the most effective Vision Statements often have an element of service.

"Joining and serving in things... you believe in while using your highest strengths is a recipe for meaning," says positive psychology founder Dr. Martin Seligman. For example, being a firefighter who saves lives is meaningful. And so is being a barista who finds meaning in connecting with the people he meets every day.

"Meaning is knowing what your highest strengths are and deploying those in the service of something larger than you," Seligman says. "There's no shortcut to that. That's what life is about."

At Mycoskie's 90th birthday party, for instance, he wouldn't want people to say: *Blake sold a lot of shoes.* He'd want others to acknowledge and be inspired by how he showed up in the world. That's why his Vision Statement draws on his values and strengths.

Here is Mycoskie's Vision Statement: **My vision is to speak, teach, and create products that will raise global consciousness to scale.**

Madefor advisor and Harvard psychiatrist Dr. John Ratey is a prolific speaker and writer—these are some of his unique strengths. His vision is to use them to help people incorporate exercise in their lives to achieve peak performance and optimum mental health.

Madefor advisor and nutritionist Evelyn Tribole is also a renowned educator and writer and she uses these strengths in her vision to empower people to connect to their innate wisdom for overall wellbeing and happiness using the framework of intuitive eating.

Madefor advisor and neuroscientist Dr. Andrew Huberman can take complex concepts and make them feel accessible and practical. He uses this unique skill in his vision to discover the scientific tools that enhance our lives, and then moves those discoveries from labs and scientific journals into people's hands.

These may seem like lofty goals, but even an empathic grocery bagger can have big dreams. She can decide, for example, to use her strengths of humor and connection in her vision to have 1 million positive encounters with people that leave them better off than they were before.

"Having clarity around what you're good at and how you're going to live your life—in alignment with your core values, your 'rules of the road,' so to speak—takes away a lot of mental distraction and uncertainty," Mycoskie says. "When you wake up each day, it becomes so easy to ask: Am I living my values or am I not? Am I living out my vision or not?"

Your Vision Statement ties together your past and future, anchoring you to a horizon that you know you can move toward now. It incentivizes you to remain on an upward growth trajectory toward a more meaningful life. And it plants a clear plan in your subconscious that your conscious mind slowly starts to work toward.

So set aside a full hour, open your Journal, and follow the three steps to creating your Vision Statement below.

Week 3: Create Your Vision Statement

Step 1. Open your Journal and complete the following statements with as much detail as possible:

1   My Top 3 Values are...

2   My unique strengths are... *(For example: I am really good at...)*

3   My biggest, most exciting dreams are... *(For example: if anything were possible, I would...)*

4   Now that you've identified your Top 3 Values, unique strengths, and biggest dreams, it's time to turn them into a Vision Statement. How could they be used in the service of something larger than yourself? If it helps, plug in a variety of strengths and dreams into this template: **My vision is to use my** *(your strengths)* **to** *(your most exciting dreams)*.

Step 2. Refine Your Vision. Refine, test, and adjust your vision. Take as much time as you need to reflect on these questions:

1   What actions do I need to take to achieve this vision?

2   Where would my vision occur?

3   When will me vision be realized?

4   Who will help me realize it?

5   Who would my vision impact?

6   What is the result of my vision?

Step 3. Write your final Vision Statement in your Journal or on a Vision Card.

When you've completed all three steps, take a moment to say your vision out loud. How does it make you feel? Would you be comfortable talking about your vision with a friend or partner? According to Phillips, a powerful Vision Statement will often...

- *Make you gulp hard*
- *Be a little embarrassing to tell others because it seems so big*
- *Feel like it exceeds your grasp*
- *Be clear*
- *Be where you really want to go*
- *Be a statement of something that isn't already a reality*
- *Have the capacity to be easily understood by a 12-year-old Honor and extend your values*

Write your final Vision Statement in your Journal or on a special Vision Card (identify your own), and keep it in an area where you see it every day. Having it front and center allows you to occasionally check in and ask yourself:

1. Am I honoring my vision?
2. Are my activities keeping me directed toward my values, strengths, and vision?
3. Am I being honest with myself?

Your Vision Statement is the foundation for all other decisions you make in life. It can underlie every personal relationship decision and career goal.

If you're deciding between two job offers, for instance, your Vision Statement gives you more clarity. If you're thinking about going back to school, or making a big financial decision, or even just getting a family pet, your Vision Statement is a strong foundation that helps you to make the best possible choices.

And, as Phillips notes, it can also give you a good reason to say "No" sometimes. Phillips finds that many people decide whether or not to take on new responsibilities and commitments based on who's doing the asking.

"They'll think to themselves, 'I like this person, so I'm going to help them,'" he says. "That's a nice way to be, but you are living out other people's visions, not your own."

On the other hand, having a razor-sharp focus on your vision helps you to instantly recognize projects that can bring you greater joy and fulfillment, because you get to align your values, strengths, and vision with activities that have meaning to *you*.

Let's Do This

Over the last nine months, you've made deep connections to your powerful internal tools. You have a stronger sense of presence, connection, gratefulness, and more. In fact, your inside-out tools have grown to the point where you have an increased capacity to take on any challenge that comes your way. So now the question is: *What will you do with your unlocked capacity?*

You deserve to experience the life you were uniquely made for. In fact, it's your responsibility to signal to your friends, family, and community what it means to pursue a vision-directed life. By identifying your Top 3 Values, imagining your 90th Birthday Party, and creating your Vision Statement, you're strategically choosing to live a life of deeper meaning.

Every so often come back to your Vision Statement and ask yourself if you are staying true to it. Just as your intention for doing Madefor may have changed, so too may your vision. But now that you've got the knowledge, you don't need a compass to tell you what to do. You already know. Now, all that's left is for you to go forth and bring your best self to the world.

Dream big.

Make your world better.

You were made for this.

It's time to take your Metrics of Change Survey!

Track key areas of change throughout the Madefor Program by completing a short five-question survey provided in the back of the book - *it will only take 5 minutes to complete!* For the most accurate results, we recommend completing the survey before your Month 1: Hydration Challenge, Month 5: Breath Challenge, and Month 10: Vision Challenge (3 times total).

Complete the survey (Tools & Resources Section).

Pat's Vision Guidance

At the outset of Madefor you set an intention for what you hope to achieve through this program—take a moment to reflect on and record how engaging this challenge might help serve your intention.

You began Madefor by setting an intention. If you're like the thousands of Members who have come before you, you've moved closer toward that intention over the course of these Challenges. You've come to realize that while the Challenges can help you to build better foundational health habits, they also help you to build a more resilient mindset—one that has a bias for action and growth, an orientation to recognize and celebrate the good, an ability to give and receive compassion and grace, an awareness of your inner landscape, and an appreciation of how the journey is the reward, no matter the destination.

As you engage with this Challenge and arrive at a vision for your life, it's important to remember that whether or not you achieve that vision is irrelevant. What matters is the daily pursuit toward becoming the best version of yourself. If your vision feels out of reach, but it inspires you to live better today, then it's right on target. If your vision feels out of reach and makes you feel less capable, then rework it until it becomes an asset to you.

If you struggle to stay on track this month, consider taking this small step—reflect on an important value and the last time you leaned into it to make yourself or someone you care about better. If one step is too hard, revisit your intention for inspiration. You got this.

For additional support, check out my Perspectives video for more information around how we designed this Challenge, recommendations on how to approach the daily exercises, and real-life experiences and perspectives from Madefor Members that have completed the journey. Or, listen to this quick Campfire Story for a little inspiration.

*Madefor Videos and Audio recordings can be found on our YouTube page (https://www.youtube.com/@getmadefor)

Congratulations, you did it!

10 Months. 10 Challenges. Many Steps.
You stuck with it and that's no small feat.
You've changed.
Not from any one tool or reading.
But, from the effort you put in.

Neuroplasticity.
Inside-out tools.
Growth Mindset.
Attention.
Intention.
No longer just buzzwords.

You are moving differently.
You have greater capacity.
You are more connected.

You elevated your baselines.
Harnessed the power of your brain.
And shifted your mindset.

This power was always within you.
You really were made for this.

A better world requires the best you.
Go show them what you're made for.

- - -

Pat and Andrew have a special Graduation Message they
wanted to share with you (https://www.youtube.com/watch?v=
vnAFUXlSd0M)

One Last Thing

I hope you've enjoyed this journey of self-discovery, and that you've arrived not at a final destination but rather at a starting point for a new way of being in and moving through the world.

If not, that's okay too—Madefor is effective at any dose, so feel free to dive back into any of the Challenges at any time. Repetition will not spoil the practice.

Just remember, how you show up today matters. It matters as much when you're 19 as it does when you're 99—you'll never fully appreciate how a small act can change the trajectory of someone's day or life, including your own.

On behalf of our team and Members all across the world, thank you for taking the time to bring out the best in yourself and the world around you.

You got this.

Cheers,
Pat

P.S. If you ever need to reach me, you can send me a message on Instagram @madefor_pat

Acknowledgements

Blake Mycoskie is not just my friend and Madefor co-founder, he has one of the biggest hearts I know of—I'm grateful he has the courage to let it guide his actions and continue to make the world a better place for all.

Lisa Sweetingham is not just an incredible writer, she is also a genuinely kind human who at times played therapist as she extracted and gave shape to the raw materials that became Madefor.

Lindsey Weening is not just an amazing teammate and leader, she is also a rockstar co-creator of Madefor who was instrumental in bringing Madefor to life and ensuring our Members were always the priority.

Andrew Huberman is not just a brilliant mind and lead Madefor Advisor, he is also a close friend whose eyes lit up when I told him my crazy idea, giving me the confidence to continue the pursuit—there is no Madefor without Andrew.

Anchored by our founding teammate, Erica Wenger, the Madefor Team has always kept our Member's wellbeing front and center. Whitney Herline, Amanda Turner, Kirsten Van Der Wey, KC Brown, Madison Sims, Patrick Wojnarowski, Margaux Giles, Gailor Large, Kelly Niethammer, Evan Sentoso, Riley Feng, Joel Parr, Jessica Lollino, Julia Ruttner, Nicole Rothschild—without your effort, Madefor would not have come to life.

Rory Cordial, Ruth Benca, Samer Hattar, Dave Phillips, Evelyn Tribole, Lisa Fitzpatrick, John Ratey, and Dan Cnossen are not just the Advisors who helped build Madefor, they are deeply committed scientists, clinicians, coaches, and practitioners whose work touches and improves millions of lives every day.

Emily, Simon, JB, Marni, Haynes, Faye, Kate, Marco, and the entire team at Red Antler were not just our partners in helping build the Madefor brand, they were instrumental in forging the experience and bringing Madefor to life.

Manami Masters is not just a bad ass community builder, coach, and teammate, she is also my last remaining teammate at Madefor and the reason you're able to read this book today.

Kim Dossett is not just my beautiful wife, she is also the best mother on the planet who gave birth and nurtured three brand new worlds while also giving me the not so gentle nudges I needed to build Madefor.

Mike Blabac is not just the world-renowned photographer responsible for the cover photo of this book, he is a kind, gentle human who uses his gifts to elevate the nature of his subjects.

To everyone who gave time, attention, and effort to Madefor, our Members, and our mission—thank you.

Program Guide

The Program

You have the power to change. Madefor is designed to fit anyone's lifestyle, with one primary goal—to equip you with the tools to take control of your life.

Our approach is radical in its simplicity, focusing on foundational practices to help you build not just better habits but more importantly, a more resilient mindset and better way of being.

There are no gurus, hype, or fads—everything we guide you to do is rooted in evidence-based research that we've distilled into doable, essential, and effective steps. When completed together, they are proven to have a positive impact on your body, brain, and life.

How it works

Everything you need to be successful in this program is inside this book.

Madefor focuses on 10 distinct 21-day Challenges designed to be completed over the course of 10 months in just a few minutes each day.

Each month, you will complete the same steps:

- **Read the Challenge Guidebook** to understand the science behind each area of focus.
- **Get offline and into action** with your 21-day Challenge (takes just 10 minutes a day!).
- **Prepare and stay on track** by leaning into the physical and digital tools as needed.
- **Take a 7-day break** between Challenges to reflect on what you've learned or catch up on steps you've missed.
- **Unlock your power and get on with life.**

PRO TIP: Anchor your Challenge start dates around a regular schedule to help you stay on track. For example, plan to start a new Challenge on the 1st of each month.

The Mindset

First, this is a program of progress, not perfection. At some point, you will experience a setback or disengage with the Challenges, and that's okay. Life gets a vote and can knock even the best of us off course, so be kind to yourself, give yourself a little grace, and when you are ready, take the smallest step possible to get back into action where you left off. Keep the Intention you set during Onboarding top-of-mind—return to it when you need extra motivation. The process of recommitting to yourself is valuable and something you will get better at with Madefor.

PRO TIP: *Whenever you feel like you have fallen behind, check out the* _2-minute video from Dr. Andrew Huberman_ *(https:// www.youtube.com/watch?v=simJUfHei2c) where he shares his perspective on how to approach setbacks (hint: get into action).*

Approach the Challenges with a beginner's mind. The areas of focus you engage at Madefor are foundational. This is part of what makes Madefor so effective, but it can also lead some to think that the Challenge is beneath them. Suspend disbelief and focus on doing the Challenges as designed—this is how you unlock the surprising benefits of Madefor. *If you don't believe us - make sure to watch the* _Founder & Member Perspective Videos_ *that are mentioned at the end of each Guidebook!*

The Benefits

The benefits people experience with Madefor are unique. Some Challenges may resonate more than others—and that's OK. Over time, you will experience shifts in your behaviors and mindset that endure past the steps you take in the program.

> *"The issue with getting into action is*
> *rarely lack of information."*
> *- Dr. Andrew Huberman*

We ask that you keep these perspectives in mind as you move through Madefor:

- **Trust the process:** We recommend completing the Challenges in the order they are laid out—no skipping ahead. Each highly-researched area of focus has been

intentionally chosen and placed in a very specific order to help build a new positive habit. When completed
together, they provide a foundation for cultivating new
mindsets and greater wellbeing.

- **Get offline and into action:** If you have to look at an
app, screen, device, or wearable—something outside
of yourself to understand how you are feeling or performing—then you've missed a critical first step. This
is why all of the Challenges at Madefor are designed to
be done offline. Approach each step with an open and
curious mindset to better understand what signals your
body is sending you and how best to respond.

- **Focus on ONE step at a time:** Madefor is designed to
help you focus on ONE thing at a time—one step at a
time. You will realize bigger benefits with focused and
intentional action, so lean in and let go.

The Tools & Resources

Throughout the book, we make recommendations for identifying physical tools or link out to digital resources that are
designed to help you get offline and remove friction so that you
can focus on getting the most out of your Challenge.

For example, we provide a 21-day tracker card, or "**Challenge
Card**", designed to help reward effort and track progress as you
cross off steps each day. We recommend finding a "**Challenge
Bracelet**" to aid you as a reminder of the practice and intention
you set at the beginning of the program—it's a simple visual
cue for the moments when you forget that you're on a journey. Numerous studies show that even the smallest of visual
cues can help nudge you to stay engaged and build positive
momentum towards your goals, which is why we recommend
these two tools in each area of focus.

When in doubt, use the tools that make the most sense for you and help you stay engaged in the Challenge. All downloadable and printable tools, as well as digital resources, can be found in the <u>Tools & Resources</u> section.

Madefor Language

Challenges: we refer to each area of focus in the Madefor Program as a Challenge. Each area of focus includes a 21-day Challenge. As an example, the Madefor Program includes a Hydration Challenge and Gratitude Challenge.

Tools: a physical or digital tool designed to help you benefit from the area of focus in just 21 days. For example, the Hydration Challenge's tool is a water bottle.

Guidebooks: the curated and relevant science behind your Challenge focus. Each Challenge's Guidebook provides you with the science and the stories to inspire you to take small steps towards the best you.

Founder & Member Perspectives: a message from Pat (Madefor co-founder & former Navy SEAL) about how we designed each Challenge, recommendations on how to approach the daily exercises, and real-life experiences and perspectives from Madefor Members that have completed the journey. You can find each Perspectives video on our YouTube, under the Founder & Member Perspectives playlist (https://www.youtube.com/ playlist?list=PLikMIQ-E2Aah8QtogFFGXAWaVD4s6AjqY).

Founder Campfire Stories: a quick story to help motivate you in your Challenge, told by Pat. You can find each Story on our YouTube, under the Founder Campfire Stories playlist <u>here</u>.

Basecamp: a long-form conversation with Pat and a Madefor Advisor(s) or other inspiring guests, designed to offer deeper insight into a certain topic and to help you get energized to complete your Challenges. We've summarized several key sessions for you at the end of the book, however you can access the complete library of all recorded conversations on our YouTube, under the Basecamp Conversations playlist (https://www.youtube.com/playlist?list=PLikMIQ-E2Aaj0j8-a5 VRZWbPXuFp99xpD).

The Community

The true strength of Madefor is in its people—and that includes you. By starting your own journey, you're joining a diverse, global community working towards a shared mission: to bring out the best in you.

Members are more successful when completing the program alongside others—bring a friend or two along on your journey and experience lasting change together.

Our digital properties allow you to learn from and engage with the global Madefor Community:

- **Engage with members.** Our social media channel (https://www.instagram.com/madefor/) connects you with Members and Alumni from all over the world. Follow us here for occasional inspiration and motivation.
- **Learn from experts.** Tap into our wealth of resources on YouTube (https://www.youtube.com/@getmadefor), including compelling conversations with world-renowned experts, short clips that inspire action, and curated content to enrich your journey.

Members have greatly benefitted from leaning into our digital resources—don't let this opportunity pass you by.

PRO TIP: *Start now! Watch your* <u>Welcome Video</u> *(https://www. youtube.com/watch?v=wiOlhn91zS8) for a complete overview of the Madefor Program and a message from Pat (Madefor co-founder) and a few of our Alumni. You won't want to miss this!*

Tools & Resources

View and download all of the printable resources available to you at ((https://www.dropbox.com/scl/fo/9jinwn2bysouig-3eyxui9/h?dl=0&rlkey=si4efwfpkggwbcyut8jsruuve))

Resources include:

- 21-day tracker cards, or "**Challenge Cards**" for each Challenge
- Phone backgrounds, or "**Challenge Screens**" for each Challenge
- 50-card **Connect Deck** (for the Connection Challenge)
- **Values Inventory** (for the Vision Challenge)
- And more!

All video resources referenced in this book can be found below or on our YouTube (https://www.youtube.com/@getmadefor).

- Madefor Program Welcome Video: a complete overview of the Madefor Program and a message from Pat and a few of our Alumni. Watch this to help kickstart your journey - you won't want to miss it!
- Founder & Member Perspectives playlist: messages from Pat about how each Challenge is designed, recommendations on how to approach the daily exercises, and real-life experiences and perspectives from Madefor Members that have completed the journey. Watch these before starting your Challenges.
- Founder Campfire Stories playlist: quick stories from Pat to help motivate you in your Challenges. Watch these when you're needing a little inspiration.

- Guided Breath Exercises: two 10-minute guided breathing exercises created for Month 5's Breath Challenge, led by advisor Rory Cordial.
- Madefor Movements Video Series: six movement videos designed for Month 6's Movement Challenge, led by advisor Rory Cordial.
- What to do when you've fallen behind: a 2-minute video from Dr. Andrew Huberman where he shares his perspective on how to approach setbacks (hint: get into action!). Watch this whenever you feel like you've fallen behind.
- Basecamp Conversations: a long-form conversation with Pat and a Madefor Advisor(s) or other inspiring guests, designed to offer deeper insight into a certain topic and to help you get energized to complete your Challenges. Watch these as needed, no pressure!
- Madefor Program Graduation Video: a short message from Pat & Andrew, congratulating you on your effort. Watch this once you've completed your Vision Challenge.

OPTIONAL: Take your Metrics of Change Survey (5 minutes)

Track key areas of change throughout the Madefor Program by completing the short survey below. For the most accurate results, we recommend completing the survey before your Month 1: Hydration Challenge, Month 5: Breath Challenge, and Month 10: Vision Challenge (3 times total).

This five-question survey is focused on your self-perceived success in areas such as cultivating a growth mindset, practicing self-compassion, being intentional, and feeling in control. Choose your level of agreement with each statement using a scale from 1 - 5 with 3 being "Neutral."

Grab your Journal and something to write with to document your answers.

Ready to begin?

1. Challenges and setbacks are inevitable, but whether or not you experience them as threats or opportunities determines how well you respond to them.

    Do you respond well to challenges?

    1 - Always a threat, 5 - Always an opportunity

2. There is nothing like having a good teammate, someone who extends you undeserving kindness and works to bring out the best in you no matter the situation and especially when you experience setbacks.

    Are you a good teammate to yourself?

    1 - I'm always critical, 5 - I'm always kind

3. A good navigator knows the destination—each step they take brings them closer to the things they care most about.

    Are you a good navigator?

    1 - Unclear on what matters, 5 - Clear on what matters

4. It's easy to get caught up in the inertia of life, feeling like you are being pulled through the day rather than actively participating in it. But, when you take the right action, you build momentum that puts you in greater control over your experience.

    Are you in control?

    1 - Never in control, 5 - Always in control

5. In your own words, please share where you are today and where you hope to be ten months from now.

    You are at the beginning of a long process of change and intentionally engaging with this writing exercise helps to reinforce lasting, meaningful change in the future. Be as detailed as possible!

Keep track of your answers at the beginning, middle, and end of the program to see how your effort through Madefor has impacted your life.

You got this!

Journaling Tips & FAQ

We know journaling is hard! Check out some of our useful techniques to help get you into the flow of putting pen to paper. **REMINDER:** This takes time, and it is a practice. Be gentle with yourself if you fall off track, and just start again.

5 Tips for Getting Started with Journaling

There are **NO RULES** to this - **EXCEPT** that you do it.

Handy Tips to Putting Pen to Paper:

1. **Make the time to take the time.** Finding 5 minutes in the morning or before you turn off your light in the evening can go a long way in creating new habits.
2. **Make this a CONSISTENT practice.** Even if you write ONE word - reflect on ONE feeling from the day - that is something worth celebrating. Bring your journal around with you for extra accountability.
3. **Be curious.** It's easy to judge ourselves and fall into what we call "analysis paralysis." See if you can create some distance by asking questions. "How does x make me feel? How did I approach that situation?" This brings room for self-compassion.
4. **Authenticity Matters.** This is all for you. So let yourself be messy. Express your genuine experience and feelings. No one is going to see this, and the more honest you can be with yourself, the more you will get out of it.
5. **Make it fun!** This is not that serious. Be playful. Make yourself a cup of tea. Can you buy yourself some fun pens? Can you bring your journal into nature?

To commit is a CHOICE. An active decision to reinforce the daily rewards you receive from small intentional acts. This attention–reward–reinforcement process is what helps facilitate the sort of sustained positive changes in the brain we are looking for!

FAQ

If you're struggling to get started or ever feel stuck, you're not alone! Here are some of the most frequently asked questions around journaling we've heard from Members going through Madefor, and our answers to help you move through that friction.

Q: I've never been able to journal. I've tried many times, but the habit won't stick. Do I have to do this part?
A: When you intentionally engage in a practice repeatedly, even at the smallest level, you create deep neural patterns that result in lasting change. That's why journaling is a crucial part of this program and you will be prompted to journal at every Challenge. Just a couple of sentences of daily reflection rewards your brain and reinforces your new habit. You're affirming your innate ability to learn—to be more plastic. The journal is designed to help you harness that power of plasticity - by putting pen to paper you are telling your brain to pay attention - which is a key element of creating lasting change.

Q: I don't know what to write, or where to start, and feel like I am being repetitive.
A: If you are having trouble, that's okay! Take it one day at a time, in small steps. Start with one word, one phrase, etc., and notice how the momentum builds. Check out our 5 journaling tips above for more inspiration.

Q: Do we experience the same benefits if we journal digitally (via phone or typing on a computer) versus writing by hand?
A: For the purposes of the program, we recommend putting pen to paper, to journal. Dr. Andrew Huberman (Madefor Lead

Advisor & Neuroscientist) talks about the benefits of forcing your brain and body to operate on the same wavelength when you write things down. You are actually engaging more parts of your brain when keeping a journal instead of saying things out loud or typing them out on a computer. Writing by hand connects you to the words, encourages you to slow down and focus on your thoughts, and helps reinforce the learnings.

> *"You can only write so fast, so it forces your brain*
> *to slow down and be present in the moment."*
> – Dr. Andrew Huberman

Q: By the time I remember to journal, it's the end of the day and I'm exhausted. I either skip the practice altogether or write just to get something down. Does it matter what time of the day I journal?

A: Nighttime journaling clears the mental decks so you can avoid a spiral of negative, default-mode thinking. Evening journaling also helps you get the most leverage out of sleep because, in addition to being a powerful recharging process, sleep is when positive brain changes happen. That said, journaling is a habit that is hard to cultivate, so while we recommend an evening practice (or at least giving it a fair shot!), we also encourage you to meet yourself where you are at and journal when it works best for you.

Remember, this is a program of progress over perfection. If you fall off track with your journaling practice at any point, just start again. You got this!

Basecamp Highlights

Basecamps are long-form conversations with Pat and a Madefor Advisor(s) or other inspiring guests around a specific topic. The information provided from these sessions is supplemental to the program and completely optional. They were designed to offer deeper insight into certain topics and to help you get energized to complete your Challenges. We've summarized several key sessions for you in this section, however feel free to check out our complete library of recorded Basecamp Conversations on our YouTube channel (https://www.youtube.com/@getmadefor)

- How to Gain a Grittier Mindset: Dr. Angela Duckworth
- How to Finally Get It Done—the Surprising Science of Motivation: Dr. Ayelet Fishbach
- The Sweet Science of Forgiveness: Dr. Everett Worthington
- Rediscovering the Joy of Movement: Dr. Kelly McGonigal
- The Science of Emotion: Dr. Lisa Feldman Barrett
- The Science of Influence: Dr. Vanessa Bohns

How to Gain a Grittier Mindset:
Dr. Angela Duckworth

Madefor co-founder and former Navy SEAL, Pat Dossett, sat down with world-renowned research psychologist, professor, and best-selling author, Angela Duckworth, to discuss her research advancing the scientific insights that help us thrive. Dr. Duckworth talked about grit, the connection between grit and happiness, the benefits of being goal-driven, and how talent and skills are not mutually exclusive to one another. Dr. Duckworth also gave the group some tips on how to gain a grittier mind-set—at any age!

> "Grit is having long-term goals that are identity-driven.
> It's not an accident that happiness and grit are correlated."
> – Dr. Angela Duckworth

The Connection Between Happiness & Grit

Can happiness and grit co-exist? Well, the argument is more one of could we find happiness without grit? According to the data, it's statistically much more likely that happiness and grit go together. In her personal opinion, Dr. Duckworth doesn't think people are happy when they don't have something to do, and people who lack goals are profoundly distressed. The research agrees. In longitudinal studies, where happiness and grit are measured overtime, it's repeatedly found that there's a virtuous cycle that happier people at time one tend to be grittier at time two. **What makes all people happy at our core, whether we would describe ourselves as ambitious or not, is because our DNA is goal-driven.**

When we talk about goals, are we only talking about things like climbing mountains or getting a Ph.D.? Absolutely not! A goal is a desired future state. This ranges from everything from a 10- or 5-year goal to something as simple as having the goal to make yourself lunch or call your mother-in-law. **There are two classifications of goals, personal and pro-social**. Personal goals are goals that when achieved, you are better off. Pro-social goals are altruistic and when we achieve them, someone else is better off. The thing that brings all this together is grit. Having long term goals that you're willing to and do work hard for. The goals are so relevant and important to you, they become a big part of your identity. Data suggests that people in general tend to be happier when pursuing pro-social goals than personal goals.

If your goals are only for you, meaning your field of view is completely taken up with yourself, it will never get you to happiness. That's something to really think about.

"People who lack goals are profoundly distressed."
- Dr. Angela Duckworth

Being Goal-Driven: Why Effort Trumps Talent

Can we gain grit and better achieve our goals at any age? Science says we can. Across the human lifespan, there's remarkable plasticity, not only neuronal growth which continues throughout the adult lifespan but also a kind of remodeling of synapses and connections. Grit is just like all the other characteristics in your personality you can intentionally change. Grit comes down to passion and perseverance. Passion leads you first, however, if you don't know what you're passionate about play and explore, learn, and be open to new experiences to figure out what light sparks in you or what really resonates or what you are just repetitively curious about. That's going to lead you to practice and ultimately result in achievement. The achievement also creates a skill.

Two things determine skill: effort and talent. When we talk about talent in this sense, it's the rate at which you're getting better. Talent does matter, but **effort counts twice**. We all have natural abilities that make skill development easy. However, we have things we want to achieve or we think we'll enjoy that we may not have a talent for at the onset of our interest. With effort – hard work and hours invested – you can develop a skill.

When you do something, again and again, you become better at it. This is the nature of human skill. Take friendships, for instance. The first time you talk to someone, it may not go great, or it can feel very surface-level. Friendship needs repetition and consistency and habit and routine, just like physical therapy. You need to put the time and effort in, and then your skill becomes stronger.

When you look at super-achievers, such as specialists and experts in various fields, they're kind of voluntarily obsessed with one thing that they think about 24/7, 52 weeks a year. These super-achievers were not always experts, they had to be willing to play and try and make mistakes to find the thing they felt truly passionate about and wanted to pursue. You can do that at any point in life from 23 to 83 (and beyond).

> *"Effort is different from talent in the sense that it takes raw potential and enables you to develop skills, and then helps you apply those skills and actually create things in the world....Effort counts twice!"*
> *– Dr. Angela Duckworth*

How to Get a Grittier Mindset

After all this talk about grit and goals, passion and persistence, it can be difficult to assess where you are as it pertains to your grittiness. What if you don't really know what you're passionate about? Maybe you are someone who stares at a wall, having a total blank, when purpose is mentioned. You're not the only one -- it just seems a lot more complicated than it is. It's actually pretty simple - start on the step that most resonates with where you are in your personal journey.

Three steps for getting a grittier mindset:

1. **Play** - So maybe you don't know what it is you are really passionate about and need some help. Embark on some playful learning. It's time to let yourself go and embrace play. If something feels really good and you feel yourself getting excited about it - notice that. If something makes you feel heavy - move away from

it. After a while, you'll start to identify areas that ignite passion and construct that passion into goals.

2. **Practice** - Growth can only come with understanding and awareness, so you need to get out there and practice achieving your goals. Yes, *practice* it. Not every effort will be a success. You need to take each mistake, misstep, or failure as a lesson - they are the key to developing grit.

3. **Purpose** - Purpose is a deep interest you have over the long-term. It's something you want to take a deep-dive in. Purpose is that thing that you want to become a part of your life. What makes you feel that way? What things are you doing in service of your purpose?

Just remember, being human makes you pre-wired for grit. Wanting to change is all you need, at any age, to make changes. Let passion lead you, embrace play, practice your passion, and grow your purpose to gain a grittier frame of mind, enhanced resilience, and an even happier life!

How to Finally Get It Done—the Surprising Science of Motivation: Dr. Ayelet Fishbach

Madefor co-founder and former Navy SEAL, Pat Dossett, sat down with author, professor, and expert on motivation and decision making, Dr. Ayelet Fishbach, for Basecamp. With nearly a month into the new year and, of course, new resolutions, they discussed why 75 percent of people don't complete their New Year's Resolutions. **Dr. Fishbach broke down the science of motivation and provided actionable steps anyone can take to bring their goals to fruition.**

Intrinsic Motivation and "The Middle Problem"

Let's start with the ten million dollar question – Why don't people stick to their resolutions? Dr. Fishbach told us what predicts how much people stick to their resolution is how much they are intrinsically motivated, that is to say, how much they found that something that feels right to them as they are doing it. Very few people set resolutions thinking, "This is going to be so fun to do!" Most people set resolutions because they think they are meaningful to their future self, i.e., "I need to work out four days each week to be healthier."

However, the problem is it doesn't matter how meaningful or important a goal is; it matters how much you are enjoying achieving it. How internally connected are you to the goal? Sure, importance is important since many goals are usually health-related, but feeling good and right while doing it is critical because it means you are more likely to keep doing it. Something to keep in mind though is the longer the time between the goal you want to achieve and the activity, the less intrinsic motivation you will have.

"It's hard to stay motivated. In the beginning, your first step is 100% of the progress. In the end, your last step is 100% of achieving the goal. In the middle, it doesn't feel like we're doing all that much, so we work less hard and cut corners."
– Dr. Ayelet Fishbach

When we start working toward our goal, it's with a lot of enthusiasm. In the middle, it's hard to stay motivated – hard to do the work, hard to invest resources, and it's also hard to do a good job. Our performance drops off. We're more likely to cheat a little in the middle. Why? Because in the middle, you don't feel like your actions have much impact.

Consider this: Let's think of a 10-step goal. Up until the fifth step, if you look back on what you've already done, your next step feels like you'll double your progress — you've come so far! From that same fifth step, if you look ahead, it feels like you have to do so much more of the work, and it doesn't feel like you're making any headway. **This is called the Psychophysics of Goals.** You can avoid that pesky Middle Problem by adjusting how you create goals. Here's a hint: take your time.

"Go slow now, so you can go fast later."
– Pat Dossett

The Right Goal Makes All the Difference

Dr. Fishbach talked about goals in terms of **two kinds of goals, approach and avoidance.** Approach goals are in pursuit of something, whereas avoidance goals are made to avoid something. Approach goals are better for the simple reason that when you try to avoid something, you check yourself by bringing the thing you are trying to avoid back to mind. It's like repeatedly inviting a pink elephant into the room. Avoidance goals do have one advantage, however, and it's that they feel urgent. There's also another interesting trend in why people make each of these types of goals. People with power set approach goals, while people who lack power set avoidance goals. Those who set approach goals are also genuinely excited about what they are doing. Which kind of goal are you making?

Another element to the success of goal progress is the Empathy Gap. When we don't care or take into consideration how our future self will feel, it can create an Empathy Gap. To avoid this, we have to consider all barriers and challenges we may face and how we can deal with them before committing to a goal. The goal also has to fit with the reality of who we are. By predicting how our future self will feel about a goal, we can anticipate challenges and have ready-made solutions, know that the goal is in line with our identity, and feel excited about not just achieving the goal but knowing ways we can be sure to enjoy the journey. This all helps us avoid that "Middle Problem" where we lose steam, performance falls off, and ultimately we quit.

Another critical part of making and realizing goals is having clarity of the bigger goals at hand. There is a hierarchy of goals and, likely, your goal is actually a sub-goal of a larger, more general goal. For example, the general goal is being healthy. Sub-goals that then would be things like improving in areas like eating, sleeping, exercising, etc. Then those sub-goals will often have activities that act as a means to achieving that goal. So if the goal is exercise, there could be many means to that end like running, yoga, weightlifting, boxing, etc.

From there we can then separate (sub)goals into two specific structures: (1) two or more activities that serve the same goal, and (2) the same activity serves several goals. This is important for a few key reasons. When we have activities that serve several goals, they can be classified as good activities that help us achieve more with fewer actions. When we think about all the goals connected to the same activity, it increases our motivation. When several activities are connected to the same goal, we call these backup plans or alternatives.

For instance, running each morning with your dog can serve many goals such as improving your health, getting out into nature, and spending time with your pup. Now let's say you injure your foot, and running is out of the question for six weeks – do you give up? No! You use one of your backup plans until you can run again. Do yoga with your dog in the backyard in the morning instead. Having those backup plans can not only give you options for when something happens, but they can also help keep you excited and fend off boredom.

Finally, you need a support system to help you achieve your goals. Reach out to others in your circle to help you stay on track, participate with you, or just serve as your cheerleaders. We as people need other people.

> *"We need to feel supported, we need to feel like this (our goal) is the right thing to do. We are looking for role models, and we find the best role model is not the one who does it well, but the one that wants you to succeed."*
> *– Dr. Ayelet Fishbach*

Dr. Fishbach's #1 Tip for Making it Happen

With so much great information from this Basecamp and in her book, *Get it Done: Surprising Lessons from the Science of Motivation*, Pat asked Dr. Fishbach, "If you were to leave everyone with one takeaway as it refers to motivation and goal setting, what would it be?" Her response was maybe a little surprising. She said, "My number one tip would be, when you are struggling with something, advise someone else who is struggling with the same thing." When you give advice, you feel motivated by your own advice. Advising another person can bring to the front of your mind everything you know about that specific area of life where you are struggling.

Make her advice actionable with these three steps:

1. Journal: Sit down and take some time to think about your goals. Ask yourself:

- What goal am I currently struggling with?
- Who do I know that is struggling with the same thing? You may need to reach out and check in with a few people, but engaging your tribe is always a good thing, right?

2. List all the advice you could give the person you selected.

3. Reach out! It could be in-person, via phone, email, or text. See how they are doing and offer advice. If you aren't sure how to give advice, use phrases like, "I find xxx helps me" or "I've been reading about (insert process/routine/regimen here), and it's working for lots of people." If the conversation goes there organically, all the better!

In closing, take your time when creating your goals before committing to them. Think out all the angles. Have backups at the ready and see where your big goals intersect. Find a support system. Be deliberate and detailed and you'll experience a higher rate of success.

The Sweet Science of Forgiveness: Dr. Everett Worthington

Madefor co-founder and former Navy SEAL, Pat Dossett, sat down with the world's leading expert on forgiveness, Dr. Everett Worthington for Basecamp. Dr. Worthington discussed types of forgiveness, why it matters so much, how we can learn to forgive others, and the cost of unforgiveness. Dr. Worthington also took us through doing the complex work of forgiving ourselves.

Forgiveness & The Benefits of Forgiveness

When we define forgiveness, we need to understand there are two different types of forgiveness. The first type is when you decide how to treat someone who's hurt or offended you. You treat them or the relationship you have with them as valuable. The second type, emotional forgiveness, is more nuanced. This type of forgiveness replaces negative emotions like resentment and bitterness with positive emotions like empathy and understanding. Forgiveness matters because whenever we experience what feels like an injustice to us, it creates automatic computing in our minds, referred to as a "justice gap." It can be large or small, and forgiveness is one of the only ways to reduce the gap.

So why do we or should we forgive? First, it's important to recognize that no one inherently deserves forgiveness when they hurt you. It's something you can give, but you don't have to. It's your choice and is an internal thing. That said, there are three types of benefits that forgiveness can bring. You can benefit relationally; after the hurt, you treat them differently, which then causes them to treat you differently. Mentally, when you forgive, it cuts down on rumination, the constant playing over and over of an injustice that only makes it worse each time. Dr. Worthington joked that rumination is the Bad Boy of Mental Health. To forgive is to stop rehearsing the negativity and stop it in its tracks. The final type of benefit is your physical health. Unforgiveness breeds stress and anxiety and can cause a lot of damage to the body. Forgiving takes your body out of the fight-or-flight internal messaging and brings your body back into balance.

> *"Rumination is the Bad Boy of Mental Health. Forgiveness can close it down so you don't feel the need to keep rehearsing the negativity and can let it go."*
> *– Dr. Everett Worthington*

In addition to giving forgiveness to others, it's just as important to give it to ourselves. However, forgiving ourselves is more complex. Why? You're coming at things from two points of view at the same time – as the offender and the offended. There's an inherent double whammy of forgiving when it's self-directed. You also have to be genuine in your self-forgiveness. You can't just casually say, "I forgive myself," when you're just letting yourself off the hook.

There's a whole extra level of having to have responsible self-forgiveness. It involves three preliminary steps before the journey to true self-forgiveness can really start. You first have to resolve things with that which you hold sacred, make things right due to the social damage you've done, and come to terms with the fact that you may have morally injured yourself by doing something you believe is in opposition to who you are as a person. Only once you've gone through those stages can you be ready to start the self-forgiveness process. Even when you finish the process, you have to do one final thing – accept yourself.

The Cost of Unforgiveness & Micro-Injustice Boil Over

Sometimes it seems like forgiving just isn't possible. Sometimes we feel like it isn't fair because someone has wronged us, and maybe they don't feel the consequences of their actions if we forgive. Pat pointed out that sometimes there's this sense that if we hold onto unforgiveness, it is a shield that we carry around. It's our armor. If we set that down, the vulnerability can be too much. Dr. Worthington mirrored those feelings back and explained that it feels like a safe place to be behind that shield of unforgiveness. However, that shield is really heavy to carry every day. It's safe for the moment, but it will take a big toll overall. To be able to lay this thing down and put it behind you, that's risky and requires a lot of courage. However, in the end, it will lead to a lot better health for you and that relationship.

Pat asked how can you forgive and still feel a reconciliation of injustice? How can you hold justice and empathy at the same time? Dr. Worthington answered that forgiveness is an internal experience and justice is an interpersonal or societal experience. Just because you forgive someone it doesn't mean they aren't accountable for their actions.

For instance, when we want to "pay someone back" for their infractions against us, we get swept into a dangerous circle of hurt. Someone hurts you, and you measure it to be a 3-units of hurt experience. You think, "I'll give them back those 3-units of hurt as payback." So you give them back, and that person feels like it's 5-units of hurt and believes they only gave you 1-unit of hurt. So now they think, "I owe them 4-units of hurt back," and so on and so on. It's a never-ending cycle because our perception of the hurt we give and get is usually different from another's perception.

> "We're entitled to hold onto whatever we want inside, but just because we have the right it doesn't mean doing so is always right. In fact, when it comes to unforgiveness, holding on imparts a cost. It's not a matter of if but when."
> – Pat Dossett

There's another way to deal with injustices – ignore or procrastinate the small ones. But that comes at a greater cost. Dr. Worthington gives a wonderful example of how micro-injustices build up over time and change our everyday lives. He said, "We need to reflect on our experiences because if it's not a big thing, I'm not inclined to pay a lot of attention to it right away. And yet, I can carry a 100-pound stone and strain under the burden, or I can carry 100 pounds of rocks in a bag. The rocks are just as heavy and straining my muscles just as much as the boulder, but I don't notice each rock as it goes in. I only notice it when I get to the place of saying: I don't know why I'm so cranky and negative and stressed all the time interpersonally and why I'm so short with people." Realizing the impact of ignoring the little injustices can be our trigger to make it a priority to examine our lives and why we feel angry or negative. Once we do that, we can start on a path to resolution and forgiveness.

How to Forgive: The Reach Practice

If we want to forgive and are unsure how to start, how can we? Dr. Worthington created the REACH Forgiveness Practice to help people find a way to forgive. There are five distinct steps and the entire process can take a while. You shouldn't hurry out of a step, for some it takes years to move to the next step. It's more important to fully complete each step before moving to the next.

The REACH Practice:

R: Recall the hurt
E: Empathize with the offender
A: give forgiveness as an Altruistic gift
C: Commit to forgiveness with a public act of some sort
H: Hold onto forgiveness

Is there a hurt you've been holding onto that you believe you can resolve with either (or both) type(s) of forgiveness? Journal on it and take yourself through the steps. You can also find this and additional no-cost resources on Dr. Worthington's website to help you on your forgiveness journey. **Remember, forgiveness is a choice and even to only emotionally forgive is to improve your health and happiness.**

Rediscovering the Joy of Movement: Dr. Kelly McGonigal

Madefor co-founder and former Navy SEAL, Pat Dossett, sat down with author, psychologist, and educator, Dr. Kelly McGonigal, to discuss her new book, *The Joy of Movement*. Dr. McGonigal talked about why we don't move more, the benefits of consistent movement, and how movement is for everybody. Learn how to change your mind and body by utilizing the "runners high" (running not required), how to use movement as medicine, and two ways to access instantaneous positive feelings when moving through music and green exercise.

Reframing How We Define Movement

It's hard to be human. We all experience pain, sadness, anxiety, loneliness, and want to be happy and experience connection, hope, and courage. How can we find an antidote to all those harder feelings and gain greater access to the inspirational ones? Surprisingly, movement is the answer.

Many of us believe that movement is exercise and vice versa.

The word "exercise" seems to be fraught with negative emotions like fear, pain, and embarrassment, but that doesn't need to be the case. We need to shift our mindset. We need to see the body not as something that needs to be fixed or controlled through exercise but to understand that the body is a vehicle for experiencing competition, strength, vitality, power and play.

Culture uses exercise as a punishment for pleasure, i.e. "I have to work off what I ate or drank." We are tracking ourselves with a sense of judgment and a lot of things in the fitness industry and culture really reinforce that. As a result, many people's experiences with movement are self-critical, punitive, and eventually avoidant. Even when someone will choose to bring movement into their life, they look for the thing that feels the worst because that's the thing they assume will be best for them. No pain, no gain, right?

Wrong.

The more you focus on controlling, perfecting, or changing your body, whether it's your appearance, your weight, or even disease prevention, the less likely you are to stick with movement or find a form of movement that you love. You're also less likely to access the physical, emotional, and social benefits of movement.

Knowing only great things will result from movement, why are we so resistant to making movement a priority in our day? While our brains and bodies reward us for moving and exertion, we also are built with an instinct to avoid overexertion, conserve energy, to rest, to avoid discomfort, and avoid failure and embarrassment. To retrain our bodies to encourage movement, we must first start with self-compassion.

We must remove the negative connotations from movement and recognize how the practice itself can be really rewarding on its own. Research shows there are three motivations that keep people moving: enjoyment, that the activity provides social community or sense of identity (i.e. "I'm a runner"), and when it's a personal challenge and meaningful to you as you're making progress toward a goal. If you can find an activity that gives you all three – you're hooked for life!

"Anytime you engage in regular activity, you're becoming this version of yourself that is more hopeful, more motivated, more energized, and better able to connect with others."
– Dr. Kelly McGonigal

The Endocannabinoid System, Chasing the "Runners High," and Movement as Mindset Medicine

One of the things that has allowed humans to adapt and survive over hundreds and thousands of years is that at some point, we found a way to persist, to hunt and gather, and to forage for food. We had to become much more active to nourish ourselves and our community and survive. We evolved all the physical characteristics to walk and run. Our brains hijacked the basic rewards systems and found a way to create a neurochemical reward for physical persistence. It kicks in when you've been engaging in a continuous effort of moderate intensity for 20 minutes or more and is mostly referred to as a "runners' high," though it can happen with any kind of movement.

When we are pursuing meaningful goals that are difficult, our brains recognize them and start releasing chemicals that increase energy and motivation. They are endocannabinoids primarily, though movement will also give you adrenaline, dopamine, and sometimes endorphins depending on what you're doing.

Endocannabinoids are a class of brain chemicals that have the ability to quiet the negative emotions in your body (stress, worry, pain, self-doubt, anger, etc.) and enhance the positives (feel confident, powerful, hopeful). Anything that is pleasurable is more pleasurable, particularly social interaction like physical touch, conversation, and shared laughter to name a few. That's the neurochemistry of an exercise high.

Research shows when you exercise, you benefit from it the rest of the day with all of your interactions. You're more likely to make progress on important goals, stressful things take less of a toll on your wellbeing, and you expand your capacity for pleasure. Research has also shown that exercise does what all known psychological treatments do for the brain. Movement can affect us and help us change our most deeply held stories about ourselves. It is a pathway to shifting our mindsets. Through the activity, we can feel more hopeful, stronger, and more capable.

"Movement is just about being in the body that you have, moving what you can, and following your own thread of joy and meaning and hope."
– Dr. Kelly McGonigal

How to Get Moving

Unlock the benefits of better brain chemistry through small, relatively low-level doses of movement. The research shows if you are serious about improving your brain health or your mental health, and treating exercise like therapy for your brain, it should be a form of exercise that feels good and challenges you to some degree. Your heart rate should go up and you should feel like you are using energy because you are going to get that persistence high.

Here are the basics:

1. Choose an activity you enjoy.
2. Do it for 20 minutes, at least 3 times per week (Dr. McGonigal recommends daily for best results)
3. The intensity should be challenging. Not so difficult that you couldn't maintain a conversation, but not so easy that your body isn't working.

PRO TIP: *One of the things that makes movement more enjoyable and meaningful for people is how they interpret the physical sensations of exercise. For a lot of people who are new to exercise, they interpret every sign as negative (sweating, breathing harder) and think, "I am so out of shape, I am so pathetic, I'm too old, I'm too big, etc." Flip the script and switch that negative self-talk to affirming statements like "I'm amazing, this is proof of how hard I'm working, I'm killing this, I'm making myself stronger." You'll become more hopeful and find more enjoyment in exercise!*

Balancing and Bettering Your Body Budget: Dr. Lisa Feldman Barrett

Psychologist and neuroscientist Dr. Lisa Feldman Barrett is one of the world's top experts in emotion. She's also the author of the books, _How Emotions are Made_ (2017) and _Seven and a Half Lessons About the Brain_ (2020). She sat down with Madefor co-founder Pat Dossett to talk about the formation and regulation of emotional states, the role we play in bringing out the best in each other, and the importance of managing our body budget.

Emotions 101: How are Emotions Formed and Regulated?

We aren't born with a default setting like a microwave or computer. When an infant is born, it doesn't have a mini-adult brain. An infant has a brain that has to finish wiring itself. The wiring instructions come from the world and its body. Dr. Barrett is quick to point out this isn't a nature or nurture issue; we have the kind of genes that require nurture. To use well-known phraseology: we are custom-made, not custom fit. Everything in our body is wired to us specifically, take our eyes for example. It takes a baby about three to four months to be able to see the world. Their wiring depends on the size of their eyes and the distance between them. This process occurs in countless other places in the body and the wiring process isn't complete until the baby human is blowing out 25 candles on their birthday cake.

Emotions, too, are built over time and form an internal model. Different interactions, experiences, and cultural influences create the model we are repeatedly running incoming data through to gauge what we should do in response. Dr. Barrett explains the receptive process as, "Your brain is trapped in a dark, silent box called your skull. It's receiving sensory data from the surface of your body. Light waves to your eyes, air pressure changes to your ear, etc....Your brain receives the sensory data which is the outcome of some set of causes."

Now here's where things get tricky, **we can't know the cause of something immediately when it happens**. Our brain fires up and predicts the cause of what is happening based on past experience, and tells us what to do next. And we're also not always right. When that happens, our brain has to process the new information and adjust our internal model.

The same occurs when we are engaging with others. You're interacting with someone and you believe you are sure about how they are feeling and act accordingly with that belief. No matter how certain we think we are, we are still always guessing. We don't read body language because movements aren't a language. There are no physical signals with universally inherent meaning.

> *"You run a model of your world, and that includes*
> *how you perceive and react to others.*
> *YOU make it meaningful."*
> *– Dr. Lisa Feldman Barrett*

Metabolic Expense: The Science of Body Budget

Our emotions both give to and take from our lives, and we measure that in metabolic expense. Feldman Barrett describes this process as body budget or how your brain budgets the energy in your body to keep you alive and well. For example, every time your brain prepares your body for a threat, it's metabolically expensive. You also pay a little extra tax for a perceived threat that doesn't manifest. When that happens enough times, it's harder for your brain to regulate your internal body systems.

Cortisol—which Dr. Barrett is quick to point out, is not a stress hormone despite its billing as such—is released into the bloodstream when the brain believes you have a large metabolic outlay. Right before you get out of bed in the morning, you have a big cortisol release. Major efforts to learn something new or move the body are all signaled by cortisol release. When you have that release repeatedly, the cells become less sensitive to it, and it doesn't work as a signal anymore, making it ultimately metabolically expensive. Over the long term, you become more vulnerable to metabolic illnesses, which can take years from your life.

We experience the state of our body budget as a mood. If we're feeling calm and happy, it's likely our body budget is doing well. If we wake up stressed, grumpy, or sad, it's possible our body budget is experiencing a deficit. When we take care of the basics like rest, hydration, practicing gratitude, and other healthy habits like those in the Madefor Program, we are depositing into our body budget.

> *"If you were to ask me, what's the one thing I can do to have better control over my mood? Sleep. Two things? Sleep and hydrate properly. Three? Add eating healthy and taking a walk every day. It makes me sound like a mom, but I'm really speaking as a neuroscientist."*
> – Dr. Lisa Feldman Barrett

We don't just affect our body budget; we also regulate each other's nervous systems for good and bad. Humans are a social species. With every interaction, we have the opportunity to make deposits and withdrawals in each other's body budgets. The words you speak can cause biological changes in another person. We influence each other. We can make it easier or harder for our fellow humans to manage a body budget.

Ask yourself: Do you want to be the sort of person who makes surprise deposits in someone's body budget or the person causing over-the-limit withdrawal fees?

Balancing your Body Budget

Let's get to the heart of the cause – how can we each balance our body budget? What if it's chronically in the red; is there no hope? There's always hope! **There are many things that can nudge your body budget, you just have to figure out what works for you.**

Here are three areas you can focus on to put your body budget back on track:

1. Physical. This one sounds easy, but if it were so easy, we'd all be doing it. Take a moment and check in with yourself:

- Am I getting enough water every day?
- Am I getting adequate rest each day?
- Am I fueling my body or just mindlessly eating and hoping for the best?
- Am I getting movement every day?
- Am I stretching every day?

If you aren't doing as well as you'd like in any of the above, choose one and focus on getting back on track. If you've done or are in the Madefor Program, revisit a 21-Day Challenge to get back on track and start depositing into your body budget. If you're not, that's ok! Pick one area you'd like to work on and commit to taking small actions every day for 21 days. Once you repair one area, pick another and do the same until you're taking care of your basic needs like a rockstar.

2. Psychological. Do another intake with yourself, this time focusing on your inner being. Feel overwhelmed, lacking confidence, or just emotionally exhausted? Choose one of the following to add more deposits under the Psychological column in your body budget by:

- Spend a few days away from Social Media.
- Practice an experience of awe for five minutes each day.

- Try to reduce uncertainty in some area of your life that seems to have a fair amount of it.
- Start (or pick back up) a gratitude process by journaling or creating a ritual that encourages you to focus on the positive.

3. Connection. Humans are pack animals. Make a deposit in someone else's body budget, and it's likely you too will make a little "interest" off it as well. Try one or more of these suggestions:

- Give someone a genuine compliment.
- Do something simple like make dinner or volunteer a night of babysitting for a friend who's overwhelmed or stressed.
- Take your mom to your favorite relaxing yoga class or invigorating dance class.
- Send a "thank you for being you" note.

Start small and slow and build over time. Dr. Barrett wants everyone to know, "You have more control than you think. You may not have as much as you'd like, but you have more than you think." It's time to balance your budget!

The Science of Influence: Dr. Vanessa Bohns

Social psychologist, award-winning researcher and teacher, and professor of organizational behavior at Cornell University, Dr. Vanessa Bohns is an expert on influence. She is the author of _You Have More Influence Than You Think: How We Underestimate Our Power of Persuasion, and Why It Matters_. During this Basecamp conversation, Dr. Bohns sits down with Madefor co-founder Pat Dossett, to talk about why we underestimate our influence, how we are unknowingly influencing others, and how to get what we want.

Why Do We Underestimate Our Influence?

We have an idea of what influence is and what it looks like, but we tend to think of more formal attempts of influence. For instance, a politician asking for money or your vote; basically, someone asking you for something. However, influence is often silent and invisible and lives in the minds of others where we can't see it. What makes it even more elusive is that it's cumulative and builds over time. Due to these factors, we often think we don't have influence if we don't see immediate tangible evidence of it such as winning a debate or getting a donation.

Since we can't see how much we influence others, we have to guess. And wouldn't you know it, we are usually guessing incorrectly and underestimating our influence. What we don't realize is we also influence the others that are watching us having exchanges with others personally or on our social media accounts. We have a much larger audience than we think and our influential reach is more far-reaching than we believe.

"When you model positive behaviors, you may not be getting through to the person you're talking to, but you might be getting through to all the people who are watching."
– Dr. Vanessa Bohns

Sorting Through The Liking Gap, Spotlight Effect, and Getting What You Want

Now that we've identified that formal influence is just a small part of the picture, why is it that we still think we don't wield the amount of influence we have? Factors such as the Liking Gap, Spotlight Effect, and the Default State of Trust all explain why we believe that we aren't liked as much as we are.

Let's begin with the Liking Gap. When we meet someone and then they eventually walk away, we think they like us less and enjoy speaking with us less than they did. Why? Because while they are thinking about the whole experience and from a high-level view, we are thinking of all of our insecurities, which is the Spotlight Effect.

Spotlight Effect happens whenever we're insecure about something about ourselves like a new haircut, weight, sound of our voice, etc. We believe everyone's eyes are on us and focus on what we perceive as a flaw or defect. We become hyper self-conscious about the root of the insecurity and think we are less likable and less influential. In reality, the person or people we are interacting with aren't paying attention to it at all. **What's especially interesting is that when we are not worried about something and just existing in our universe, thinking no one is paying attention to us, we are even more influential.** People are paying attention to us more than we think. They see us on social media, with friends, or just in repose with ourselves. Upon observing us, they wonder why we're doing what we're doing and if they should do it too, often mimicking us. This shapes the social norms our society lives by.

We can't discuss influence without talking about why it's important, and let's be frank, we want to be influential because it aids us in getting the things we need. We often count on our influence because coming out and just asking someone is plain old scary, and we brace ourselves for rejection. In truth, we really shouldn't be worried about the ask. We believe the default setting people have when asked for something is to reject us, so we tend to tiptoe around what we want and not be clear or direct in our ask. The opposite is true; we have a Default State of Trust where we want to help others and be agreeable naturally. **To get what we want, we simply need to be direct and honest along the lines of, "Here's what I'd like and why."** For the best results, you want to make these requests in person, but if that isn't possible video or phone chat is the next best thing.

People are more inclined to do something for you than you think. It feels good to be able to help someone. Think back to the last time you were about to help someone, in a small or big way, it felt great, right? As humans, we are centrally motivated to feel good about ourselves and connect to other people. Doing something for someone satisfies both of those internal needs.

"A better world really begins with a better you."
– Pat Dossett

How to Stop Underestimating Your Awesomeness

Now that you're armed with all of this information, how do you use it? Are you more influential than you've been believing? Ready to harness that power for yourself and the world? Try these three tips to bask in your own uniqueness, up your influencer status, make others feel good about themselves, and put more positive vibes out into the world.

1. Practice Getting Perspective. It's easy to assume we know what people are thinking; however, we are often wrong. The next time you are in a situation where you observe yourself falling into this trap, stop! Ask the person you're interacting with what they are feeling and experiencing instead of assuming you know. They'll appreciate you asking them, and you just upped your influence quotient!

2. Reframe. When we think about ourselves, we tend to focus on the negative. The next time you catch yourself having those "nobody likes me" or "I don't really matter" thoughts, take to your journal and write down three reasons you feel that way. Now turn those negatives into positives by reframing them.

For instance, maybe you think others are less likely to befriend you because you're opinionated. Make it positive by realizing some people like you for that exact reason – they can count on you to give an honest, informed opinion of the topic of conversation.

3. Pay it Forward. The next time you think a nice thought about someone, tell them. It can be in person, by phone, text, email, or in a note. Bonus: it'll give you both the warm fuzzies!

Like everything in life, it's a practice. You won't lose insecurities overnight, but when you work on them consistently, you'll start to see how influential you are. Then you can apply that knowledge to living your best life and helping others lead theirs.

Scientific Keywords

Active-constructive responding (ACR): a communication style that's proven to accelerate the deepening of relationships; simply about coming alongside another person with enthusiasm and delight as they tell you about a win; active listening.

Attention Restoration Theory (ART): according to ART, attending to softly fascinating stimuli not only requires little effort but also leaves mental space for reflection; walking in nature is perceived as softly fascinating, and therefore restorative, whereas watching television is a source of hard fascination.

Circadian rhythm: the internal cyclical, biological process that has a pivotal impact on sleepiness, wakefulness, temperature, digestion, hormonal fluctuations, and more; responds primarily to light and dark (the rise and fall of the sun).

Cognitive reappraisal: when you take an event that's fraught with negative emotions and choose to respond in a neutral or positive way; a strategy for down-shifting your emotional reactions.

Growth mindset: the belief that your talents can be cultivated through greater effort, new strategies, and help from others; your abilities are ever changing and you lean towards learning and curiosity; persistent in the face of setbacks.

Interoceptive awareness: the ability to detect and interpret sensations arising within the body, such as a full bladder, changes in heart rate, muscle contractions, and more; increased interoceptive awareness leads to greater overall wellbeing.

Mindfulness-based stress reduction (MBSR): evidence-based, stress-reducing practices and/or techniques; ex. loving-kindness and mindfulness.

Neuroplasticity: the different ways the brain can modify itself in order to process and respond to external stimuli; the brain's ability to learn and grow.

Positive emotional contagion: that experience or uplifting moment when you "catch" another person's good mood.

Founding Advisory Board

Our diverse collective of experts, scientists, and clinicians are all dedicated to helping you achieve greater wellbeing.

As leading experts in their respective fields, our advisors have helped develop every Challenge and ensure each is built on the strongest scientific foundation. As part of the program, you will be exposed to their life's work and the positive benefits their findings can have in your life.

Neuroscience

Andrew Huberman, PhD
Neuroscientist and Head of Huberman Lab at Stanford and Madefor Advisory Team

Dr. Andrew D. Huberman is a neuroscientist, tenured professor, and principal investigator/head of the Huberman Lab in the Department of Neurobiology at the Stanford University School of Medicine, and host of the Huberman Lab Podcast. He has made numerous important contributions to the fields of brain development, brain plasticity, and neural regeneration and repair. Dr. Huberman was awarded the McKnight Foundation Neuroscience Scholar Award (2013), a Biomedical Scholar Award from the Pew Charitable Trusts, and a 2017 ARVO Cogan Award for his contributions to the fields of vision science. His work on the use of noninvasive methods to enhance regeneration of damaged retinal neurons, leading to partial recovery from blindness, has been covered extensively in the popular press (Time, Scientific American), and is part of the National Eye Institute's Audacious Goals Initiative to restore vision to the blind.

In 2017, the Huberman Lab created a state-of-the-art virtual reality platform to induce fear and anxiety under controlled conditions and study the neuroscience underlying these responses. Creating it involved collecting authentic 360-degree video of stress-inducing scenarios such as heights, claustrophobia, and swimming with great white sharks.

In 2018, the lab published a study in Nature reporting the discovery of two new mammalian brain circuits: one that promotes fear and paralysis, and another that promotes a "courageous" / confrontational reaction to visually evoked threats. This discovery has prompted ongoing exploration of how these brain regions may be involved in phobias, generalized anxiety, and PTSD—along with coping tools for reducing irrational fears.

Human Behavior

Ruth Benca, MD, PhD
UC Irvine Chair of Psychiatry & Human Behavior

Dr. Ruth Benca is a professor and chair in the Department of Psychiatry & Human Behavior at the University of California Irvine School of Medicine. Previously, she was director of the University of Wisconsin Center for Sleep Medicine and Sleep Research and medical director of Wisconsin Sleep, where she treated patients with a broad range of sleep disorders.

Widely published in her field, Dr. Benca is an internationally recognized authority on the relationship between sleep and psychiatric disorders, and she has served as principal investigator for a number of basic and clinical research studies, funded by agencies including the National Institutes of Health and the Department of Defense. She has served as president of the Sleep Research Society and on the board of directors of the American Academy of Sleep Medicine. Dr. Benca received her undergraduate education at Harvard University and her MD and a PhD in Pathology from the University of Chicago, where she also completed a residency in Psychiatry and a fellowship in Sleep Medicine.

Health Literacy

Lisa Fitzpatrick, M.D., M.P.H
Epidemiologist & Chief Executive Officer and Founder, Promoting Practical Health, Inc.

Lisa Fitzpatrick, M.D., M.P.H., is a CDC-trained medical epidemiologist and board-certified infectious diseases physician with both domestic and global experience in public health. She was recently named as a member of the Institute of Medicine/National Academy of Sciences Roundtable on Health Literacy.

Although Dr. Fitzpatrick's career has traversed clinical medicine, research and public health program implementation, she is most passionate about improving the nation's health literacy and demystifying health information. Her goal is to inspire greater and more effective disease prevention and health promotion action in communities by making practical and useable health information more accessible to ordinary citizens.

Dr. Fitzpatrick's skills and experiences are diverse. She is a medical doctor who began her public health career in 1998 as a medical epidemiologist at the nation's premier public health agency, the Centers for Disease Control and Prevention (CDC) as a member of the CDC's elite Epidemic Intelligence Service. She has served a foreign diplomat in the Caribbean while representing the US government CDC Global AIDS Program under PEPFAR.

Psychiatry

John Ratey, MD
Psychiatrist at Harvard and
Author of "Spark" and "Go Wild"

Dr. John J. Ratey is an associate clinical professor of psychiatry at Harvard Medical School and an internationally recognized expert in neuropsychiatry. Dr. Ratey's groundbreaking "Driven to Distraction" series on attention deficit disorder, written with Dr. Edward Hallowell, is considered one of the bibles of ADD, with over two million copies in print. His book "Spark: The Revolutionary New Science of Exercise and the Brain," established Dr. Ratey as an authority on the brain-fitness connection and set him on a mission to re-engineer schools, corporations, and individual lifestyle practices to use exercise to achieve peak performance and optimum mental health.

His 11th and most recent book, "Go Wild," explores how to achieve optimal physical and mental health by getting in touch with our caveman roots and "re-wilding" our lives. Dr. Ratey has served as a consultant to the President of Taiwan and the Minister of Education in South Korea, a co-head of the Advisory Board of the California Governor's Council on Physical Fitness and Sport, a consultant to ANTA Kids in China, and an Ambassador for Active Kids with BOKS, Reebok's nonprofit school fitness program. Dr. Ratey's own nonprofit, Sparking Life, has a mission to promote exercise in the treatment of mental health challenges. Recognized by his peers as one of the Best Doctors in America since 1997, Dr. Ratey was honored as "Outstanding Psychiatrist of the Year for Advancing the Field" in 2016 by the Massachusetts Psychiatric Society.

Married, with two children and two grandchildren, Dr. Ratey maintains private practices in Cambridge, Massachusetts, and Los Angeles, California.

Nutrition

Evelyn Tribole, MS, RDN, CEDRD-S
Registered Dietitian and Co-Author of "Intuitive Eating"

Evelyn Tribole, MS, RDN, CEDRD-S (Certified Eating Disorders Registered Dietitian-Supervisor), is co-author of the bestselling "Intuitive Eating," a mind-body self-care eating process, which has given rise to over 90 studies showing benefit, and more than 800 certified intuitive eating counselors in 22 countries. Tribole has written nine books on healthy eating and runs a busy nutrition-counseling practice in Newport Beach, California. Previously, she was the nutrition expert for Good Morning America, a national spokesperson for the American Dietetic Association, and a contributing editor for Shape magazine, where her monthly column appeared for 11 years. Tribole has been quoted in hundreds of media outlets, including CNN, Today, MSNBC, Fox News, USA Today, The Wall Street Journal, The Atlantic, and People magazine. As a highly sought-after speaker and college lecturer, she trains the public and healthcare professionals on how to cultivate a healthy relationship with food, mind, and body. Tribole received her master's in nutritional science and her bachelor's in dietetics from California State University, Long Beach. In 1984, she qualified for the Olympic Trials in the first-ever women's marathon (with a time of 2:51:15!). Although she is no longer a competitive runner, Tribole is a wicked ping-pong player and avid hiker. Her favorite food is chocolate—when it can be savored slowly.

Chronobiology

Samer Hattar, PhD
Chronobiologist at National Institutes of Health (NIH)*

Dr. Samer Hattar is a senior investigator and chief of the Section on Light and Circadian Rhythms at the National Institute of Mental Health, the lead federal agency for the research of mental disorders, under the auspices of the National Institutes of Health. A leading chronobiologist in his field, Dr. Hattar's research focuses on how light affects behavior.

For years, it was assumed that when light struck the retina, only two kinds of cells responded: rods and cones. However, research by Dr. Hattar and others uncovered a third type of photoreceptor cell called intrinsically photosensitive retinal ganglion cells (ipRGCs). This discovery has spurred further research into how light influences circadian rhythms, sleep, learning, and mood, potentially leading to more effective treatments for seasonal affective disorder.

Dr. Hattar was previously an associate professor in the Department of Neuroscience and the Department of Biology at Johns Hopkins University, where he established the Hattar Lab. He received his PhD from the University of Houston in Texas, and was a postdoctoral fellow at Johns Hopkins University School of Medicine and the Howard Hughes Medical Institute. He is married to Rejji Kuruvilla, a neuroscientist and professor at Johns Hopkins.

Dr. Hattar is serving in his personal capacity.

Movement

Rory Cordial, DPT
Physical Therapist

Rory Cordial, a doctor of physical therapy (DPT) and certified strength and conditioning specialist (CSCS), is an international speaker and leader in the field of sports medicine, rehabilitation, and sports performance. Cordial's clients include professional athletes, dancers, entertainers, CEOs, and health-conscious entrepreneurs who seek to optimize performance while preventing or mitigating injury.

He received his doctorate degree at the University of Montana, a bachelor of science in sports science at the University of Idaho, and spent years studying experts in the fields of sports medicine, strength and fitness, spirituality, human movement, psychology, and philosophy. He credits his father, a physical therapist with 30-plus years of experience, for honing his treatment skills. More recently, Cordial added to his extensive knowledge of biomechanics, physiology, anatomy, and human movement by spending time in Thailand learning Thai massage, in Bali learning yoga, and he sought out a Shaolin monk to learn Qi Gong and mindfulness.

As a lifelong learner, Cordial's methods are based in science but his methodology allows for the vast complexity and unknowns that surround the workings of the human body and mind.

Human Performance

Dan Cnossen
Navy SEAL officer (retired) and Paralympian

Cnossen was raised on a fifth-generation family farm in Topeka, Kansas. After successfully completing basic SEAL training in 2003, Cnossen deployed numerous times in support of global special operations. As a SEAL platoon commander, he was severely injured in 2009 in Afghanistan, resulting in the amputation of both legs above the knees.

Turning to sport for recovery, Cnossen began training full-time for the U.S. Paralympic ski team in 2011 as a cross-country skier and biathlete. Before his injury, he had never skied. But he has since competed for Team USA in the 2014 and 2018 Winter Games and is the first male athlete to win a gold medal for the United States in biathlon, a sport that combines cross-country skiing with precision shooting.

Cnossen holds a bachelor of science degree in English from the U.S. Naval Academy, a master's in public administration from the Harvard Kennedy School of Government, and a master's in theological studies from the Harvard Divinity School.

Mindset

Dave Phillips
Executive Mentor, Speaker, and Author

Dave Phillips is an executive mentor for high-performance CEOs and business leaders who seek an authentic life purpose. He works with clients on topics ranging from the boardroom to the bedroom and some of the most challenging areas of leaders' lives.

Phillips is an entrepreneur, columnist, talk show host, and the author of "Three Big Questions," a book that helps everyone to answer critical questions about purpose, mission, and vision. Previously, he was a member and coach of Canada's National Freestyle Ski team, a stuntman, and a professional ski-show performer. Phillips broke two Guinness World Records for ski duration and was also awarded the Bronze Medal for Bravery from the Royal Canadian Humane Association for his part in a life-saving effort.

Phillips is married to Ontario native and Olympic gold medalist in Alpine skiing, Kathy Kreiner-Phillips. They live in Vancouver and have three grown children, Nelson, Liam & Michela.

About the Author

As co-founder of Madefor, Patrick Dossett worked alongside a team of subject matter experts in the fields of neuroscience, positive psychology, and health and wellness to deliver world-class programming designed to help individuals unlock hidden potential.

Prior to Madefor, Dossett served in various leadership roles, first as an officer in the US Navy SEAL teams and later in the fields of technology and non-profit to create positive change at .scale.

Dossett holds a bachelor of science degree in Oceanography from the U.S. Naval Academy, a master's in business administration from the Wharton School of Business and is the recipient of numerous awards and commendations for his service and leadership. Dossett currently resides in Los Angeles, CA with his wife, three children and their cat, Kula.

Source Notes

Onboarding

For more than 150 years
"Learn The Knowledge of London," Transport for London. bit.ly/2SPfsiR.

Researchers at University College London
Maguire, E.A., Gadian, D.G., Johnsrude, I.S., Good, C.D., Ashburner, J., et al. (2000). Navigation-Related Structural Change in the Hippocampi of Taxi Drivers. *Proceedings of the National Academy of Sciences of the United States of America.* 97(8), 4398-403. bit.ly/2SQdONE.

scanned the brains of bus drivers
Maguire, E.A., Woollett, K., Spiers, H.J. (2006). London Taxi Drivers and Bus Drivers: A Structural MRI and Neuropsychological Analysis. *Hippocampus.* 16(12), 1091-101. bit.ly/2TNsVI5.

These groundbreaking results
"Cache Cab: Taxi Drivers' Brains Grow to Navigate London's Streets," by Ferris Jabr. Dec 8, 2011. *Scientific American.* bit.ly/2TIC2K4.

Scientists used to think that our brains
Degeneration and Regeneration of the Nervous System, by Santiago Ramon y Cajal. 1928. Haffner Publishing Co. New York, NY.

we now know that the adult brain
Fuchs, E., Flügge, G. (2014). Adult Neuroplasticity: More Than 40 Years of Research. *Neural Plasticity.* Article ID 541870. bit.ly/2SB0Ymi.

Neuroplasticity is a scientific concept
Neuroplasticity, by Moheb Costandi. 2016. The MIT Press. Cambridge, MA.

Madefor's lead advisor Dr. Andrew Huberman
Dr./Professor Andrew Huberman's contribution to this publication was as a paid consultant, and was not part of his Stanford University duties or responsibilities.

86 billion to 100 billion neurons that communicate
Neuroplasticity, by Moheb Costandi. *Ibid.*

Will Smith talks about the mindset
Interview on *Charlie Rose*, March 13, 2002. bit.ly/2GTnSnR.

when we multitask
See Make Your Brain Smarter, by Sandra Bond Chapman. 2013. Simon & Schuster, New York, NY; and Ophir, E., Nass, C., Wagner, A.D. (2009) Cognitive Control in Media Multitaskers. Proceedings of the National Academy of Sciences of the United States of America. 106(37):15583-87. bit.ly/2sRQHHu; and "A Decade of Data Reveals That Heavy Multitaskers Have Reduced Memory, Stanford Psychologist Says," by Sofie Bates. Oct 25, 2018. *Stanford News*. stanford.io/2GQKeWL.

something called a "positive growth mindset."
Mindset: The New Psychology of Success, by Carol S. Dweck. 2016. Ballantine Books, New York, NY.

In a study at Dominican University
"Goals Research Study." Matthews, G. Dominican University of California. bit.ly/2FsWOth.

helps to keep your mind attuned
"The Science of Smart: How the Power of Intention Can Help You Learn Better." Oct 29, 2013. Nova/PBS. to.pbs.org/2Vt9RQU.

A reminder: Madefor is a program that engages your mind and body in positive practices that are safe and effective for the vast majority of people. But if you have any medical issues or health concerns, consult with your primary care doctor before beginning this or any program.

Hydration

BUD/S pushes about 75% of candidates
"FAQ's About Becoming a Navy SEAL," by U.S. Navy SEAL + SWCC Scout Team. June 18, 2015. Official Naval Special Warfare Site. bit.ly/2EWTs1t.

Water comprises 45% to 75%
Riebl, S.K., Davy, B.M. (2013). The Hydration Equation: Update on Water Balance and Cognitive Performance. *ACSM's Health & Fitness Journal.* 17(6), 21-28. bit.ly/2TUyHaP.

and 80% of your brain
Brain Food: The Surprising Science of Eating for Cognitive Power, by Lisa Mosconi. 2018. Avery, New York, NY.

Water transports nutrients, regulates
Riebl, S.K., Davy, B.M. *ibid.*

for a month or two without food
"Dehydration: Risks and Myths," by Jane E. Brody. May 9, 2016. *New York Times.* nyti.ms/2sz3u14.

more than a week without water
"How Long Can the Average Person Survive Without Water?" by Randall K. Packer. Dec 9, 2002. *Scientific American.* bit.ly/2VXg3AS.

releases the equivalent of 6 to 13 cups
Riebl, S.K., Davy, B.M. *ibid.* This study estimates 1500–3100mL/d total output for adults in temperate climates, which is equivalent to 6.35 to 13.10 cups.

found that 43.7% of Americans drink less
Goodman, A.B., Blanck, H.M., Sherry, B., Park S., Nebeling L., Yaroch A.L. (2013.) Behaviors and Attitudes Associated With Low Drinking Water Intake Among US Adults: Food Attitudes and Behaviors Survey. 2007. *Prev Chronic Dis.* bit.ly/2RRmAxW.

In 2004, the Institute of Medicine
"Dietary Reference Intakes for Water, Sodium, Chloride, Potassium and Sulfate." Institute of Medicine of the National Academies. 2005. National Academy Press, Washington, D.C. bit.ly/2S33yEH.

thirst is triggered in the brain
Riebl, S.K., Davy, B.M. *ibid.*

a new and growing body of evidence
See Riebl, S.K. et al., and "Off Your Mental Game? You Could Be Dehydrated," by Alison Aubrey. July 30, 2018. National Public Radio. n.pr/2QUiLU8.

accelerate the brain shrinkage
Brain Food, ibid.

The early signs of mild dehydration
"What is Dehydration? What Causes It?" May 2, 2017. WebMD. wb.md/2W0INsv.

Chronic dehydration
"What Does It Mean When Dehydration Becomes Long-Term and Serious?" Healthline. Accessed Dec 20, 2018. bit.ly/2FVKku9.

In severe cases
"What is Dehydration? What Causes It?" *ibid.*

electrolytes, the essential minerals
"Fluid and Electrolyte Balance." Medline Plus. NIH: U.S. National Library of Medicine. Last updated Oct 23, 2018. bit.ly/2RAKuhy.

When Dossett began to convulse
Nardone, R., Brigo, F., Trinka, E. (2015). Acute Symptomatic Seizures Caused by Electrolyte Disturbances. *Journal of Clinical Neurology* (Seoul, Korea). 12(1), 21-33. bit.ly/2FBL6xp.

For athletes, as little as a 2%
Popkin, B. M., D'Anci, K. E., & Rosenberg, I. H. (2010). Water, Hydration, and Health. *Nutrition Reviews.* 68(8), 439-58. bit.ly/2swdgkD.

Madefor's lead advisor Dr. Andrew Huberman
Dr./Professor Andrew Huberman's contribution to this publication was as a paid consultant and was not part of his Stanford University duties or responsibilities.

Drinking water sheds
Daniels, M.C., Popkin, B.M. (2010). Impact of Water Intake on Energy Intake and Weight Status: A Systematic Review. *Nutrition Reviews.* 68(9), 505-21. bit.ly/2RV9lMy.

Water is the secret to
See Wolf, R., Wolf, D. Rudikoff, D. Parish, L.C. (2010). Nutrition and Water: Drinking Eight Glasses of Water a Day Ensures Proper Skin Hydration— Myth or Reality?" *Clin Dermatol.* 28 (4): 380-3. bit.ly/2Dlc4H3; and "Dehydration: Risks and Myths," by Jane E. Brody. May 9, 2016. *New York Times.* nyti.ms/2sz3u14; and "Does Drinking Water Cause Hydrated Skin?" by Lawrence E. Gibson. Nov 7, 2015. Mayo Clinic. may-ocl.in/2DkAel2.

Dark urine is a sure sign
"10 Colors That Suggest Urine Trouble," by Scott LaFee. April 21, 2014. UC San Diego Health. bit.ly/2UcU1ly.

Only water can hydrate
"Dietary Reference Intakes for Water..." *Ibid.*

Okay, but coffee and tea
The most interesting science debunking this myth can be found in: 1. Killer S.C., Blannin A.K., Jeukendrup A.E. (2014) No Evidence of Dehydration with Moderate Daily Coffee Intake: A Counterbalanced Cross-Over Study in a Free-Living Population. *PLoS ONE.* 9(1): e84154. bit.ly/2Wec96Q; 2. Armstrong, L.E. (2002). Caffeine, Body Fluid-Electrolyte Balance, and Exercise Performance. *Int J Sport Nutr Exerc Metab.* 12(2):189-206. bit.ly/2FVMs; 3. "Coffee Myth-Busting: Cup of Joe May Help Hydration and Memory," by Allison Aubrey. Jan 13, 2014. National Public Radio. n.pr/2WbHzut; and 4. "Science Just Debunked a Coffee Myth That's Been Around Since 1928," by Alexa Erickson. Accessed Dec 20, 2018. *Reader's Digest.* bit.ly/2Ug7n79.

How about beer?
"Beer as a Post-Workout Recovery Drink? Not as Crazy as It Sounds," by Linda Poon. March 5, 2014. National Public Radio. n.pr/2RIF9F8.

A pinch of salt
"Get the Facts: Sodium and the Dietary Guidelines." Centers for Disease Control and Prevention. Accessed Dec 20, 2018. bit.ly/2FNahwS.

and if you're a mouth-breather
Svensson, S. Olin, A.C, Hellgren, J. (2006) Increased Net Water Loss by Oral Compared to Nasal Expiration in Healthy Subjects. *Rhinology.* (1):74-7. bit.ly/2B86Mgz.

Gratitude

In a 2015 Scientific American article
"Which Character Strengths Are Most Predictive of Well-Being?" Aug 2, 2015. *Scientific American.* bit.ly/2C2kORp.

the 24 character strengths and virtues
These are based on *Character Strengths and Virtues: A Handbook and Classification,* by Christopher Peterson and Martin E. P. Seligman. 2004. American Psychological Association/Oxford University Press.

thanks to decades of scientific research
Wood, A.M., Froh, J.J. Geraghty, A.W.A (2010). Gratitude and Well-Being: A Review and Theoretical Integration. *Clinical Psychology Review.* 30(7), 890-905. bit.ly/2EJwKYV.

In a 2009 study, scientists used functional
Zahn, R., Moll, J., Paiva, M., Garrido, G., Krueger, F., et al. (2009). The Neural Basis of Human Social Values: Evidence from Functional MRI. *Cerebral Cortex.* 19(2), 276-283. bit.ly/2EI60ro.

the "find, remind, and bind" emotion
"The Science of Gratitude." A white paper prepared for the John Templeton Foundation by the Greater Good Science Center at U.C. Berkeley. May 2018. bit.ly/2HpA1zB.

A 2015 study of 186 people with heart
Mills, P.J., Redwine, L.S., Wilson, K., Pung, M.A., Chinh, K., et al. (2015). The Role of Gratitude in Spiritual Well-Being in Asymptomatic Heart Failure Patients. *Spirituality in Clinical Practice*. 2(1), 5-17. bit. ly/2NJyHbR.

A study of 115 women at University
Jackowska, M., Brown, J., Ronaldson, A., Steptoe, A. (2016). The Impact of a Brief Gratitude Intervention on Subjective Well-Being, Biology and Sleep. *Journal of Health Psychology*. 21(10), 2207-17. bit.ly/2H6IWHC.

Another study of 962 Swiss adults
Hill, P.L., Allemand, M., Roberts, B.W. (2013). Examining the Pathways Between Gratitude and Self-Rated Physical Health Across Adulthood. *Personality and Individual Differences*. 54(1), 92-96. bit.ly/2H4MIjA.

In a classic gratitude study from 1998
McCraty, R., Barrios-Choplin, B., Rozman, D., Atkinson, M., Watkins, A.D. (1998). The Impact of a New Emotional Self-Management Program on Stress, Emotions, Heart Rate Variability, DHEA and Cortisol. *Integrative Physiological and Behavioral Science*. (33)2, 151-170. bit.ly/2XH4635.

Research has exploded since this early study
"The Science of Gratitude," *ibid*.

the underlying mechanism of gratitude
Schache, K., Consedine, N.S., Hofman, P., Serlachius, A. (2019). Gratitude: More Than Just a Platitude? The Science Behind Gratitude and Health. *British Journal of Health Psychology*. 24(1), 1-9. bit.ly/2SQbGoF.

"Some people claim that gratitude is just
"Five Myths About Gratitude," by Robert Emmons. Nov 21, 2013. *Greater Good Magazine*. U.C. Berkeley. bit.ly/2UmUsRe.

evening gratitude practice promotes better and longer sleep
Emmons, R.A., McCullough, M.E. (2003). Counting Blessings Versus Burdens: An Experimental Investigation of Gratitude and Subjective Well-Being in Daily Life. *Journal of Personality and Social Psychology*. 84(2), 377-389. bit.ly/2C7fhJp.

After all, if you're focusing on
Wood, A.M., Joseph, S., Lloyd, J., Atkins, S. (2009). Gratitude Influences Sleep Through the Mechanism of Pre-Sleep Cognitions. *Journal of Psychosomatic Research*. 66(1), 43-48. bit.ly/2TqmwqB.

weekly gratitude journal were 25% happier
Emmons, R.A., McCullough, M.E. (2003). Counting Blessings... *ibid.*

individuals who exist in chronic states of stress
See Mariotti A. (2015). The Effects of Chronic Stress on Health: New Insights Into the Molecular Mechanisms of Brain-Body Communication. *Future Science OA*. 1(3), FSO23. bit.ly/2TjXj0U; and Kubzansky, L.D., Kawachi, I. (2000). Going to the Heart of the Matter: Do Negative Emotions Cause Coronary Heart Disease? *Journal of Psychosomatic Research*. 48(4-5), 323-337. bit.ly/2HjvEpw.

Gratitude blocks the toxic emotions
"Gratitude is Good Medicine," by Robert Emmons. Nov 25, 2015. UC Davis Health Medical Center. bit.ly/2UnWVej.

Silver Lining Essay is an evidence-based
See Garland, E., Gaylord, S., Park, J. (2009). The Role of Mindfulness in Positive Reappraisal. *Explore (NY)*. 5(1), 37-44. bit.ly/2HjWPAA; and Watkins, P. Cruz, L., Holben, H., Kolts, R. (2008). Taking Care of Business? Grateful Processing of Unpleasant Memories. *The Journal of Positive Psychology*. (3)2, 87-99. bit.ly/2HI5UZL.

cognitive reappraisal, a strategy for
Troy, A.S., Wilhelm, F.H., Shallcross, A.J., Mauss, I.B. (2010). Seeing the Silver Lining: Cognitive Reappraisal Ability Moderates the Relationship Between Stress and Depressive Symptoms. *Emotion*. 10(6), 783-95. bit.ly/2HhycVb.

he's boiled marriage success down to a 5:1 ratio
"The Magic Relationship Ratio, According to Science," by Kyle Benson. Oct 4, 2017. The Gottman Institute. bit.ly/2EHUFrr.

Negativity bias is a survival mechanism
See "Our Brain's Negative Bias," by Hara Estroff Marano. June 20, 2003. *Psychology Today*. bit.ly/2XHSWem.

Fuel

In America, we rely on nutrition-policy
"Crumbling, Confusing Food Pyramid Replaced by a Plate," by Patrick J. Skerritt. Jan 28, 2016. Harvard Health Blog of Harvard Medical School. bit.ly/2UfIBDH.

We make impulse buys at the supermarket
"Rigged: Supermarket Shelves for Sale," a report from Center for Science in the Public Interest. Sept 28, 2016. bit.ly/2XiTvuh.

Americans spend $70 billion a year
"The Diet Industry: Executive Summary," by Lisa Rabasca Roepe. March 5, 2018. Sage Publishing. bit.ly/2D3z4tG.

Tribole and her colleague Elyse Resch
Intuitive Eating: A Revolutionary Program that Works, by Evelyn Tribole and Elyse Resch. 1995; 3rd edition in 2012. St. Martin's Griffin. New York, NY.

a pioneering book that's given rise to over
See: "What Is Intuitive Eating?" by Evelyn Tribole. Sept 12, 2018. Author's website. bit.ly/2Inr36a; and Bruce, L.J., Ricciardelli, L.A. (2016). A Systematic Review of the Psychosocial Correlates of Intuitive Eating Among Adult Women. *Appetite*. 96, 454-472. bit.ly/2KjDClC.

This isn't hyperbole. Research indicates
See: Khalsa, S.S., Adolphs, R., Cameron, O.G., Critchley, H.D., Davenport, P.W., et al. (2018). Interoception and Mental Health: A Roadmap. *Biol Psychiatry Cogn Neurosci Neuroimaging*, 3(6), 501–513. bit.ly/2Gf4srf; and Farb, N.A.S., Daubenmier J., Price C.J., Gard T., Kerr C., et al. (2015). Interoception, Contemplative Practice, and Health. *Front. Psychol.* 6:763. bit.ly/2YXzHOG.

Reviews of the scientific literature
Mann, T., Tomiyama, A.J., Westling, E., Lew, A.M., Samuels, B., et al. (2007). Medicare's Search for Effective Obesity Treatments: Diets Are Not the Answer. *American Psychologist*. 62(3), 220-233. bit.ly/2UpOK5h.

in a famous study at Kansas State
See "K-State Nutrition Expert: Many Dieting Theories Are Just Junk," By Gabriella Dunn. Sept 27, 2015. *The Wichita Eagle.* bit.ly/2VNnnhQ; and "'Twinkie Diet': A Physician's Take on What Really Happens," by David Katz. Nov 13, 2010. huffpost. bit.ly/2GsHAn1.

A yearlong study at Stanford University
See "Low-Fat or Low-Carb? It's a Draw, Study Finds," by Hanae Armitage. Feb 20, 2018. Stanford Medicine News Center. stan.md/2ZfFuPB; and Gardner, C.D., Trepanowski, J.F., Del Gobbo, L.C., Hauser, M.E., Rigdon, J., et al. (2018) Effect of Low-Fat vs Low-Carbohydrate Diet on 12-Month Weight Loss in Overweight Adults and the Association With Genotype Pattern or Insulin Secretion: The DIETFITS Randomized Clinical Trial. *JAMA.* 319(7), 667–679. bit.ly/2Xx2Dvm.

believe that dieting is harmful
See Camacho S., Ruppel A. (2017). Is the Calorie Concept a Real Solution to the Obesity Epidemic? *Glob Health Action.* 10(1), 1289650. bit.ly/2UI1yD5; and "Death of the Calorie," by Peter Wilson. March 16, 2019. *The Economist.* econ.st/2G9VZFq.

a fascinating study of competitors on The Biggest Loser
See Fothergill E., Guo J., Howard L., et al. (2016). Persistent Metabolic Adaptation Six Years After 'The Biggest Loser' Competition. *Obesity (Silver Spring).* 24(8), 1612–1619. bit.ly/2UJo6U2; "After 'The Biggest Loser,' Their Bodies Fought to Regain Weight," by Gina Kolata. May 2, 2016. *The New York Times.* nyti.ms/2P3MQ4k; and "A Lesson From the Biggest Losers: Exercise Keeps Off the Weight," by Gina Kolata. Oct 31, 2017. *The New York Times.* nyti.ms/2KnsJPF.

Numerous studies show that chronic dieters
"Why You Can't Lose Weight on a Diet," by Sandra Aamodt. May 6, 2016. *The New York Times.* nyti.ms/2GcdULT.

1,838 Finnish male Olympians
Saarni S.E., Rissanen A., Sarna S., Koskenvuo M., Kaprio J. (2006) Weight Cycling of Athletes and Subsequent Weight Gain in Middle Age. *Int J Obes (London).* 30:1639-1644. bit.ly/2uVVqIY.

While there's no single approach
The Blue Zones, by Dan Buettner. 2012. National Geographic Partners. Washington, DC.

It takes time, but listening to hunger
The Intuitive Eating Workbook, by Evelyn Tribole and Elyse Resch. 2017. New HarbingerPublications. Oakland, CA.

A quick trick from Tribole
Ibid.

Connection

a 2005 study of more than 1,000 older adults
See Giles, L.C., Glonek, G.F.V, Luszcz, M.A., Andrews, G.R. (2005). Effect of Social Networks on 10-Year Survival in Very Old Australians: The Australian Longitudinal Study of Aging. *Journal of Epidemiology & Community Health*. 59:574-579. bit.ly/2WKJAOa; and "Survival of the Social," by Michelle Flythe. Sept 1, 2005. Greater Good Magazine. bit. ly/2Ywph7F.

lowers your risk of depression and anxiety
"Social Interaction Is Critical for Mental and Physical Health," by Jane Brody. June 12, 2017. *The New York Times*. nyti.ms/2Hq72en.

greater odds of surviving serious illness
See Scheffler, R., Brown, T., Syme, L., Kawachi, I., Tolstykh, I., et al. (2008). Community-Level Social Capital and Recurrence of Acute Coronary Syndrome. *Social Science & Medicine*. (66) 1603-13. bit.ly/2Qi4jXr; and "How Social Connections Keep Seniors Healthy," by Jull Suttie. March 14, 2014. Greater Good Magazine. bit.ly/2YCdTXJ.

A 12-year study of 1,100 seniors
James, B., Wilson, R., Barnes, L., Bennett, D. (2011). Late-Life Social Activity and Cognitive Decline in Old Age. *J Int Neuropsychol Soc*. 17(6), 998-1005. bit.ly/30ougJv.

Researchers at the California Institute
See Zelikowsky, M., Hui, M., Karigo, T., Choe, A., Yang, B., at al. (2018). The Neuropeptide Tac2 Controls a Distributed Brain State Induced by

Chronic Social Isolation Stress. *Cell.* 173(5), 1265–1279. bit.ly/2Qbe6hD; and "How Social Isolation Transforms the Brain," by Lorinda Dajose. May 17, 2018. CalTech. bit.ly/30r7zUJ.

We know that oxytocin, a neuropeptide
Algoe, S.B., Kurtz, L.E., Grewen K. (2017). Oxytocin and Social Bonds: The Role of Oxytocin in Perceptions of Romantic Partners' Bonding Behavior. *Psychological Science.* 28(12), 1763–1772. bit.ly/2Q6jYZw.

Stanford University neuroscientist Dr. Andrew Huberman
Dr./Professor Andrew Huberman's contribution to this publication was as a paid consultant and was not part of his Stanford University duties or responsibilities.

We naturally glean information about
"The Psychology of Eye Contact, Digested," by Christian Jarrett. Nov 28, 2016. The British Psychological Society Research Digest. bit.ly/2EjuWGC.

when we avoid eye contact
See Khalid, S., Deska, J.C., Hugenberg, K. (2016). The Eyes Are the Windows to the Mind: Direct Eye Gaze Triggers the Ascription of Others' Minds. *Pers Soc Psychol Bull.* 42(12), 1666–1677. bit.ly/2W9Jld2; and "Why Meeting Another's Gaze is So Powerful," by Christian Jarrett. Jan 8, 2019. BBC. bbc.in/2Q8rdjT.

even complete strangers who are
See Kellerman, J., Lewis, J., Laird, J. (1989). Looking and Loving: The Effects of Mutual Gaze on Feelings of Romantic Love. *J Res Pers.* (23) 145-161, bit.ly/2YBxibg; and "Here's One Powerful Sign You're With the Person You Trust Most," by Kate Hakala. Mar 10, 2015. Mic. bit.ly/2HnpBjb.

noted social neuroscientist John Cacioppo writes
Loneliness, by John T. Cacioppo and William Patrick. 2008. W.W. Norton & Company. New York, NY.

A 2014 study of more than
Sandstrom, G.M., Dunn, E.W. (2014). Social Interactions and Well-Being: The Surprising Power of Weak Ties. *Pers Soc Psychol Bull.* 40(7), 910–922. bit.ly/2VtM81S.

Cacioppo and other scientists have found
Loneliness, ibid.

survey of more than 20,000 Americans
"Americans Are a Lonely Lot, and Young People Bear the Heaviest Burden," by Rhitu Chatterjee. May 1, 2018. NPR. n.pr/2WQhf9g.

Studies show that chronic isolation
See Yang, Y.C., Boen, C., Gerken, K., Li, T., Schorpp, K., et al. (2016) Social Relationships and Physiological Determinants of Longevity Across the Human Life Span. *Proc Natl Acad Sci.* 113:57883. bit.ly/2VIZ0Gd.

Try active-constructive responding
See Gable, S.L., Gonzaga, G.C., Strachman, A. (2006). Will You Be There for Me When Things Go Right? Supportive Responses to Positive Event Disclosures. *J Pers Soc Psychol.* 91(5):904-17. bit.ly/2VA8ONH; "Capitalizing on Positive Events," by Greater Good Science Center. bit.ly/2HEMeP4; and "Try This At Home: Building Positive Relationships Through Active Constructive Responding," by Dr. Martin Seligman. Coursera. bit.ly/2LN7RC3.

study at the University of California
Gable, S.L., Will You Be There... *ibid.*

Breath

Decades of scientific research
See Zaccaro, A., Piarulli, A., Laurino, M., Garbella, E., Menicucci, D., et al. (2018). How Breath-Control Can Change Your Life: A Systematic Review on Psycho-Physiological Correlates of Slow Breathing. *Frontiers in Human Neuroscience.* 12, 353. bit.ly/2G17b78; and "Proper Breathing Brings Better Health," by Christophe André. Jan 15, 2019. *Scientific American.* bit.ly/2XCmCIV.

Cnossen and teammate Kendall Gretsch
See "Dan Cnossen, A Navy SEAL Veteran and Double-Amputee, Wins Paralympic Biathlon Gold," by Robert Gearty. Mar 10, 2018. Fox News. fxn.ws/30g46ro; and Cnossen Team USA bio at go.teamusa.org/32cT8Vk.

Stanford neuroscientist Dr. Andrew Huberman
Dr./Professor Andrew Huberman's contribution to this publication was as a paid consultant and was not part of his Stanford University duties or responsibilities.

reduce symptoms associated with anxiety
For an exhaustive review of the benefits, see Altered Traits, by Daniel Goleman & Richard J. Davidson. 2013. Avery. New York, NY; Zaccaro, A., Piarulli, A., et al., ibid.; Twal, W.O., Wahlquist, A.E., & Balasubramanian, S. (2016). Yogic Breathing When Compared to Attention Control Reduces the Levels of Pro-Inflammatory Biomarkers in Saliva: A Pilot Randomized Controlled Trial. *BMC Complementary and Alternative Medicine.* 16, 294. bit.ly/2G2q0Xf; Ma, X., Yue, Z.Q., Gong, Z.Q., Zhang, H., Duan, N.Y., et al. (2017). The Effect of Diaphragmatic Breathing on Attention, Negative Affect and Stress in Healthy Adults. Frontiers in Psychology. 8, 874. bit.ly/2LKacfl; and "Breathe. Exhale. Repeat: The Benefits of Controlled Breathing," by Lesley Alderman. Nov 9, 2016. The New York Times. nyti.ms/2NIbKJD.

For example, your nasal passageways
See Trabalon, M., & Schaal, B. (2012). It Takes a Mouth to Eat and a Nose to Breathe: Abnormal Oral Respiration Affects Neonates' Oral Competence and Systemic Adaptation. *Intl J of Pediatrics.* 207605. bit.ly/32eOWnU; and Dallam, G., McClaran, S., Cox, D.G., Foust, C. (2018). Effect of Nasal Versus Oral Breathing on Vo2max and Physiological Economy in Recreational Runners Following an Extended Period Spent Using Nasally Restricted Breathing. *Intl J of Kinesiology and Sports Science.* (6) 22. bit.ly/2LKINdm; "Could Nasal Breathing Improve Athletic Performance?" by Jae Berman, Jan 29, 2019. *The Washington Post.* wapo.st/2LNGJBD; and *Jaws: The Story of a Hidden Epidemic,* by Sandra Kahn & Paul R. Ehrlich. 2018. Stanford University Press. Redwood City, CA.

mindfulness-based stress reduction, or MBSR
See "History of MBSR," Center for Mindfulness in Medicine, Health Care, and Society. University of Massachusetts Medical School. bit.ly/2JvOidf; Lamothe, M., Rondeau, E., Malboeuf-Hurtubise, C., Duval, M., Sultan, S. (2016). Outcomes of MBSR or MBSR-Based Interventions in Health Care Providers: A Systematic Review with a Focus on Empathy and Emotional Competencies. *Complementary Therapies in Medicine.* 24, 19-28. bit.ly/2YI2MNo; and Hölzel, B.K., Carmody, J., Vangel, M.,

Congleton, C., Yerramsetti, S.M., et al. (2011). Mindfulness Practice Leads to Increases in Regional Brain Gray Matter Density. *Psychiatry Research.* 191(1), 36–43. bit.ly/2XFH8NH.

In fact, among the 200 "billionaires, icons
"The One Routine—Yes, One!—Common to Billionaires, Icons and World-Class Performers," by Tim Ferriss. Dec 6, 2016. *Observer.* bit.ly/2XA1Pub.

According to its creator Kabat-Zinn
Irving, J.A., Dobkin, P.L., Park, J. (2009). Cultivating Mindfulness in Health Care Professionals: A Review of Empirical Studies of MBSR. *Complementary Therapies in Clin Pract.* 15, 61-66. bit.ly/2JoBbvL.

a lifetime that's relatively free of pain
Altered Traits, pgs 165-190.

For example, just three days of mindfulness
Rosenkranz, M.A., Davidson, R.J., Maccoon, D.G., Sheridan, J.F., Kalin, N.H., et al. (2013). A Comparison of MBSR and an Active Control in Modulation of Neurogenic Inflammation. *Brain, Behavior, and Immunity.* 27(1), 174–184. bit.ly/2L7ptHP.

Mindfulness can also help sharpen
Gorman, T.E., & Green, C.S. (2016). Short-Term Mindfulness Intervention Reduces the Negative Attentional Effects Associated with Heavy Media Multitasking. *Scientific Reports.* 6, 24542. go.nature.com/2YHkzEx.

improved their GRE
Mrazek, M.D., Franklin, M.S., Phillips, D.T., Baird, B. & Schooler, J.W. (2013). Mindfulness Training Improves Working Memory Capacity and GRE Performance While Reducing Mind Wandering. *Psychological Science.* 24: 776-781. bit.ly/2LJqZzk.

Loving-kindness sidebar
For more variations on this practice, see *Altered Traits* and *"Loving-Kindness Meditation,"* by Dr. Emma Seppalla. Greater Good Science Center. UC Berkeley. bit.ly/32fypQB.

In a 2008 study at Stanford
Hutcherson, C.A., Seppala, E.M., Gross, J.J. (2008). Loving-Kindness Meditation Increases Social Connectedness. *Emotion.* 8(5), 720-724. bit.ly/2JtVtme.

Researchers at the Max Planck
See Klimecki, O.M., Leiberg, S., Lamm, C., Singer, T. (2013). Functional Neural Plasticity and Associated Changes in Positive Affect After Compassion Training. *Cerebral Cortex.* 23(7), 1552–156. bit.ly/2JyS6u6; and "When Empathy Hurts, Compassion Can Heal," by Adam Hoffman. Aug 22, 2013. Greater Good Magazine. UC Berkeley. bit.ly/2XvfVgm.

As Klimecki explains
Singer, T., Klimecki, O.M. (2014). Empathy and Compassion. *Current Biology.* 24(18): R875-R878. bit.ly/2Jngpwn.

reverse the effects of excessive empathic distress
Klimecki, O.M. (2015). The Plasticity of Social Emotions. *Social Neuroscience.* 10(5) 466-473. bit.ly/2L7fhPu.

default-mode cycle
See Hamilton, J.P., Farmer, M., Fogelman, P., & Gotlib, I.H. (2015). Depressive Rumination, the Default-Mode Network, and the Dark Matter of Clinical Neuroscience. *Biological Psychiatry.* 78(4), 224–230. bit.ly/2NHo4cY; and Judson Brewer, J.A., Worhunsky, P.D., Gray, J.R., Tang, Y.Y., Weber, J., et al. (2011). Meditation Experience is Associated with Differences in Default Mode Network Activity and Connectivity. *Proceedings of the National Academy of Sciences.* 108 (50) 20254-20259. bit.ly/2Jq7dWl.

Movement

"The best workout I had
Dr./Professor Andrew Huberman's contribution to this publication was as a paid consultant, and was not part of his Stanford University duties or responsibilities.

"Just walking once a day will make
Spark, by John J. Ratey with Eric Hagerman. 2008. Hachette Book Group. New York, NY.

Add to that list: proteins that play pivotal
Spark, ibid.

In a 2014 study at Stanford University
M. Oppezzo and D.L. Schwartz. (2014). Give Your Ideas Some Legs: The Positive Effect of Walking on Creative Thinking. *Journal of Experimental Psychology: Learning, Memory, and Cognition.* 40 (4), 1142–1152. bit.ly/2GGzGaq.

inventive thinkers from Aristotle to Richard Branson
"How Jeff Bezos, Steve Jobs, and Richard Branson Run Efficient Meetings," by Bryan Adams. Jan 11, 2018. Inc. bit.ly/2OAs9jV.

And if you're among the 1 in 8 American adults
Pratt L.A., Brody D.J., Gu Q. (2017). Antidepressant Use Among Persons Aged 12 and Over: United States, 2011–2014. NCHS Data Brief #283. Hyattsville, MD: National Center for Health Statistics. bit.ly/2MwwEcn.

In a 2016 study of 8,100 adults over age 45
See Diaz, K.M., Howard, V.J., Hutto, B., Colabianchi, N., Vena, J.E., et al. (2016). Patterns of Sedentary Behavior in US Middle-Age and Older Adults: The REGARDS Study. *Medicine and Science in Sports and Exercise.* 48(3), 430–438. bit.ly/2GFxVKH; and "Yes, Sitting Too Long Can Kill You, Even If You Exercise," by Susan Scutti. Sept 12, 2017. CNN. cnn.it/2LWMeys.

150 minutes a week
Physical Activity Guidelines for Americans, 2nd Edition. 2018. U.S. Department of Health and Human Services. Washington, DC.

"Text neck" refers to
"'Text neck' is Becoming an 'Epidemic' and Could Wreck Your Spine," by Lindsey Bever. Nov 20, 2014. The Washington Post. wapo.st/2ZnwTKF.

Research indicates that after 30, men and women
"Bed Rest and Immobilization: Risk Factors for Bone Loss." The National Institutes of Health Osteoporosis and Related Bone Diseases National Resource Center. Last reviewed Nov 2018. bit.ly/2YlVwuI.

In a study at New Hampshire University
M.J. Biondolillo & D.B. Pillemer. (2015). Using Memories to Motivate Future Behaviour: An Experimental Exercise Intervention. *Memory*. 23(3), 390-402. bit.ly/2yyTfwE.

Nature

immunologist Dr. Qing Li wanted to
Forest Bathing: How Trees Can Help You Find Health and Happiness, by Dr. Qing Li. 2018. Viking. New York, NY.

But by the early '90s
"In Japan, Mired in Recession, Suicides Soar," by Stephanie Strom. July 15, 1999. *The New York Times*. nyti.ms/2IFsALD.

By 2004, the government began funding
See Introduction to the Japanese Society of Forest Medicine. bit.ly/2IN7drE.

healthcare-design expert Roger Ulrich
Ulrich, R. (1984). View Through a Window May Influence Recovery from Surgery. *Science*. 224(4647), 420−421. bit.ly/2m3fs31.

Natural Killer (NK) cells
Narni-Mancinelli, E. & Vivier, E. (2014) Delivering Three Punches to Knockout Intracellular Bacteria. *Cell*. 157(6) 1251-1252. bit.ly/2IGvJuP.

Researchers are racing
See: "Engineered Natural Killer Cells May Be the Next Great Cancer Immunotherapy," by Mitch Leslie. Sep 13, 2018. *Science*. bit.ly/2IOBAOo, and "Natural Killer Cells for Prostate Cancer Immunotherapy." May 14, 2019. Prostate Cancer Foundation. bit.ly/2m7SJmt, and "'DIY Cancer Treatment' May End Fatal Outcomes from Disease," by Sarah Knapton. Dec 29, 2018. *The Sydney Morning Herald*. bit.ly/2IGRcDU.

Li found that after just two days
NK cell activity rose from 17.3 to 26.5%; NK cell numbers rose from 440 to 661; granulysin was up by 48%, granzyme A by 39%, granzyme B by 33%, and perforin by 28%. For more, see: Li, Q., Morimoto, K., Nakadai, A., Inagaki, H., Katsumata, M., Shimizu, T., ... Kawada, T. (2007).

Forest Bathing Enhances Human Natural Killer Activity and Expression of Anti-Cancer Proteins. *International Journal of Immunopathology and Pharmacology*. 20(2_suppl), 3-8. bit.ly/2m4FpPH; and Li Q. (2010) Effect of Forest Bathing Trips on Human Immune Function. Environ Health Prev Med. 15(1):9–17. bit.ly/2ksY47G; and *Forest Bathing*, by Dr. Qing Li. 2018. Viking. New York, NY.

As geobiologist Hope Jahren describes
See *Lab Girl*, by Hope Jahren. 2016. Vintage Books. New York, NY; and Rhoades, D. (1983) Responses of Alder and Willow to Attack by Tent Caterpillars and Webworms: Evidence for Pheromonal Sensitivity of Willows. *ACS Symposium Series*. (208)4, 55-68. bit.ly/2lHaUiQ.

for three nights they slept
Li, Q., Kobayashi, M., Wakayama, Y., Inagaki, H., Katsumata, M., Hirata, Y., Shimizu T., Kawada T., Park B.J., Ohira T., Kagawa T., Miyazaki, Y. (2009). Effect of Phytoncide from Trees on Human Natural Killer Cell Function. *International Journal of Immunopathology and Pharmacology*. 22(4), 951–959. bit.ly/2lJkilU.

global scientific inquiry
See "Forest Policy and Forest Healing in the Republic of Korea." Oct 10, 2015. Minister of Korea Forest Service. International Society of Nature and Forest Medicine. bit.ly/2k9A09t; and The Forest Bathing Institute, bit.ly/2lIr7Ek; and "How Much Nature Is Enough? 120 Minutes a Week, Doctors Say," by Knvul Sheik. June 13, 2019. The New York Times. nyti.ms/2maoKKN; and ParkRx.org; and *Forest Bathing: How Trees Can Help You Find Health and Happiness*, by Dr. Qing Li; and *The Nature Fix: Why Nature Makes us Happier, Healthier, and More Creative*, by Florence Williams. 2017. W.W. Norton & Company. New York, NY.

In 2008, the World Health
United Nations, Department of Economic and Social Affairs. bit.ly/2m7TvQp.

Humans have lived in nature
Mesopotamia, the first city, was established between 4,000 to 3,000 BC. See "Humans Are Becoming City-Dwelling 'Metro Sapiens,'" by Sarah Zielinski. Nov 24, 2014. Smithsonian.com. bit.ly/2lP66Yv.

Research shows that a wide
Shannon, G., McKenna, M.F., Angeloni, L.M., Crooks, K.R., Fristrup, K.M., Brown, E., ... Wittemyer, G. (2015). A Synthesis of Two Decades of Research Documenting the Effects of Noise on Wildlife. *Biological Reviews.* 91(4), 982–1005. bit.ly/2mbo6wJ.

If the brain were a computer
"Why It's So Hard to Pay Attention, Explained by Science," by Daniel J. Levitin. Sept 23, 2015. Fast Company. bit.ly/2mapEqF.

"We have evolved to
Dr./Professor Andrew Huberman's contribution to this publication was as a paid consultant, and was not part of his Stanford University duties or responsibilities.

Countless studies tell us that excessive
Elhai, J.D., Dvorak, R.D., Levine, J.C., Hall, B.J. (2017). Problematic Smartphone Use: A Conceptual Overview and Systematic Review of Relations with Anxiety and Depression Psychopathology. *Journal of Affective Disorders.* (207) 251-259. bit.ly/2m9sWKL.

we spend nearly 12 hours a day
"Time Flies: U.S. Adults Now Spend Nearly Half a Day Interacting with Media." July 31, 2018. Nielsen Insights. bit.ly/2m2PVaa.

One in ten admit to See
"One in 10 People Checks Their Phone During Sex: Survey," by Jane Ridley. June 7, 2018. New York Post. bit.ly/2kaJvoW; and "How Much Time Do We Spend on Social Media." Dec 15, 2016. MediaKix. bit.ly/2IJFXue.

Harvard psychiatrist and Madefor advisor
Go Wild, by John J. Ratey, MD and Richard Mannin. 2014. Little, Brown and Company. New York, NY.

Dr. Qing Li recommends using at least
Forest Bathing: How Trees Can Help You...

Even brief exposures have strong benefits
White, M.P., Alcock, I. Grellier, J. Wheeler, B.W., Hartig, T. Warber, S.L., Bone, A. Depledge M.H., & Fleming, L.E. (2019). Spending at Least

120 Minutes a Week in Nature is Associated with Good Health and Wellbeing. *Scientific Reports.* 9(7730). go.nature.com/2IMCV8M.

Attention Restoration Theory
Basu, A., Duvall, J., & Kaplan, R. (2018). Attention Restoration Theory: Exploring the Role of Soft Fascination and Mental Bandwidth. *Environment and Behavior.* 1-27. bit.ly/2IN3c6A.

Let your attention drift
Sullivan, W.C., Kaplan, R. (2015) Nature! Small Steps that Can Make a Big Difference. *Health Environments Research and Design.* 9(2) 6-10. bit.ly/2k8gb2k.

researchers at Stanford University
Bratman, G. N., Hamilton, J. P., Hahn, K. S., Daily, G. C., & Gross, J. J. (2015). Nature Experience Reduces Rumination and Subgenual Prefrontal Cortex Activation. *Proceedings of the National Academy of Sciences.* 112(28), 8567-8572. bit.ly/2IFv3pn.

Physicist Richard Taylor
University of Oregon bio. bit.ly/2k8gKcs.

In 1999, Taylor worked
"Order in Pollock's Chaos," by Richard Taylor. Dec 2002. *Scientific American.* bit.ly/2k8h4ba.

More recently, Taylor has studied
"Why Fractals Are So Soothing," by Florence Williams and Aeon. Jan 26, 2017. *The Atlantic.* bit.ly/2kFJWb9.

Clarity

"I bought a four-story,
"Living with Less. A Lot Less," by Graham Hill. Mar 9, 2013. *The New York Times.* nyti.ms/2Mx7WHt.

a typical American consumer
"We Are All Accumulating Mountains of Things," by Alana Semuels. Aug 21, 2018. *The Atlantic.* bit.ly/2VzNgCx.

Stanford neuroscientist Andrew Huberman
Dr./Professor Andrew Huberman's contribution to this publication was as a paid consultant and was not part of his Stanford University duties or responsibilities.

According to Belk's "extended self" theory
Belk, R.W. (1988). Possessions and the Extended Self. *The Journal of Consumer Research*, (15) 2. 139-168. bit.ly/35v4DJA.

But as we age and our self-concept evolves
Belk, R.W. *ibid.*

a vocal advocate for essentialism
See: *Essentialism*, by Greg McKeown. 2014. Currency. New York, NY.

Researchers at Princeton University found
McMains S, Kastner S. (2011) Interactions of Top-Down and Bottom-Up Mechanisms in Human Visual Cortex. *J Neurosci.* 31(2):587–597. bit.ly/33joUQ4.

UC Los Angeles scientists found
See: *Life at Home in the Twenty-First Century: 32 Families Open Their Doors*, by Jeanne E. Arnold, Anthony P. Graesch, Enzo Ragazzini, and Elinor Ochs. 2012. The UCLA Cotsen Institute of Archaeology Press. Los Angeles, CA; and "The Clutter Culture," by Jack Feuer, July 1, 2012. UCLA Magazine. bit.ly/2OH76KD.

A study out of Cornell and Syracuse universities
Vartanian, L.R., Kernan, K.M., & Wansink, B. (2016). Clutter, Chaos, and Overconsumption: The Role of Mind-Set in Stressful and Chaotic Food Environments. *Environment and Behavior*, 49(2), 215–223. bit.ly/317W2ZV.

Rest

investigators of the 2017 collisions
Comprehensive Review of Recent Surface Force Incidents. Oct 26, 2017. U.S. Fleet Forces Command. bit.ly/2p1RAi8.

two-thirds of troops who served
"Nap for High Performance," by Debbie Vyskocil. June 2018. *Proceedings*. U.S. Naval Institute. bit.ly/33zvaUm.

Dr. Ruth Benca
See Dr. Benca's page at UC Irvine for more: bit.ly/34P5P9w.

Dr. Andrew Huberman
Dr./Professor Andrew Huberman's contribution to this publication was as a paid consultant and was not part of his Stanford University duties or responsibilities.

In a 2011 Stanford study
Mah C.D., Mah K.E., Kezirian E.J., Dement W.C. (2011). The Effects of Sleep Extension on the Athletic Performance of Collegiate Basketball Players. *Sleep*. 34(7):943–950. bit.ly/33tZG22.

Hattar was among a small team
See Dr. Samer Hattar's Biography at NIMH for more: bit.ly/2qExJ94.

For thousands of years, human physiology
Wright K.P. Jr., McHill A.W., Birks B.R., Griffin B.R., Rusterholz T., et al. (2013). Entrainment of the Human Circadian Clock to the Natural Light-Dark cycle. *Curr Biol*. 23(16):1554–1558. bit.ly/2NZchUf.

studies at the University of Colorado, Boulder
See Wright... ibid; and Stothard E.R., McHill A.W., Depner C.M., et al. (2017) Circadian Entrainment to the Natural Light-Dark Cycle across Seasons and the Weekend. *Curr Biol*. 27(4):508–513. bit.ly/34FM1Fg.

late circadian and sleep timing
Stothard, *ibid*.

the actual number of minutes you need depends
In one study, just milliseconds of light sufficed: Zeitzer, J.M. et al. Millisecond Flashes of Light Phase Delay the Human Circadian Clock During Sleep. (2014) *Journal of Biological Rhythms*. (29) 5: 370-6. bit.ly/2CHMLhb.

Those benefits, according to Hattar and

See Fernandez, D.C., Fogerson, P.M., Lazzerini Ospri, L., Thomsen, M.B.,... Hattar, S. (2018). Light Affects Mood and Learning through Distinct Retina-Brain Pathways. *Cell.* 175(1), 71–84. bit.ly/2NvXzp0; and LeGates T.A., Fernandez D.C., Hattar S. (2014). Light as a Central Modulator of Circadian Rhythms, Sleep and Affect. *Nat Rev Neurosci.* 15(7):443–454. bit.ly/2WXUAZz.

71% of people who go to bed with their phones

"Is Your Smartphone Ruining Your Sleep?" The National Sleep Foundation. bit.ly/34DBiv8. A study at Brigham and Women's Chang, A., Aeschbach, D., Duffy, J.F., Czeisler, C.A. (2015). Impact of Light-Emitting eBooks Before Bed. *Proceedings of the National Academy of Sciences.* 112(4), 1232-1237. bit.ly/2Nvq3PF.

Ten more ways to get better sleep

For more in-depth information on sleep hygiene, see *Sleep Disorders: The Clinician's Guide to Diagnosis and Management*, by Dr. Ruth Benca. 2011. Oxford American Neurology Library. Oxford University Press.

About 15% of Americans use wearable

"Sleep Trackers Can Prompt Sleep Problems." Rush University. Feb 26, 2017. bit.ly/2NwVCIH.

Researchers at Rush University Medical School

Baron K.G., Abbott S., Jao N., Manalo N., Mullen R. (2017) Orthosomnia: Are Some Patients Taking the Quantified Self Too Far?. *J Clin Sleep Med.* 2017;13(2):351–354. bit.ly/2NygeAI.

Vision

Values are scientifically defined

See: Vyskocilova, J., Prasko, J., Ociskova, M., Sedlackova, Z., Marackova, M., et al. (2016). Values and Values Work in Cognitive Behavioral Therapy. *European Psychiatry.* 33, S456–S457. bit.ly/2PVGkgA.

Psychological research finds

Cohen, G.L., Sherman, D.K. (2014). The Psychology of Change: Self-Affirmation and Social Psychological Intervention. *Annual Review of Psychology.* 65(1), 333–371. bit.ly/35L0yQS; and "Values Clarification:

How Reflection On Core Values Is Used In CBT," by Joaquín Selva. Nov 20, 2019. Positive Psychology. bit.ly/2MdTPXY.

report from Ohio University
Clark, B.C., Mahato, N.K., Nakazawa, M., Law, T.D., Thomas, J.S. (2014) The Power of the Mind: The Cortex as a Critical Determinant of Muscle Strength/Weakness. *J Neurophysiol.* 112: 3219–3226. bit.ly/2PCzEoU.

professional athletes use it
"Seeing Is Believing: The Power of Visualization," by AJ Adams. Dec 03, 2009. *Psychology Today.* bit.ly/36QBvMA.

When Team USA Winter Olympians practice
"Olympians Use Imagery as Mental Training," by Christopher Clarey. Feb 22, 2014. *The New York Times.* nyti.ms/2rUQVAK.

Dr. Martin Seligman
See: Flourish, by Martin E.P. Seligman. 2011. Free Press. New York NY; and "Positive Psychology," by *Psychology Today*, bit.ly/38TMOpc; and "Eudaemonia: The Good Life. A Talk with Martin Seligman," by John Brockman. March 23, 2004. The Edge. bit.ly/2Ps9mWg.

Printed in Great Britain
by Amazon

24426125R00209